PERSON TO PERSON

The Simple Guide to Mastering Your Social Self

Nika Domi

10-10-10
Publishing

Front cover image by waqas@bookcoverartist.com
Cartoons by maciej.jurkiewicz@gmail.com

Printed in Canada and the United States of America
First printing edition 2021

Publisher
10-10-10 Publishing
Markham, Ontario, Canada

Table of Contents

Foreword

Do you believe that great communication is one of the most important keys to success? I definitely think so! Would you like to improve your skills in this area? *Person to Person: The Simple Guide to Mastering Your Social Self* will help you increase your knowledge of basic human mental processes, and cultivate the power to directly improve your life's outcomes and incomes.

I am excited to endorse this book, especially in a time when your person-to-person experiences may have become more distorted than ever before. Nika takes you on a surprisingly smooth ride through the complicated study of human interconnection. While progressing through the chapters, you will become engaged in the discovery of your inner being, and look past the layers of social learning that threaten to cover it up. You will become more empowered to manage your response to things that appear contradictory in nature.

I appreciate the clever way in which Nika utilizes research-based academic content that you can apply in your daily life. This is one of those books that may cause you to actually want to take notes. Do you ever wonder why the "law of attraction" hasn't really been effective for you? Perhaps you have given too much power to the "automaton" within your mind, which causes many costly mistakes like ruined relationships, friction in your professional life, missed opportunities, or a decrease in your overall well-being.

It doesn't matter who you are. *Person to Person: The Simple Guide to Mastering Your Social Self* will be useful to you in many ways, if you are ready to take greater control of your life.

Raymond Aaron
New York Times Bestselling Author

CHAPTER 1

THE PERSON-TO-PERSON PHENOMENON

"Know thyself, then thou shalt know the Universe."

– Temple of Apollo, Delphi

You Are Here for a Reason

S ocial interactions have always been central to the existence and evolution of us humans. If you were an alien visiting Earth, one of the first things you would easily notice is humans interacting together on many levels, in various ways. Person-to-person encounters are embedded in every aspect of daily life. Our earliest ancestors, just like us now, have been obliged by various physical and emotional needs, a satisfaction of which happens to require the participation of other people. We have always collaborated in search of necessities like food, shelter, safety, and of course, in creating more humans. Although the visible basics of survival help us see the next day, our desires to fulfill that which may not be visible to the eye sets us on a perpetual journey through various emotional experiences together. We need each other for the basic things in life, as well as the more extraordinary ones.

Have you ever wondered why people simply can't get along? If you look at the various levels of conflicts, misunderstandings, and disappointments, which often happen during human social encounters, things don't always go so smoothly. Most of the time, humans get a failing grade in the lesson of seeing things from the perspective of others, seeing through mere appearances, or sometimes even simply seeing the big picture. Many pieces of your past experiences make up your unique perspective, which in turn shapes the creation of your convictions (or beliefs, feelings, attitudes). Despite our often-misestimated mental capacity, as humans, we are incorrect about many things we think we know. Your mind unfortunately builds many inaccurate convictions because, as Joseph Jastrow profoundly stated, *"Conviction is the rivalry between reason and emotion."*[1] Often, the emotion wins the bid to build that conviction, because they're already associated through the memory process. Social-psychological knowledge is here to expose the common processes of the human mind as it encounters various social interactions throughout the path of life. Knowledge of how and why we operate the way we do, will eliminate the obstacles that stand in your way to the mastery of self. It will pull you out of the darkness of misconceptions, which can lead you down the wrong path. Are you tired yet of wasting time on mistake after mistake? I know I was, and then I found this knowledge. The right knowledge utilized is central to the quality of your life, and that of the world around you.

Mastering the social part of your earthly experience is crucial to your basic survival and beyond. Those who are skillful in the craft of social interaction are most likely among the winners in many areas of their life, as compared to those who are not as skillful. They are often pretty good at disallowing emotions to distract their judgement. I've always admired movie or story characters who were impressive in dealing with other people, and knew exactly how to remain ahead of the game in every social situation. I'm sure you can already imagine which types of characters I'm talking about! *Sherlock Holmes, Tony Stark, Alice from Resident Evil, Hermione Granger in Harry Potter, even Fresh Prince of Bel Air or Bugs Bunny.* They were keen listeners and observers, had exceptional awareness of their environment, and were almost psychic in their ability to predict the behaviour of others. They always had the perfect response for pretty much anything, and others looked to them for solutions in tough situations. This skill inspired me to get to know the human mind as much as I can, and to work on overwriting my own inopportune mental programs to achieve the highest level of mind mastery in this lifetime.

What truly impressed me about these characters was how hard it was to fool them. Such people are a minority in our world. Did you know that most people cannot spot a lie in real time when interacting with someone who is lying? Researchers, Bond and DePaulo, found that the average person here in the Western world is roughly 54% accurate in discriminating lies from truths when judging the liar's behaviour at the time when the lie is being told.[2] That is pretty much like scoring a wild guess, because people's minds are often automatically inclined to judge lies based on peripheral cues, which are the superficial factors. Attention is swayed by things such as incorrect stereotypes about what a liar does, or looks like. Less often, people look to the inconsistencies in the liar's message. The trick here is that the mind is designed to make you operate most efficiently, and chooses actions that save time and energy. Highly blinding effects of emotions, desires, or accepted social norms can also work against you. Intelligent people who were assumed to be highly diligent, have lost big money because someone has been able to talk them into a bad investment, and even top-level spies have allowed themselves to be fooled by the enemy. The autopilot within you happens to be a terrible lie detector.

From a young age, many of us are taught various behaviours, such as to be nice and polite in social settings. We adapt this automatic assumption that other people will also be nice to us, or that they should have our best interest in mind. It is important to value good manners, kindness, and be a nice person, but if niceness is not mindfully managed, it can make you hesitant to stick up for yourself when needed, or deter you from questioning the motivations of others. I was that person for a long time. As smart as I thought I was, it was during my study of psychology when I truly realized how vulnerable I was to the sources that manipulated my perception of them, in order to gain some material or emotional goal. I also realized that my desire to automatically be overly friendly towards everyone, was often putting me in a disadvantaged position. Seeing how many people fall for simple manipulations, and extreme scams, has inspired my mission to share this essential knowledge with nice people world-wide, who are tired of getting the short end of the stick, as well as those who have been doing quite well and do not want to jeopardize all the hard work due to the mismanagement of that one unresolved vulnerability hiding within them. Social-psychological knowledge will train you to skillfully avoid being misled in the world full of various levels of deceit. It is said that knowledge shall set us free, and it may be true because, often, it happens to be the naive who make it possible for the malevolent to achieve their goals.

I am sure you would probably agree that you don't take enough time to sit quietly and detach from your surroundings to deeply reflect on your thoughts, feelings, behaviours, attitudes, or beliefs. Most people don't. Interestingly enough, a psychological research study, by Timothy Wilson and colleagues, revealed that "participants typically did not enjoy spending 6 to 15 minutes in a room by themselves with nothing to do but think, that they enjoyed doing mundane external activities much more, and that many preferred to administer electric shocks to themselves instead of being left alone with their thoughts. Most people seem to prefer to be doing something rather than nothing, even if that something is negative."[3] This adds even more evidence for the sociability of humans. It is likely that you have dipped into some mindfulness concepts, listened to motivational speakers, tried meditation, or are part of some like-minded group, but you still feel like something is missing. Have you ever thought that it would be great if you could just find that missing piece so you can finally move to the next level? I'm quite certain that you were led to this book for a reason. Now the time has finally come to perfect your knowledge of self, and your knowledge of others, so that you can flow with greater ease towards total mastery of life.

I'm glad you have the desire to learn about the mind! Your mind directs your whole life, and often people reach for great heights of knowledge but forget to learn the basics of how this main operating station of theirs operates. It doesn't matter what background or level of knowledge you come from, or how old you are, this book will help to fill in the blanks of what you may have missed in your own learning trajectory, or it will spark new dimensions of thought about some topics that are relevant to you. The aim of this book is to set and reinforce proper mental foundations of knowledge of self, and knowledge of others. Reading the information contained here will help you elevate your mind's processes to a whole new level, improve your social outcomes, and make you laser-sharp in the art of understanding others. As a bonus, you will move much closer towards fully getting to know your very best friend: your own self. This somewhat simple but broad review of basic social-psychological theories, thoughts, and examples will prepare you for the next levels of your rise. I'm certain that the more people learn about the mind in a social context, the higher chance we will have to improve our world by straightening out human interactions, so that we can finally move in the direction of social harmony. After a couple of thousand years of social discordance, it's about time to elevate into a higher state of being as a species.

This first chapter is just a brief overview of the vibes we will be getting into throughout this book, so keep that in mind before you get discouraged by a slight information overload in this first chapter! If you must, then feel free to skip to the second chapter—I'll forgive you in advance! If you are one of those people who thinks they picked up just another gimmicky self-help book, I want you to note that this book contains fluff-free, university-level knowledge, and at the same time, it does not ignore the energetic forces present in all things—otherwise, self-mastery would once again be incomplete.

The Daily Diplomat

Are you seated comfortably? Well, let's begin! Did you know that you happen to be a full-time diplomat hard at work? Whatever age you are, that's how many years of diplomatic experience you have. Each day, you negotiate the terms and conditions of your mutual connection with various others. There is an exchange that goes on between people, whether it is material or non-material. You may require things from others, and others may require things from you. Such is the nature of this world.

You don't just communicate in order to pass on information, but as professor Jerzy Bralczyk explains,[4] you want to form a connection, which is the most difficult in all of this. You also want to be viewed as credible, so people believe you, and you want to efficiently get your point across without accidentally saying what you don't want to say. Communication becomes an art of negotiation. *Wikipedia* defines **negotiation** as an interaction and process between entities who compromise to agree on matters of mutual interest, while optimizing their individual utilities.[5] They also list conflict as part of this definition, but I must challenge them on this point because many negotiations don't involve any conflict. Your daily life is a platform for many negotiations, big or small. They can happen anywhere, and we don't really consider them as such, because they hide under the guise of normalcy, or more specifically, under the guise of **social norms** (we will discuss them more in depth throughout this book) by which we guide our behaviour when sharing spaces and experiences with other people. It takes a great deal of effort, and mental energy, to negotiate with other people daily. The constant "dressing up" of our words in a proper way, in order to ensure the most favourable response, can be really exhausting, especially with the latest preoccupation with political correctness filtering the spontaneity out of our communication.

For example, when a waiter is attending to a table of clients, he is focused on behaving in a way that will result in a bigger tip. He is not literally negotiating that tip by saying to the clients, "How much will you give me at the end of my service to you?" or, "It will be $2 extra per joke; how many would you like today?" The negotiation is happening through both parties' mutual understanding of this social norm of keeping it cool as they participate in the norm of giving a tip. The norm requires them to kind of pretend it doesn't exist, and the negotiation is playing out somewhere within that dynamic. Behaviours, emotions, and thoughts, combined, form themselves into the frequency that aligns with a specific monetary amount to be awarded to the waiter.

Somehow, **influence** finds its way into our daily negotiations. To get others to assist you in anything, you must use some form of influence. Whether we want to acknowledge it or not, people are motivated to a large extent by **self-interest**. The waiter wants a substantial tip, so they have to act in a way that will help them receive it. The result of your negotiations with others usually is meant to equate to something that benefits you, or benefits something else that is important to you. Self-interest sounds selfish, but it is not to be taken literally as a bad thing, because it is incorporated into the design of human life, as every human at some point realizes that they themselves, above all, are responsible for whether they eat or not. Every human should be prepared for having their own life in their own hands, even if in this moment that may not be a necessity. There are levels to all of this, you see. Self-interest has a scale. You may not have thought that a simple thing such as stopping to pet someone's dog is motivated by self-interest. If you look deeper, this action is driven by the desire for a pleasurable experience, which emanates from feeling the soft fur of this cute animal, and hopefully having the dog confirm to your ego that you are an awesome person because dogs like you.

Have you ever had to run into a store, right at closing time, wanting to quickly purchase something you need, so you tried to influence or convince the cashier to process this one last transaction just for you? You had to influence the cashier to give you that favour. More serious influence can be found in situations like parents influencing their children's career decisions or marriage decisions, or some law representatives influencing defendants to plead guilty in order to get a better deal in their sentence and end the case. Self-interest is at the core of all humans because we all have a main goal: to keep ourselves alive in the most pleasant and efficient way. Survival is the one thing that life all over surely has in common. It may not always appear that humans are motivated to act in a manner that is most pleasant or efficient, but even those who consciously sabotage their own good are often driven by something that satisfies some part of them, giving them the perception of a continuum.

Not just in today's world, but all throughout time, the right social capital has been a valuable commodity, and can be a huge asset in your life's portfolio. *Social capital* refers to the people within your reach, who can be a valuable link to something that benefits you, your family, or your business. Everyone relies on other people for many things. On a deeper level, it is actually the thoughts, feelings, and behaviours of other people that you rely on, and those must be recognized for what they really are, not just what they appear to be. There are **intrinsic** (internal) and **extrinsic** (external) traits, and the former only come out in specific situations, and often after some time, making them much harder to size up. That understanding must also be applied to yourself. When you remember to check with your inner "guru" for guidance in various decisive life situations, you will be less likely to buy someone's junk, especially when you are caught off guard, distracted, or put on the spot.

Whether you consider yourself to be outgoing, or prefer to keep to yourself, personality shouldn't decide for the quality of your interactions with others. Everyone needs to eat, and everyone needs to become as familiar as possible with the playing field of their lives. You don't have to be a social butterfly in order to achieve a pleasant and beneficial social life. When you increase your psychological awareness, and continue to equip yourself with interesting knowledge that expands your basic interests, you will be able to tailor your social results to your very own personality. Moving into a greater state of consciousness will increase the ability to attract more like-minded people into your life who suit your needs.

You are continuously lobbying for your access to many aspects of this life, and sometimes also lobbying in favour or disfavour of others. It also happens that you may NOT be lobbying for yourself enough, and miss out on many benefits simply because of things like shyness or limiting cultural beliefs. Some people shy away from approaching strangers to network with. Many people also demote themselves subconsciously and have a hard time promoting themselves because they don't want to be accused of bragging; although, no matter the personality, it is important to keep in mind that whatever you want to achieve, it will involve not only talking to others, but talking to them in a way that will be effective for you. Even in something as common as getting a job, or a deal, an overwhelming majority of what happens is by word of mouth! The *Small Business Trends* website reports that the majority (about 70%) of "employers feel most comfortable with word of mouth job candidates—when a friend or acquaintance of a current employee or someone in their circle applies for a job."[6] This is why person-to-person interactions are so crucial to the proper functioning of society and its economy, just as they are crucial to your quality of life. Might as well become a master of your social world, enjoy the benefits, and leave disappointments in the past. Increased knowledge of the mind will illuminate your future, one day at a time.

Needs Like Weeds

Our lives came with a bag of needs and wants, some of which are material in nature, such as clothes to cover and warm up our bodies; and some being non-material, such as hugs to warm up our hearts. Other people represent various pieces to your puzzle of needs; in turn, you also serve as a piece to someone's life puzzle. This puzzle requires people to constantly exchange these pieces with each other in order to complete the full picture, and who even knows if it can ever be complete. That's why emotions are represented in astrology by the element of water.

I must keep warning you, there are huge benefits to learning psychology, but there are also downsides! You may start looking at others from a different mindset than before. In my experience, it feels something like seeing what's behind their words, and recognizing some things about them that they don't even realize themselves, that I never noticed previously. Knowledge of psychology awards you this strange mental x-ray vision, which sees through words and exposes the deeper reasons for other's behaviour, their moods, needs, and beliefs. Many people are not ready to face their inner selves, and often it's important to find a careful way to suggest your realizations to others in your life, without the tone of judgement, just leading them to water by asking them more questions. As they answer questions, they will start feeling more engaged in their own transformation, which will remove much of their resistance to that realization. For example, if your friend Ann says to you that she doesn't like your other friend Kate, instead of saying, "Well, she's nice; I like her," you can ask Ann, "How did you come to that opinion? Tell me some things Kate did to cause you to come to that conclusion." If Kate didn't do anything to deserve not being liked, Ann, by not being able to answer with legitimate reasons, will have no choice but to move closer towards the realization that she was acting out of some inner reasons of her own, which may not have much to do with Kate as a person—it can be driven by things like jealousy, need for attention, fear of abandonment, or just simply lack of trust towards newly met people. Esther Hicks, a famous motivational teacher, once said, *"People will love you, people will hate you, and none of it will have anything to do with you."*[7] This is something that you will realize more and more, as you flow through the pages of this book. And while I agree with this quote, because I have seen this happen many times, I wouldn't want people to feel excused from not working on themselves, end up acting out of balance, and then reject criticism with this same idea by saying they don't care what anyone thinks of their behaviour.

The more I kept learning about our psychology, the more I started becoming convinced that the biggest human flaw is the need to feel special. This topic is important enough to be brought to light on a greater scale in our society. An accomplished hypnotist and mind coach, Luca Bosurgi, after 30 years of his experience with clients, suggests that we (as a society, or as therapists) have been focusing on the wrong causes of mental illness and distress, causes such as traumas and bad habits. In fact, it is something else that is probably the biggest problem affecting people's mental health. That which is responsible for much of anxiety, fear, and addiction, which dramatically affect our society, lies in a condition still largely unexplored. That condition is the **Adult Emotional Dependency**, an adult version of what Bosurgi defines as "an instinctual behaviour, hardcoded in our minds to protect and stimulate our emotional development during childhood. Its main function is to compel children to gain parental protection, guidance, and emotional fulfillment."[8] Attachments to other people's validation of our value or safety, can take up a large capacity of the body's energy, and decrease your overall efficiency. For those who are on a quest towards greater success, this can prevent that precious flow of valuable energy from being channelled into something more beneficial.

People show real strength when they are on a quest to fulfill their emotional needs. Some people will leave everything behind to travel across the world to fulfill some strong desire. **Belongingness** is another major human need, right next to the need to satisfy hunger, according to the findings of Abraham Maslow, a famous social psychologist.[9] Do you know in what type of situations you may be driven by this need for belongingness? I am now better at recognizing what this need looks like, but I wasn't years ago when I was controlled by it. When I was a teenager, I was drawn to people who had the same taste in music as myself, and now that I have studied this psychological knowledge, I realize it was a desire more driven by this need for belongingness and solidarity with like-minded others, than it was about the music. What is interesting is that this desire for emotional gain, in some cases, can be stronger than the desire for material gain. Some people stay in the same boring job for years because they feel like they belong to a "family" of co-workers, and maybe they don't have a crowd that would play that role outside of work. Sarcastically speaking, even people who consider themselves anti-social satisfy their need for belongingness by being part of the "anti-social club," and chatting with other anti-social people on social media (pun kind of intended).

The need for belongingness is an emotion, often happening on the unconscious level, unless you make it conscious and then gain the ability to control it. That particular mastery can put you within 5% of society. Emotional behaviour is often wrongfully attributed just to women, but men also act out of emotions; it just appears in different ways. According to Harvard Business School professor, Gerald Zaltman, "95 percent of our purchase decision making takes place in the subconscious mind."[10] mentions that people's shopping choices are guided mostly by their emotions. This is so powerful that many big companies invest in research about how to make their product or service more attractive to consumers. Zaltman mentions that "the basic idea of connection is central to the product's value proposition and becomes a more profound basis for developing marketing strategy than, say, technical superiority or long-lasting benefits." When you are aware of why you are making the choice you are making, then you can save yourself from making mistakes, which can slow down your progress and put you off track. When a financially broke teenager buys a designer piece of clothing, but doesn't have a driver's licence, they need to look within and ask themselves the reason why they spent $500 or more on a piece of clothing rather than on a licence that can have long-term benefits. It was likely a fast way to relieve the desire to feel accepted and admired for having something that they see their musical idols flash in their face, conditioning them to recognize such things as symbols of respect. When I worked in the fragrance industry, I remember people asking for the celebrity branded perfumes, which our stores didn't carry because their quality was too low. Such celeb name perfumes are typically made up of cheaper ingredients, and therefore can potentially be even harmful to your health. When it comes to perfume, you often get what you pay for, although the customers who were asking for these celebrity fragrances didn't have quality in mind at all; they just liked that particular celebrity and wanted to bask in their energy by way of this fragrance, despite the negative aspects of their emotionally driven choice. There is much more to the topic of youth and marketing, so stick around as we will discuss it in one of the further chapters, including some shocking study results done by my ex-professor.

Communications within the dynamic of emotional, physical, or material dependency can be a significant contributor to stress. Misunderstandings, disappointments, changes of heart, shame, rejection, or aggression... Those are popular reasons why many people can't sleep at night, or function during the day. You can be dependent on others for things like tangible resources, collaborative project results, and even time, because time is like money. You can also be dependent on others for non-material things such as others liking, admiring, or respecting you, though the **physical** and the **emotional** are quite connected. People can be dependent on others to fulfill their emotional satisfaction, while often even sacrificing their material resources. There are many women, as well as men, who get scammed by romance fraudsters just because their emotional needs dazed and confused their minds. The *Federal Trade Commission* writes that "scammers create fake online profiles using photos of other people—even stolen pictures of real military personnel. They profess their love quickly. And they tug at your heartstrings with made-up stories about how they need money, for emergencies, hospital bills, or travel. Why all of the tricks? They're looking to steal your money."[11]

Some people want to avoid the stress that comes with becoming a boss of their current co-workers, so they actually deny a job promotion. Sudden change in how one is viewed by people whose opinion they care about can be painful to whoever holds such emotional values dear. Other than the sense of authority, some people may be jealous that you got the higher position, or may count on you to award them preferential treatment. I have been through a similar situation, back when I was a manager to a few of my friends. It was not easy, but those friends happen to still be around today! I hope that means I have mastered this tough test that is feared by many. There surely were moments when my superiors expected me to act in harsh ways, but somehow I was able to work my magic to distract them away from the topic, as I coached my friends on how to improve. Always look for ways in which you can turn a negative into a positive. Instead of creating a report on the weak performance of my co-worker, I created a list of things that they were improving in, and things that were achieved during the extra coaching. Also, what many new managers fail to do is to make sure the people who they weren't previously close with, feel cared for just as much as the people they're closer with. The new manager should make sure to give those people a bit more positive attention, so they don't assume that they will be treated worse than the manager's buddies. If you want to be better at reading and understanding others, you must take yourself out of the equation and figure out what their needs are. Always remember my quote from above: that people like to feel special. To win their sympathy or respect, you must make sure to act like they are special. After all, when it comes to careers, also keep in mind that friends don't pay your bills... But on the contrary, in some cases, a crappy job may not be worth your integrity either.

You live in a social matrix made up of various daily encounters that shape your reality. Various needs, your own or other people's, can become a great cause of stress if they're not managed. Most of this stress comes from expectations we put on our social ties with others, and how they can sometimes take unexpected turns. Familiarizing yourself with this psychological knowledge will help you straighten out any skewed ways in which you place unbalanced expectations on others, and vice versa. This increased ability to see the actual, and not just the perceived desires and emotions of others, will smooth out your path towards greater positive results.

Like a Sponge

The **brain** is an extremely complex organ, which has been providing researchers and philosophers with plenty of work for hundreds of years, and it still manages to maintain its mysteriousness. *The Human Memory* website writes that the brain has "an estimated 100 billion neurons passing signals to each other via as many as 1,000 trillion synaptic connections. It continuously receives and analyzes sensory information, responding by controlling all bodily actions and functions. It is also the centre of higher-order thinking, learning, and memory, and gives us the power to think, plan, speak, imagine, dream, reason, and experience emotions."[12] It is also subject to the constant shaping and modification by your environment. Most of the programming happens in the child stage, when you encounter and record all kinds of new stimuli. What you absorb from your surroundings can be anywhere on the scale from beneficial to destructive, from true to false, from happy to sad, and on. Just like when being outdoors can be both beneficial and not, your skin absorbs the sun's healing rays, as well as the damaging free-radicals floating in the air of polluted places. Your mind absorbs much of what is around you—the good, the bad, and the ugly—and it's not asking for your permission.

Did you know that if you live in a city, you encounter thousands of advertisements per day? You may not remember the exact advertisement you saw, but your mind has surely stored pieces of the program presented by those advertisements. For example, it's hard to deny that there is an oversaturation of TV advertisements that show older people taking medicine. This constant pairing of these two things has the power to cause you to automatically view old age as inseparable from sickness. Only you have the power to monitor and reshape programs within your mind, so that your stored information is pretty close to accurate and beneficial to your well-being. Just try to catch and examine the thoughts that appear automatic when they jump into your mind. Don't give them a lifetime pass, because many don't deserve that privilege. For example, you can consciously affirm a correction to yourself that goes something like this: "I may see older people taking medication on advertisements, but I understand that there are many older people staying very healthy, and I know it is possible, so I commit to staying active and healthy myself." The more you do it, the more you will be able to break up the discordant narratives before they get absorbed too deep into your being, and become much harder to fix.

We will talk a lot about the powerful influence of **social norms**, the invisible rules that most members of a specific society agree on, based on their shared beliefs in things like fairness, or respect, without them being specified by the formal laws of the specific country or state. When you stand behind the last person in a line-up at the cash register, and you don't step in front of those who got there before you, then you're performing one of the social norms. You automatically do it without even thinking about it. When you travel anywhere else in the world, you will expect the line-up rule to apply in the same way. It can be quite challenging to escape some of the influences that are programmed into your physical existence. Assessing them from time to time is a good idea, since it's your responsibility to ensure that you're not blindly following rules that are outdated or need to be questioned, such as the norm of not challenging the opinions, actions, or demands of your elders, which can be a dangerous rule in my view because it presumes that all elders are smart and have your best interest in mind, which is not the case. Just because someone is older doesn't exactly mean that they deserve to be awarded authority over others.

Also, following social norms in extreme situations can sometimes work against you. The particulars of the situation can influence your emotional and mental processes, and that is why it is actually quite easy to predict your behaviour in a set scenario. You may think you know exactly how to behave properly in specific situations, but when you are distracted, overly emotional, bound by commitments to others, or maybe mesmerized by others' personal charms, your inner guidance gets clouded, and it all simply "throws you off." When a street thief tries to steal something from an unsuspecting person, they often have someone else distract the unsuspecting victim, with something like asking for directions, while the thief digs into their bag. The whole situation depends on whether the victim suspects foul play right away and secures themselves, or whether they will allow their mind to wander off into questioning that "iffy" feeling in their core. That feeling is often accompanied by conflicting thoughts, such as, "Should I tell them the directions or guard my purse," and, "Will it look weird if I guard my purse; they may take offence—what if they're nice people?" In such a situation, it is crucial to forget social norms, and block this battle of thoughts that will only steal valuable time, already well calculated by your adversary. Of course, I'm not saying to never help out strangers in need, but be fully aware of yourself, your inner vibe, and your surroundings while you're at it.

I once saw a YouTube news clip that really made me think about how dangerously unaware people can be. It demonstrated the ultimate distraction while a purse was stolen in a restaurant.[13] This situation was pretty bad because there was no direct interaction with the thief. The boyfriend of the woman (victim) was facing this thief as he was standing super close to the woman, but the boyfriend failed miserably in protecting the purse and the personal space of the woman he was with. His attention was possibly too fixated on the girl, and he really didn't see what was happening, or maybe he had a glimpse of thought regarding this strange guy standing so oddly close to her, but he convinced himself that maybe there was a valid reason why he was there and that it was nothing, or maybe he just didn't want to say anything to the strange guy, in fear of breaking some social norm, like maybe not wanting to offend him. Check out the video linked on my website; you'll be shocked too!

The interesting human phenomenon, and a major point of this book, is that an overwhelming percentage of people share the same types of responses. Have you seen the comedy programs on TV where they prank random unsuspecting people on the street? The reason why the pranks are funny is that you already expect a specific reaction from the person who's being put on the spot. You are most likely surprised when the rare person doesn't give into the prank, and deep down you wish to be that person if someone was to prank you. You may assume you would stand the test of being fooled, but there is a large chance that when under certain pressure of the situation, you would bend too. Falling for a prank is not as dangerous as falling for a scam. But the source of both actions come from someone having an advantage of knowledge over you in that particular situation. They say that knowledge is power, and you're increasing yours as you continue to read further, so... let's move on!

Flight Through the Unconscious

The Buddha apparently said that the cause of all pain and suffering is ignorance. **Ignorance** is defined in *dictionary.com* as lack of knowledge, and one of its synonyms is the state or place of "unconsciousness."[14] **Consciousness** refers to the mental faculties being fully active. **Unconsciousness** is when that activity is limited or gone, or as if it was asleep. When something is unconscious, it lacks awareness, or cognition (thought).

You may have heard the saying that most people are operating on "autopilot." It is actually quite true. This autopilot is stationed in your unconscious mind. The word "unconscious" is similar, if not the same, to the word "subconscious." This still confuses people a hundred years after Sigmund Freud, who was a world-renowned psychoanalyst, famous for work in this topic. He decided to stick with the term "unconscious" just to be more consistent and avoid confusion. This word has remained the choice of scholars, although even today's neuroscientists are still confused about this term, just as they are still puzzled by these mysterious unconscious mental processes, maybe because they don't seem to actually have a specific place in our brain structure; at least it hasn't been found yet. Could it be that they may very well be looking in the wrong place?

A person complaining about someone else being on **autopilot** probably got frustrated at some point with their behaviour, which seemed as if it was enacted without much conscious control; maybe they did something that was unthoughtful, clumsy, or ignorant. Maybe this person simply didn't know any better, was under the influence of someone or something, or was "zoned out," which is a pretty suitable term to illustrate a temporary lack of full mental control. People are in an unconscious state; for example, when rushing to work, worried that they are late for an important meeting, and they didn't think to hold the door for the person walking behind them, causing them to spill their coffee as they were hit with the door. Is that first person terrible, or is it that their perception of other people at that particular moment was being handled by their autopilot? Their conscious mind has blocked everything that isn't directly related to being on time for work, and all thought capacity at that time had to be channelled to that task in order to move the person there more efficiently. In that case, all other factors in the environment were dealt with from the auto mode, just enough to get them by. Therefore, in my view, it is fair to associate unconsciousness with the main "character" of this book, the **autopilot**. I want to refer to this phenomenon as the "autopilot," to make it easier to identify these automatic psychological processes that all humans are wired with to a varying extent.

It's not something commonly realized how much this autopilot is involved in our movement through life, without requiring permission. Dr. Michael Craig Miller writes in a *Harvard Health* newsletter that "a good deal and perhaps most of mental life happens without our knowing much about it."[15] This so-called autopilot's purpose is to direct your body through this highly detailed world in an efficient way, especially when you are not able to pay attention. It takes care of the slightest and the biggest decisions, whether it's leading you to take a step up the stairs while you're talking on your cell phone, or being able to think about what groceries to buy while you're driving a car. It's built on the foundation of habit: Once you do something more often, it becomes natural and automatic. You would not be able to get anything done if you had to consciously process each detail every time you encountered it. It also helps you feel more comfortable in your surroundings.

It is not here to cause harm; the human mechanism is an intelligent creation, and all of the parts are given a function to serve the goal of your survival. Sometimes the autopilot can cause great trouble when it gets too much leeway, especially when a person is distracted, emotionally charged, under the influence of substances or people, or in a rush. Would you cross the road on a green light without looking both ways to make sure you can rely on that green light? I bet not, but some people do so, and they often even have headphones on, or worse, as I have seen such careless road crossers even pushing a child in a stroller! They seem to walk onto the road without checking if it's safe to do so, and something else is probably taking up their attention.

You are the one in charge of selecting what deserves your attention in a given situation, and what can be delegated to the autopilot. You're the CEO of your body and your life, so allow the autopilot to be your employee. To ensure a greater level of conscious control, the mind must be exercised, just like the body. Mental faculties have to be used to remain active and serve you well in the latter parts of your life, so it's good to expand your mind by learning psychology, as well as other new and exciting things. Breaking habits and repetitive actions on purpose will snap your mind out of the comfort of unconscious processes, while getting the inactive areas of your mind sparked up with renewed life force energy. Be in control of your reality, and don't let reality control you!

As I mentioned earlier, each person collects information from personal experience, and their mind stores it in the form of **schemata** or **heuristics**, which can be both conscious and unconscious. A **schema** is a generalized mental model, or mental picture of some object that got stored in your memory after you had an experience with it. It will then continuously get retrieved later when you experience similar things, which your mind will try to match up and categorize with some already held old schema. For example, your schema of a chair is probably an image of a wooden square with a back and four legs, and in the future, when you encounter something that looks similar to that image, you will categorize it as a chair as well. This includes stereotypes, but stereotypes are generally more applied to social groups and tend to exaggerate differences, while a schema prefers to categorize similarities. *Schemata* (plural) are formed when you are getting to know the world around you as a child, and can be edited throughout life, but generally they're quite hard to change or erase. This concept was introduced by a British psychologist, Sir Frederic Bartlett, in the late 1800s, and what's interesting is that later in the 1970s, it was rediscovered by *Marvin Minsky,* who was a computer scientist working on artificial intelligence.[16] Minsky saw the cognitive categorization process as something that can be applied to machines in order for them to recognize their environment.

Schemas also include *heuristics*, which are various rules of thumb developed from your past experience with a similar situation. They are stored in your mind to help you make faster decisions or snap judgements, as your mind automatically brings up the most readily available heuristic as a guide. It saves you from having to stop and examine every situation again and again. *Heuristics*, like *schemas*, are actually helpful to your success, according to *Psychology Today*, as they write that "navigating day-to-day life requires everyone to make countless small decisions within a limited timeframe. *Heuristics* can help individuals save time and mental energy, freeing up cognitive resources for more complex planning and problem-solving endeavours."[17]

Fast decisions are important in all kinds of life situations, especially in the financial markets. *Investopedia* explains that "analysts in every industry use rules of thumb such as intelligent guesswork, trial and error, process of elimination, past formulas, and the analysis of historical data to solve a problem."[18] Though, this kind of thinking can also cause trouble, because past performance doesn't necessarily guarantee future results, and there may be information that can get overlooked because of this **heuristic** confidence. This type of thinking must be consciously checked, but how?

The more you strive towards greater consciousness by studying your own mind, you will be much quicker in recognizing when your intuitive radar, or gut feeling, tries to point you away from that set heuristic. Your inner guidance system will alert you to switch back to manual mode at a crucial time, and the more skilled you are in listening to your inner self, the more you will notice these alerts. Regular practice of meditation is also key to such mastery because it clears the clutter that blocks the paths of communication. People who sometimes act irrationally are blind to their inner alert system. They trust the comfort of the past, which can pose as "common sense," so they continue sailing on autopilot, straight into troubled waters. The autopilot may simply get you through your situation, but it may not be capable of managing the situation in a masterful way.

Sigmund Freud actually not only saw the unconscious as containing things like mental shortcuts and heuristic models, but his main focus involved the notion that repressed feelings and emotions also get stuck in this thing called **the unconscious**. This repressed baggage can influence your decision making, and weigh on your pilot's ability to move you smoothly through your situations. A manager who yells at an employee in front of customers or co-workers, is allowing emotions to guide their behaviour, as it is ignited by the heuristic in their mind that this employee has been messing around previously, so they are led to think it's happening again. These emotions may be triggered by deeply rooted anxiety regarding an upcoming conference call with their boss to discuss negative financial results; or they may be angry over the fight with their partner at home, or maybe they're just simply a terrible person. Becoming aware of our darkest aspects that obstruct the way for light to pass, can be very liberating and healing, even for the most terrible of humans.

The Butterfly Effect

My desire is to bring attention to the importance of understanding social psychology, because I see how beneficial it has been in my life, and how beneficial it can be to you, and the whole world! Theories of psychological knowledge are so simple, and so compelling and life changing that they need not be hiding in scholarly articles and just "preached to the choir" of academics. It even appears that the public officials don't even bother utilizing this science to better balance out our society. During my studies, I couldn't stop wondering why I hadn't heard these basic concepts of the human mind throughout the many years of my schooling. Even by growing up in two different cultures, countries, and even continents, I thought I had a pretty good idea of myself, the world, and myself in the world—but boy, was I ever wrong! That is why I had to create this book! I was way too eager to share this knowledge and its processes with the world, with those who are guided and ready to elevate, who will pass it forward to others. Each one, teach one. When I first started learning about all of these social theories, and noticing so many misconceptions I used to hold regarding so many things in life, I realized that I was literally living in the dark. Despite being deeply interested in politics since my teenage days—college education, always being around very diverse people, and gaining experience from growing up on two sides of the planet—I had to pull back all my knowledge and now try to fit it into this psychological mould. Gladly, all of this was followed by this super liberating feeling of finally getting over a huge obstacle, or solving a puzzle, and moving on to the next level.

I bet that you share my desire for the world to be one where people are more inclined to understand others, rather than make judgements based on their own automatic perceptions. Also, if people understand themselves and behave more consciously, it can potentially reduce many personal imbalances, such as depression, aggression, social inhibitions, and criminal activity, while increasing the quality of life for everyone. Many acts of aggression spiral from the perpetrator's frustration with being misunderstood, and not being able to manage their own inner processes because of their lack of awareness of them. Such awareness has the power to diminish many of the crises we experience personally, as well as collectively.

One specific true story really made me realize how important it is to get this knowledge out of the university books and into the minds of all people, because it can literally save lives. It is the story of a young woman who was fatally attacked by a man outside of her New York apartment a few decades ago. This case became so controversial because there were many witnesses to her attack; people stood by and watched but no one helped. This is what sparked the research into the concept of **altruism**, a concept that refers to the goodwill of humans.

It is often mentioned in conversations that people are just evil, which may be based on the stories about people walking by someone lying on the ground and not stopping to check what happened. What you must keep in mind is that being in groups affects people's behaviour in various ways that you may not even expect. When learning how to predict people's behaviour, keep in mind to consider the context they are in. **Bystander effect** takes place when people are placed within a crowd; they tend to look at the reaction of others around them first, and assume that someone else is more qualified to help. All of these things delay getting help, because of the mental shock and attempt to make sense of the situation, while looking around for others to act, which prevents people from acting fast enough. This tendency is called the ***diffusion of responsibility***. In an extreme case of needing help from a crowd of people, the best way to get someone to help is to point to a specific person from that crowd, and ask them directly for help or to call emergency, if the situation permits. How awesome would it be if more people knew what's best to do in case of a big emergency, as well as the numerous mini emergencies or dilemmas of daily life that require the right decision? Knowledge of various mental processes will stick in your mind, and later will provide you with a higher chance of quicker decision making if you're placed in a sudden situation.

There are studies that prove this as well. Beaman and colleagues put together a study where they assigned random participants into two groups. One group was told to listen to a lecture about bystander intervention, which talked about how people tend to react in an unclear situation. The second group was to listen to a lecture about something unrelated. The study required the participants to come back two weeks later to take part in what they thought was another unrelated study. There, they encountered a student lying on the ground, and it was unclear to them whether he was hurt, fell, or was so tired that he fell asleep—they had no idea. When the researchers examined this situation later, they found that 25% of the participants that heard the unrelated lecture, stopped and helped the student; and 43% of the ones who had heard the "bystander intervention lecture," stopped to help.[19]

I will reveal more of such group behaviour theories further in this book, but what this simple study reveals is the critical need to educate people about social-psychological knowledge, so its value can be put into action while making our world a better place, one mind at a time.

Order Out of Chaos

There are things about the human mind that can easily shatter what is left of our positive view of humanity. Though, if you keep in mind that knowledge of self can set you free, you will be able to use it to your advantage rather than despair.

I realized, after reviewing lots of social research, that humans are quite inaccurate in their assumptions, and are unaware of true reality most of the time. We absorb, hold, and perpetrate numerous misconceptions. And you may be shocked that common sense—that glorious thing that many people call upon—is not all that accurate after all. In one of my first psychology courses, the professor said that the most important tip for new social psychology students is to never assume that we know the answer to a question, and that we must throw what we consider to be common sense, right out the window. That is why, usually, there are in-depth experiments done to test every hypothesis to see if it's actually true or just a myth. The professor highlighted that we cannot pass an exam without studying for it, because many people are convinced that human behaviour, thoughts, or feelings are common sense, but often it turns out that the truth is twisted and your assumption can be far from it.

The famous fictional character, George Costanza, from the TV show *Seinfeld,* said in one of the popular episodes, that if everything that he normally does seems to go wrong, then he will start doing the opposite of what he would normally do, to get better results in his interactions with other people. (I can just see Seinfeld fans laughing as they recall this skit. It's pretty funny. I have linked it on the website, so check it out!)[20] There is a profound ancient text taken from *The Egyptian Book of the Dead: The Book of Coming Forth by Day,* by Muata Ashby, and it says, "Never forget, the words are not the reality, only reality is reality; picture symbols are the idea, words are confusion."[21] It may be deep, but take a moment to meditate on the meaning of this ancient message. Then take a deep breath, clear your mind, and rush over to the next chapter to find out about the surprising, and not so surprising, effects of your environment on your life!

CHAPTER 2

POWER OF YOUR ENVIRONMENT

*"The simple act of paying attention
can take you a long way."*

– Keanu Reeves

2

Since You Were Born

To understand and predict the behaviour, thoughts, or feelings of those you come in contact with, as well as your own, try to look through the lens of ***socialization***, which refers to the process of people learning and internalizing the norms of a culture that they have been engaged with for a longer period of time. It integrates the individual into a particular society or group. It's not to be confused with the term "socializing," which is simply the act of communicating with others, or "enculturation," which focuses on acquiring cultural traits. Socialization is the reason why we can do basic things like waving hello, eating with utensils, or folding clean clothes, as well as bigger things like getting married, or moving over to the side of the road when driving, for emergency vehicles to pass. You learn all of this from sources outside of yourself that are present in your environment—from parents, or anyone you encountered in your life—directly or indirectly. When you start a new job, you will likely even try to speed up the process of socialization into that workplace, because you may not want to feel like an outsider, or make mistakes by not knowing the rules.

The study of **social psychology**, which helps us understand how people are affected by the presence of others, is buddies with the study of **sociology,** which helps us understand how societal structures affect people. Basically speaking, in order to know how humans operate, we can't ignore the effects of external things. In his article about **socialization** in adolescence, L. Steinberg breaks down socialized knowledge into three basic things. He talks about it in relation to the adolescent life stage, but I think it can help us understand the basics of socialization as it relates to all of us, at any age. First, according to Steinberg, we must consider to what extent adolescents are influenced by different agents of socialization, such as the family or peer group; second, which aspects of adolescent development (e.g., school performance, drug use, prosocial behaviour) are most influenced by these various socialization agents; and finally, which of their characteristics (e.g., age, gender, upbringing) make them more or less susceptible to different sources of influence.[22]

Next time you happen to wonder why some people just don't click together, or why someone is behaving in a way that seems strange to you or others (but to that person, it seems normal), remember to think back to the concept of socialization. How did this person's upbringing, family, culture, peer group, or maybe even a past life, contribute to their current behaviour? I once had a coaching client who was a big subscriber of the idea that you should enjoy life while you can, and didn't mind spending money on fun things such as trips.

He came from a family of business owners, and he learned how to make money as well as how to spend it. He was becoming unhappy with his wife because she had a different approach to money; she came from an upbringing where money was treated in a conservative manner, and every extra penny was saved for a rainy day. She typically wanted to stay home and relax, while he wanted to travel the world. The couple didn't consider and discuss important factors of their individual socialization when they decided to get married, which seemed to show up as clashing personality traits, or incompatible lifestyle goals.

Paying attention to the effects of socialization on others will improve your social relations with them. It will give you a chance to modify things accordingly, and to make more informed decisions. To be able to figure out what a specific person likes, how they think, or how they will behave in some situations, you have to try to understand where they are coming from, and where they are heading. No one is spared from socialization; your experiences in the world, program your mind from the beginning. I call it the "Tarzan Effect." I assume that you are familiar with this story character, who was raised by jungle animals from a very young age, and in turn became socialized into their ways of life. When he finally encountered humans for the first time, their behaviour was strange to him, and he didn't have much in common with them besides appearance. We are all Tarzans in our own reality, shaped by the environmental stimuli that we happen to be around. But it doesn't have to hold you captive; under free will, you actually have agency over your own socialization, and can choose the environment that speaks to your soul.

There are people who place much emphasis on the power of genes, who often set aside the concept of environmental effects on the psychology of a human. The medical field most often represents a school of thought that analyzes human behaviour by focusing primarily on the biology of the brain; although the biology bubble bursts when you examine the numerous studies, which prove that your current genetics are affected by all kinds of environmental factors that not just you but even your ancestors were exposed to. I see it as a mutual relationship of genetics and environmental conditioning—two factors affecting each other, stuck in a constant back-and-forth cycle. Just look at the adaptation of species to their environment; you will see that they tend to change through time. Change has been an ongoing process that stems from our need for survival.

A *BioNews* article describes **epigenetic processes** as the chemical processes that can be influenced by environmental factors to switch genes on or to switch them off.[23] Environmental factors that can cause changes in how genes express themselves "may occur in the womb or in the outside world. They could include psychosocial influences as well as exposure to food, drugs, and toxins." A study done by Joslin Diabetes Center, along with the University of Cambridge, also agrees that **epigenetic** effects are passed down from generation to generation.[24] In another *BioNews* article, Dr. Aarathi Prasad talks about various findings in this new field of study, which has benefitted from recent technological advancements, and reiterates the observations of other researchers who found that DNA differences are visible in adults in relation to prenatal starvation, childhood abuse, and childhood socioeconomic circumstances, and may be transmitted through families over several generations. She also mentions other strange findings where "the age at which a man starts smoking affects the birth weight and early growth of his sons—an effect not correlated to maternal smoking. The earlier a father starts smoking, the larger the body mass index (BMI) of his future sons. However, there was no significant effect in daughters."[25] Many psychological disorders have their connection to epigenetic effects as well, but the topic is still in the fresh stages of being explored.

You literally absorb your surroundings on many levels. Next time you travel to another country that is much different from your own, you will notice a contrast. Try to then think about how you would have turned out if you had grown up in that country. Think about how many beliefs, habits, and behaviours you have picked up from the culture you spend most of your life in. If you were born somewhere else in the world, would you still like the same things? Believe the same beliefs? Dress the way you dress?

I recently travelled to beautiful Rome, Italy. I have been living in Canada for many years, and I've also spent lots of time in

Poland, where I was born. What particularly impressed me about Rome was the genuine friendliness radiating from the people on the streets and in businesses, to a much higher extent than in Poland or Canada. Just by walking around the old town on a hot August evening, without much effort, I chatted with numerous strangers, who just said hello, just like that, out of nowhere. People seemed less apprehensive towards starting conversations with just about anyone, as compared to the other two countries, where coming in contact with random strangers noticeably emanates much less warmth. What's interesting is that both Poland and Canada are often rated quite high on the scale of street safety, as well as friendliness of the general society, but there is much less spontaneity and overall positive energy personally felt from people, when compared to a country like Italy. Maybe it's the effect of the sun, as warmer places seem to affect the personality of the people residing in them, in a much different way than colder ones. So now imagine the children who grow up in a socially colourful environment, like the example of Italy, where they will be exposed to lots of attention from their highly social family, friends, and neighbours. Such socialization will likely result in more highly developed communication skills and an extrovert personality. Now, if they move to a country like Canada, and live in more secluded suburbs—where they barely know who their neighbours are—their children, or their children's children, will become more shaped by this new environment to some degree, and may lose that trait over time. As *The National Association for the Education of Young Children* states in their article, "Of all that brain science has taught us over the last 30 years, one of the clearest findings is that early brain development is directly influenced by babies' day-to-day interactions with their care-givers."[26] We could get more into the biological effects of the environment over generational time frames, but I think you get the basic idea that the environment and genetics are in a very tight relationship, and need to be considered together. Further in this book, we will get into more detail about the importance of a child's environment on their romantic relationships later in life.

Objects in the Mirror

What you see in the mirror is not always a true reflection of reality. You may look in the mirror on two different days, or in two different change rooms while trying on clothes, and feel good about your appearance in one setting, and then feel bad in the next, depending on many things, such as the outfit you're wearing, the lighting, the type of mirror, or the emotions you're feeling. So if you can't stay consistent with the description of your own self, then imagine how many variations of perspectives can be expected from other people!

Try to recall a time when two or more people looked at the same object, or have witnessed the same situation, but they each described it totally differently. Of course, it's a no-brainer that two very different people, such as you and your mother for example, may describe the same outfit in opposing ways, looking at it from the perspectives of someone older and younger, or who grew up in a different culture, possibly. Or let's take speed, for example: When I drive with my mother in my car, despite going the speed limit, she always comments that I'm going too fast. There are many cognitive biases that can affect a person's memory, and people can deliberately or unknowingly convince themselves of something that didn't exactly happen that way. My mother can convince herself that I was going too fast just because she worries about my safety, and that worry will strive to convince her, to convince me, to drive really, really slow just in case. It may also be the case that drivers are used to the feeling of being in control of the car, and switching to the passenger seat can feel much different, as you're no longer feeling that sense of control coming from your own foot being on the pedal, and it may exaggerate your perception of speed.

Biases can have really serious implications when someone's well-being is hanging on a thin string of someone else's perception. There are way too many criminal cases where various witnesses later describe the situation differently than what it really was. Brandon Garrett writes in his book, *Convicting the Innocent: Where Criminal Prosecutions Go Wrong*, that faulty eyewitness testimony has been implicated in at least 75% of DNA exoneration cases, and that is more than any other cause![27] Why do you think this happens? What are the factors that shape the way people perceive and interpret things? Why do we see something not as it plainly is, but through a filter made up of the information you picked up along the way, from the path filled with your personal life experiences? How you see something is unique to you because only you have seen, felt, and internalized the numerous things you've encountered. Knowing this pattern gives you power to be able to recognize your own biases and work on them, so they don't skew your vision.

Social interpretation draws on the associations from the past, or the feelings of the interpreter, and can sometimes result in serious outcomes. Many years ago, Thomas and Thomas wrote in their book what became **Thomas theorem**, stating that "if men define situations as real, they are real in their consequences."[28] People tend to assume a position on a situation, from their own point of view, and very often there is a large discrepancy between how the actor and observer see the same situation from each of their own points of view. The authors write that an example of child behaviour, when being examined by therapists, should include the child's own account of the situation, as well as the account of the parents and teachers, and be verified by unrelated investigators in order to be able to define the situation as close to reality as possible.

The long awaited legalization of cannabis has recently shaken the governments of the world, causing them to finally accept the will of the majority, and recognize the wide range of benefits it brings to people and the economy. But the definition of cannabis that was spread throughout many societies, was unfortunately negative, and it provided a guidance for social norms and written laws. Many things influenced that narrative, one of the major players being the popular media, which often associates cannabis with things like extreme partying, low social status, or even the mighty devil, as we have heard that this is a plant with roots in hell, in some old public service advertisements. Now just imagine a court trial where a person is in trouble for possessing cannabis, and someone who comes from a stricter belief system happens to be the judge. That judge's decision may likely be somewhat influenced by their own definition of this situation, and it may result in a harsher sentence. Such a narrative has sent millions of people to jail for simple possession of a few green leaves, exposing them to great dangers of the prison system, as well as a hard reality of living with a criminal record.

The world is changing fast! Just a few years ago, I would have never expected to see marijuana being produced by huge companies that are traded on the stock market! What is especially interesting is that many older people, who we would assume were against it, are becoming accustomed to it after legalization came to pass. Statistics Canada states that cannabis consumption among seniors has been accelerating at a much faster pace than it has among other age groups.[29] Maybe people just didn't want to be seen as doing something that was labelled as illegal, and all this time it was just assumed that they were against it. That's a question of group conformity—a group behaviour concept that we will talk about later on!

Maintaining a state of **objectivity** has always been very challenging for us humans because it requires seeing things from all possible viewpoints. When a person has trouble considering more than one viewpoint, it is representative of the capacity of a young child who hasn't yet fully developed an ability to step into another person's shoes. In other words, anyone who refuses (or simply isn't able) to consider the position of others is acting in an under-developed manner, equal to a child under the age of 6—except a child has a good excuse. There is a study designed by a famous developmental psychologist, Jean Piaget, called "The Three Mountain Task." Children of various ages were seated at a table with a model of three mountains. A doll was seated across from the child, and the child was asked to describe what the doll sees. The purpose of the study was to determine at what age children are able to see a situation from the perspective of another. They found that up to age 6, children take an **egocentric perspective**, meaning they only can imagine what they themselves feel or see. There actually is a bit of an excuse for those adults who tend to be low on this noble ability, and that excuse is based in our human design intended to make us energy efficient, which we already talked about earlier when describing schemas. If you had to think deeply about every single thing you encounter all day, that is not mentally efficient, and it would take you forever to process all bits of incoming information. Looking from all possible viewpoints would require your mind to take a hike up and around the whole mountain each time you are prompted to assess other people, situations, or things. In our busy and distracted lifestyles, that is not easy to do... unless you train your mind.

Power of the Situation

The **context** of situations is a simple thing that gets misused, thanks to your autopilot's efforts to conserve fuel. When judging the actions of other people, when defining the situation, we usually give more weight to the personal dispositions first, before we consider the **situational (environmental) factors**, located outside of that person, which could have played a role in their behaviour. Daily interactions with other people force you to constantly make **attributions** about them, or in other words, make judgements. How is it that people come to explain the behaviour of others, and how do they explain their own?

If you have brothers or sisters, you may remember situations when you both did something bad, and they blamed you while making excuses for themselves. It may be the one trait most people never really grow out of. It often happens that a parent will come in and make **internal attributions** towards the perceived troublemaker, telling them that they're clumsy or irresponsible, often without checking what really went on. Internal attribution is when you see someone's behaviour as their own fault, as something to do with their internal flaws.

WHO PUT THIS POLE HERE ?!

KEEP YOUR EGO PROTECTED WITH A CALMING DOSE OF EXTERNAL ATTRIBUTION.

External attribution is when you refer to a person's behaviour as being caused by something outside of the person's control, which may not be visible or obvious. Most people excuse their own behaviour with external attributions, pinning the blame on something else that caused their situation. Researchers Mirowsky and Ross, who study the psychology of human sense of control, confirmed what is actually quite obvious: that people often claim responsibility for good outcomes, and deny responsibility for bad ones. They also suggest that it's not a healthy thing to do, as it may affect their psychological well-being.[30] This finding adds to the notion that humans are a bit self-centred. On the contrary, it is not good to keep blaming yourself either; this is one of those tricky parts to learning our human lessons: You must master the balance of solution-focused constructive criticism, towards yourself and towards others, rather than falling into the dark depths of victim mentality. When you admit to yourself that you made a mistake, you will give yourself a chance to learn from it while clearing up your further path.

I am reminded of a good example of **attribution theory** from my experience while managing luxury cosmetics brands located in shopping centres. When the particular location was lacking customer traffic, the management very often blamed the sales-floor employees for lack of productivity that day, and even began to question their work ethic, suggesting that they were not doing their jobs. Special meetings, individual performance reviews, and task sheets to hand in at the end of the shift, just like school children, became implemented, beating into the minds of the employees that they themselves must do more to sell more. In turn, the leaders didn't have any innovative business-oriented strategies of their own, such as coming up with new marketing ideas.

The baffled employees continuously dreaded expressing their external attribution to their management, which seemed to them as a legitimate argument because there was simply no one to sell to, and they were not responsible for going outside of the store and soliciting customers off the street to come in. Management continued to harass the sales crew to sell, sell, sell, even if it meant selling to ghosts. In the managers' excuse, if we were to apply the external attribution approach, we would then have to recognize that they are often under a lot of pressure from their own bosses, so their automatic re-action in this case was to move the blame onto their employ-ees' internal dispositions, away from their own lack of imagination, motivation, or skill. Isn't it interesting how peo-ple are able to put in the effort of considering the power of the situation for their own benefit, but find it harder to do the same when referring to others?

Consideration of the situational factors gets even more im-portant when there are less visible parts of a story hiding un-derneath the surface, away from your perception. Police officers are expected to be very careful not to make assump-tions about an incident, and gather all available points of view for their investigation. After a car accident, they have to con-sider everything: if the driver was messing around with his phone, or was drowsy, impaired, or sick; or something hap-pened to the car, or affected the road. What if the police would use the same automatic process as the above-men-tioned managers, and just make internal attributions about the person to assess what happened at the accident? Officers are not exempt from their human processes, and don't re-ceive enough psychological training to counter that, but the system of procedures that they follow is in place to make sure they get as close to the truth as possible.

In our daily lives, we go around throwing judgements around many times in a day, often without actually thinking if what we said or thought was actually accurate. When someone is driving super slowly in front of you, do you automatically think to yourself, "What a terrible driver," or do you think, "I wonder what is causing that person to go so slow?" And then you look inside their car and see an elderly person who is so focused on being careful that they forgot about keeping up with the expected speed. Our world has become a bit more understanding; we attempt fair trials rather than burning people at the stake in the city centre, for mixing herbs or dancing under the full moon, like some time ago. This still happens today, just in different ways. Many times, I see naturopathic doctors be ridiculed in the mainstream medical world, and it makes me sad, because a naturopathic doctor actually saved my life—I wish those who take part in this bullying would objectively consider various standpoints, rather than pass simple judgement. Without putting some effort into considering the depth of a situation, you fall into the dark trap of ignorance. People of our modern societies consider themselves as highly civilized, but the thought mechanisms we enact every day are still quite primitive.

Situation changes everything, and yet it's the thing people either try to purposefully escape, forget about, or just don't have the mind capacity to comprehend without being prompted by others. How often do you go through some degree of investigation before you make an assumption about a person or situation? It's beneficial to put on these invisible attribution-balancing glasses and penetrate through the layers of what appears before you, so you can avoid creating a negative vibe, or even make the wrong call in a crucial situation. Automatic assumptions can also cost you valuable accuracy, and make you seem closed minded or ignorant in a social setting.

Your Feelings Colour Your World

Situational factors such as **mood** are also a huge determinant of whether you will perceive something more positively or more negatively. There are skilled persuaders among us who are capable of priming the situation in a way that will be conducive to their agenda. Scott Adams, the cartoonist who created *Dilbert* comics, who is also into the study of persuasion, writes in his book that "pre-suading, or setting the table, is about creating mental and emotional associations that carry over. If you get the mood right, and your credibility is high, you're halfway done with your persuasion before anyone knows you started."[31]

Creating a setting that elevates the mood is a tactic often used by clever businesses who understand the importance of making their guests feel good. When positive mood is induced in a store or an office, clients are likely to leave positive reviews, and be more agreeable. Many studies have shown that people will suspend their caution when they are in a happy mood, and therefore spend more. Some businesses, such as spas and hotels, play soothing music in the background, and have a nice fragrance in the air. If you are a real estate agent, consider bringing a flavourful scent into the property you are about to show, something warm and sweet, to make the property feel like home. The pleasure of a pleasant scent may reduce any feelings of tension or nervousness within. Such seemingly insignificant things can really make a big impact and increase your success rate.

One of the most detrimental things a business can do, in my opinion, is to keep a television screen switched to the news channel, like we often see in waiting rooms or even restaurants. The news channels thrive on emphasizing negative stories, which can quickly ruin the moods of their clients, whose unconscious minds will associate that business with a negative feeling, even if they received a decent service. Recently, I was at a dentist's office, and they had the news on, not just in the waiting room but also in the procedure room. One of the people in the waiting room couldn't resist making a rude comment about a politician who appeared on the screen, which caused others to give her a dirty look. What if that sparked an argument in the waiting room? To avoid such things, make sure you eliminate the negatives and replace them with positives—you can't go wrong with that. I actually suggested to the office personnel that the news may not be an ideal channel, especially at a place like a dentist's office, a place associated with pain, where most people arrive already stressed to some degree. Putting on the news channel in that context is like pouring gas onto a flame. As a social psychologist, I couldn't help but ponder these facts as I was sitting in the dentist chair, waiting for my not so pleasant procedure, having no choice but to look at the news on the screen, which insisted on showing me crime and bloodshed. Your business should take the well-being of your clients seriously, and provide a bit of an escape from daily life so that they will gladly want to come back. This can also be said about the employees who have to be distracted from their work, with negative news for hours. They often say that they tune it out, but that's just what they tell themselves. If you know anything about the unconscious mind, you know it's a "quick picker upper," like the Bounty paper towels.

Television can be used to create a positive effect as well. I have learned a valuable trick from the famous author and success coach, Jack Canfield, during our interaction at an event in Toronto. He came up with a brilliant idea, which helped a particular business successfully motivate their team of employees to reach their sales quota, and win a vacation. Jack saw that they had a few TV screens scattered around the hallways and lunchrooms of the company building. He instructed the managers to strictly use those TVs to play videos featuring that particular travel destination throughout the day. This served as a reminder to the employees to focus on their goal and recharge their energy with a positive vision of themselves on that beach, which provided a sub-conscious reinforcement of that desired outcome to their brain. They did in fact succeed in reaching their goal, because the motivation to do so increased, causing them to get more creative and active at work. The positive affirmations radiating from these televisions most definitely served their purpose. We will go deeper into the topic of luck, in the last chapters—and I know you're going to make it to the end, because why not be part of the statistical bracket among the very few special people who tend to finish the whole book they set out to read?!

Just like socialization factors, emotions also have a significant influence on your ***memory***. Have you ever been to a dance club, or some other fun social location, with a friend, and you happened to attract attention from some good-looking guy or girl? Unfortunately, your friend didn't seem to be having much luck, and if that wasn't enough, a drink spilled on their new shoes. Later on, when you both meet up with a third friend, who asks you both about your opinion of the club, you both may describe the whole thing in a completely different light. You may say that it was so much fun, and your friend may contradict you and say that the club actually wasn't that good. The third friend will definitely wonder why one of you liked the club experience, and the other didn't. They may assume that the person who didn't like the club has a reason for this negative memory attached to it; possibly because of their disappointment in not meeting anyone, unlike their friend.

Scientists who studied emotions and memory, have found that situations you experience become associated with emotions, and then get stored as memories in your brain. But the interesting thing is that the memory apparently is not stored as a whole. Susumu Tonegawa, one of the authors of the study, explains that the info from the physical location where a situation takes place (such as the club), gets stored in the area of the brain called the **hippocampus**. The emotional part gets stored separately, in the part of the brain called the **amygdala**.[32] So, experience + emotion = memory. When the memory is recalled, the two have to be matched up again. Gladly, nature often gives us an opportunity to take control in shaping our reality when things may not be going so great, providing ways of undoing damage, and balancing the imbalance, and so this study also found that there is a possibility to fix the negative contextual memory by re-associating it with something positive.

The brain region responsible for your emotions, the **amygdala**, is overactive and enlarged in people who are prone to aggressive behaviour (explained in the further chapter about aggression). This brain region can be literally altered by continuous negative emotions that are often linked to unpleasant memories. A therapy such as meditation has the ability to repair that imbalance, with the focus on replacing unpleasant memories with pleasant ones, through affirmations, which will slowly start reshaping the brain back to its balanced state.

All of these findings boil down to emotions literally colouring your world, as well as affecting the world around you. They have lasting effects that are powerful enough to imprint biological changes in your physical body. Unmanaged, and left purposefully forgotten within the dark corners of your mind, suppressed and negative feelings, emotions, and memories can contribute to harmful behaviours—harmful to yourself or others, directly or indirectly. Unnecessary or harmful behaviours that explode out of unbalanced emotions, are something that most people later regret. When a parent yells at their child, for no other reason than being tired from working too hard, it can later result in feelings of guilt in that parent. Regret or guilt can remain in the memory for a long time, and many people struggle with such thoughts of regret stashed somewhere within their being, without ever bringing them to the surface.

The Psychology of Homes

It sometimes occurs to me that, really and truly, every single thing around us—every person, animal, thing, space, and place—is influencing our human psychology. Such is the process of life. I'm about to present you with a concept that is often overlooked in conversations about the well-being of our society, but it has been a major part of societies since the very beginning. That is the psychology of the buildings in our lives, especially our homes, which are the objects of our aspirations and dreams, and serve as reflections of our entire lives. Sometimes they're just a roof over our heads, and to some people, they're also something highly unachievable. Buildings are a reflection of human adaptation to the constant motion of social change. It has never occurred to me that buildings have significant influence over our lives and our interactions with others. Their inner and outer structure and design, as well as the streets, parks, and other physical structures, are something we must move through daily, and everything about their qualities shapes us, just as much as we shape them.

Being from one of the top tourist cities in Europe—Wroclaw—I have learned the value of art, colour, and fanciness of old European architecture, and the positive psychological effects it brings to the residents and visitors. One major factor in this result was the famous Wroclaw dwarfs. They are these cute little dwarf statues made of bronze by a local artist. They started appearing mounted into the ground or other objects all around the city centre. They are adored by kids, and tourists, because they can have fun following the dwarf map and try to find each one of them. The city was awarded the title of European Capital of Culture in 2016. The city has been lucky to have mayors who really made aesthetics a priority. It created a positive atmosphere for residents, and brought in increased tourism. Toronto has an area called the Kensington Market, which was not meant to look classy but rather extremely artsy, with an overload of funky elements scattered everywhere as they decorated artisan shops and unique restaurants. It's one of those areas that enchants the city's visitors as well as residents, and it should be treasured. Though, in an honest critique, I must say that many Canadian and American leaders can learn a thing or two when it comes to city aesthetics and the integration of art, culture, history, nature, standards of cleanliness, and most importantly, child-friendly public spaces into the daily experience. Especially important outside of the downtown area, in places where people live their family lives. Lately, with the events of the year 2020 and the destruction it is leaving behind, the downtown area of a city like Toronto has filled up with tents of the homeless. The epidemic of substance addiction and poverty is filling the void that aesthetics didn't get to fill. Outrageous rent prices have chased out many of the cutest shops, many of which have been icons in the local culture for a long time. Outside of the core, instead of colourful playgrounds and gardens, what bloomed was gangs full of kids whose only option for outdoor activity was a dirty parking lot of a nearby plaza. Instead of modern colour schemes adorning new and old buildings, you have all shades of ugly red brick which haven't been updated for decades as it irritates the eyes of residents each day they must pass it, as they try to block it out of their focus. In Poland, red brick is usually associated with jails.

Unfortunately, it has taken too long. We do not need science to tell us that surroundings, which are created with a touch of care, can surely socialize their inhabitants into a higher level of well-being, as compared to plain ones that lack character or are visibly unattended to. People pay big money to travel to places that are aesthetically attractive, for the reason that such places nourish our inner spirit that is hungry for beauty.

Lack of care attended to physical properties and their surroundings, seems to further perpetuate negativity. When something is already broken, it seems natural to not care for it as much—kind of like when you decide to paint your room; you will likely wear some old clothes that are already a bit ruined. It is something that goes on within that mysterious unconscious of ours. There was a popular study done years ago, which wanted to test how people will react to damaged objects in their neighbourhoods, with the intention to prove that property that is uncared for eventually gets destroyed even more, regardless of the demographic that lives there, whether it's a poor neighbourhood or rich, inhabited by a certain group of people versus another group, etc. Could it be that a dirty basket can spoil the apples within it? Philip Zimbardo, a Stanford psychologist, tested what he called **the broken-window theory,** through his own field experiments. He placed a car with a broken window, on the side of the street in two varying classes of neighbourhoods, and found that in both of them, the residents looted that car even more. James Q. Wilson and George L. Kelling later wrote an article called "The Police and Neighbourhood Safety: Broken Windows," to communicate to the governing forces the importance of maintaining the quality of neighbourhoods on all levels, rather than just treating the major issues that arise from lack of maintenance.[33] They wrote that "social psychologists and police officers tend to agree that if a window in a building is broken and is left unrepaired, all the rest of the windows will soon be broken. This is as true in nice neighbourhoods as in run-down ones ... one unrepaired broken window is a signal that no one cares, and so breaking more windows costs nothing."

As we are on the topic of communication in this book, it's important to note that this particular research has a bit of an unfortunate controversy attached to it, because it was utilized by the mayor of New York at the time, Rudy Guiliani, but apparently misinterpreted by the police departments, who took it as a suggestion to crank up their efforts in the criminalization of minor issues in the city's neighbourhoods, such as selling loose cigarettes or loitering. They interpreted this theory with the idea that if you take care of small misdemeanours, it will prevent major crime, because it is likely the same people involved in both. They seemed to ignore the suggestions of the original study, and Wilson and Kelling's paper, which seemed to encourage combatting crime in a positive way, by things like making living spaces a bit more pleasant. It's unfortunate that such sociological findings were misused, instead of being focused on repairing the quality of life, uplifting the aesthetics of the run-down areas of the city, as well as fostering positive relationships between the representatives of the law and the citizens in these communities.

Do we shape buildings, or do buildings shape us? It's likely both. Let's go a bit deeper and examine how buildings can regulate human interactions by influencing how we move throughout them. **Architecture** provides a system of passages through which you move about in your daily life. No matter where you may live in the world, there are buildings that you and others use for various purposes, and there are roads leading to them, as well as physical and social barriers around and within them, which are set up to regulate access.

This spatial system is built through the continuous interactions among its users and the natural world around them. It is a reflection of cultural and social trends of the time and place in which they happen to reside.

Some homes have been around for generations and have been slowly transformed, or left in their original state by various inhabitants who continue to make them their personal castle. Imagine your, or someone else's, family home, for example. In a modern society, chances are that most kitchens you encounter are attached to the dining room, which makes it easy to move food from the kitchen to the dining room table. In the olden days, the kitchen and living room were one and the same general living space for people of the lower class, as it provided warmth in the cold days, and a possibility for a mother to cook and watch the kids at the same time because they did not have caretakers. The upper classes often enjoyed a separate kitchen, away from the guest and family rooms, with maids and cooks who worked there and lived in special rooms close by. When electrical power became more widely available, it became more common for people to utilize more rooms in their homes. For upper classes, living rooms were often maintained just for visitors. If you're older, you may recall some really picky family members covering their living room furniture with plastic or sheets, and only using that room to show off to their guests. Children were definitely not allowed to play there.

As time goes on, human interactions with each other, and with the material structures in their lives, continues to change. Lately, in a regular family home, we see that visits don't happen as often as they used to back in the day, so the living room became a place for the family to just chill out and engage in television programming. The bedrooms placed upstairs give members of the family some privacy. Having rooms on the higher floor serves to hide objects like beds, clothing, and personal items from the eyes of visitors hosted downstairs.

Whether there are visitors or not, walls serve as a means of communication on many levels. It was David Halle who studied how people communicate their culture, beliefs, values, or desires to others, by what they choose to put on their walls. His research involved examining 160 homes located in various neighbourhoods of New York City, all of which he has documented in his book, *Inside Culture – Art and Class in the American Home*.[34] This strange but extremely interesting study tries to make sense of what represents modern North American culture, by looking at what drives people to choose the types of items they wish to display in their private spaces. Among numerous observations, the differences in social status and choice of art were quite apparent. The white upper-middle classes seemed to have a taste for abstract and exotic art, while the working class Catholics displayed religious icons and family photos. If you thought that the dominant higher classes have a special interest in high arts, you may be surprised that the author didn't find enough evidence to support that popular theory, and he states in his book that in both America and France, "it is true that survey data we have, shows that dominant classes are more likely than subordinate classes to participate in high culture, and items of high culture do not in fact appear of great interest to most of the dominant classes." Often, expensive and exclusive participation in high arts seems to only appeal to a minority within the high status groups.

Higher status does seem to have a connection to the desire for privacy, and in most modern neighbourhoods, this desire has only increased. The continuous political instability, as well as an overwhelming display of crime in the media, has increased the narratives about the home's role as a fortress, shielding us from the outside threats. This started mainly in Victorian England. In his work on this topic, Mike Hepworth talks about how the middle class created an ideal image of the home, which represented respectability through bordering off the deviant outdoors. The ability to have security measures to block out the outside world was a symbol of morality. He writes that "the moral barricades of the Victorian home were much more than the structural defences of walls and fences, doors, locks, and keys. The defences against deviance extended into the home itself to include ... rules governing standards of conduct in different rooms in the house and relationships between the residents."[35] Because life has moved inside and to the back of the house, behind fences and blinds, away from the view of strangers, the situation worsened for victims of domestic abuse, because their cases were hidden from the view of the community.

In most North American homes, the yard is in the back of the house, and the nicely designed lawn is in the front for display to other people, but not really for any other use. In the past, and in some places still today, people would sit in front of the home and socialize with others in the community. Long ago, and in some close-knit communities today, a backyard party would be seen as impolite because it projects an exclusive vibe, excluding others in the community from joining. A good example of such ideology can be found in the Netherlands, where people don't believe in window coverings—not just to let lots of sunlight into their apartments, but also to show others in the community that they have nothing to hide.

One of my former professors, Lisa-Jo K. van den Scott, spent five years living in Nunavut, the northern part of Canada, where she had the chance to experience what it's like to live in such a remote land, among its people. This experience inspired her decision to do ethnographic research there, which she describes in her work, "Mundane Technology in Non-Western Contexts: Wall-as-Tool."[36] Her study focused on the concept of permanent walls among the Inuit communities, their interactions with such modern technologies, and what consequences such technologies have on their culture. Walls are referred to as "technologies," because they are an invention of modern cultures, which allowed for improvement from the olden-style dwellings with one common space. They serve for separating, creating rooms with special purposes, allowing multiple floors, and more. Lisa writes that "until the early 1960s, a nomadic lifestyle, with ingenious and creative survival-based technology, provided the basis of Inuit culture. They lived in igluit (snow houses), and tupik (caribou-skin tents), according to the season. Once the authorities rounded up the nomadic Inuit and forced them "off the land," into the newly-created town, which persists today, they introduced the Inuit to permanent structures." It has been a challenge for them to adapt to these structures as a true home, because they have been built for them by members of a different culture, according to their own ideas of what a family home looks like.

The Inuit are used to having one large space to hang out in, to cater to the extended family that often live in the same place, or visit often. Since the temperatures can get cold in the northern parts of Canada, it is easier to stay warm by being together in one room. The kitchen is too small and not tailored to accommodate their culinary traditions, so the preparation of food sometimes also gravitates towards the living room, as family members collaborate in the work. Lisa also discovered how the Inuit people like to make use of those walls so that they are not just in the way. Making lemonade out of lemons, many of them decided to use them as storage space for hanging important items and documents that they don't want to lose or damage, as well as for hanging cultural and non-cultural items that mean something special to them, or serve as some reminder. The plan of the house shapes how we conduct our lives, and affects how we behave in a family setting. Or not even necessarily family, as a large number of people (Inuit and others) live with roommates, who are likely strangers, and that situation changes the boundaries between people, applied to their movement throughout that building, but that's another story.

Social Walls

There are physical walls as well as invisible walls, and both make up a maze through which you move about your life among other people. In Professor Lisa's course on the psychology of spaces, I have also discovered the depth of invisible walls between humans, the *social boundaries* and *symbolic boundaries*.

Michele Lamont and Virag Molnar, from Princeton University's sociology department, define social boundaries as "objectified forms of social differences manifested in unequal access to and unequal distribution of resources (material and nonmaterial) and social opportunities." *Symbolic boundaries* are somewhat on a level invisible to the eye, described by these researchers as "conceptual distinctions made by social actors to categorize objects, people, practices, and even time and space. They are tools by which individuals and groups struggle over and come to agree upon definitions of reality." When a majority of the particular group agrees on these symbolic boundaries, they can become social boundaries. For example, one famous political boundary of our times was the Berlin wall, a guarded concrete barrier that physically and ideologically divided Berlin, from 1961 to 1989.[37] The physical wall itself was that social boundary dividing people, and the conflict of ideologies between the residents of both East and West is the symbolic boundary. Even when the wall was destroyed, and freedom was celebrated, it didn't completely destroy the negative perceptions and vibes between the two sides. A *Financial Times* article seems to agree that "today, Germans in East and West not only vote differently, think differently, and feel differently, but those differences seem to be growing more pronounced."[38] Although the time when the wall was taken down was a beautiful display of human unity and love, it was all sparked by a major miscommunication served by one special man, as if it was orchestrated by some divine power. You must read up about this story; it was quite a profound event in world history, to say the least.

Would you ever think that the way buildings are designed can have an effect on how people live their daily lives in each other's company? By looking deeply into the **dynamics of spaces** around us, it can be noticed that even complex things like equality among people, or simple things like the construction of our daily routines and activities, can be shaped by such dynamics. Spaces are created by people, and changed along with their needs, but they also shape and re-shape people's lives in ways that we overlook almost completely. For those who are still a bit confused as to how such a topic is rel-

www.persontopersonbook.com

evant to improving and mastering the art of social interaction, think of it this way: If you want to be a master of your mind, a master of your life, and have greater control over yourself within any environment, you must be in control of that which can control you, or at least be conscious of it. To be in control, you must have an understanding of how the environment affects your thoughts, feelings, and behaviours. You must also have an understanding of how it all also affects other people, to be able to predict and understand their behaviour in a more enlightened way. That is how you will have a greater chance of always being steps ahead. But when you let your autopilot lead you, it is easy to move throughout the buildings and structures in your daily life, without noticing their effects, and without making favourable adjustments, while allowing them to master you instead.

Let's talk about how spaces are distributed among people and use the example of **power divides,** which exist as separators of people in macro-level societal contexts, and also in our micro-level personal contexts. Power divides have a way of managing your movement through common space, and they depend on things that describe you, such as your social status, age, background, gender, and so on. In a micro-level example such as a family setting, the father figure may naturally put his stuff—like accessories or tools—in the shed or in the garage, and that automatically becomes his space within these walls. He naturally assumes that he belongs there the most, and takes over the space, which limits others from freely using it. If the kids play in there, they may get in trouble for making a mess or touching the tools. In this example, the father naturally gravitating towards these spaces is a result of ideas planted in our minds by living in a society that substantially awards authority to an adult figure within the family, as well as suggests to men that their interests should include things like cars and tools.

I am not suggesting that it is wrong for men to have such interests by any means; rather, I'm just pointing to the effects of socialization on our daily life choices, out of the desire for people to be aware of what shapes them, as well as to be aware of how conflicts arise, which could be prevented through such higher understanding. If, for example, a child in that family happened to be a gifted percussion player, and wasn't allowed to place their giant instrument in the garage, the only place in the house where it could fit, that is a power struggle within the family, while both individuals live there and should have rights to that space. However, many people often argue that kids don't pay for the bills, and therefore they have no say in the distribution of family resources.

Probably the most annoying thing to hear, for any child, is the popular "until you live under my roof, you will abide by my rules." I'm not sure if such regime-style communication is an ideal way to motivate a kid towards anything beneficial to them, other than making them want to move out of the home as soon as they are able to, for better or worse. I must challenge that idea, as in my view, a kid's responsibility is not to pay bills, but to do well in school, clean up after themselves, discover their talents, and learn proper social skills. They are doing their jobs, sometimes even better than the adults who are raising them. Some still have to help with housework, provide childcare for younger siblings, and even go out to work at a very young age. Children who live on farms are likely helping around the home from a very young age. Therefore, why should they be so often told that they don't deserve to be treated equally, or to have their desires and opinions valued? Age can serve as a power divide, where the older child gets the bigger room, and no one can just walk in there. In contrast, the younger child often gets the smaller room or has to share it with other younger children. Age creates a power divide because we tend to give more power to those who are older. I am not saying that it is not often a legitimate power because of things like greater skill or more experience. Understandably, kids should not be left with a burden of certain crucial decisions that they don't fully understand. A child's intelligence should not be ignored. I can think of many examples where the simplicity of their thought, and an impressive connection to intuition, enables them to often give correct advice to adults on complicated matters. Check out the linked video![39]

It is important to recognize that some barriers are necessary and make sense to uphold, as they help to reinforce rules and regulations, and maintain social order so an equal chance is given to all people, ideally. There are power divides that exist in public contexts, and as much as we talk about maximizing inclusivity in our society, there are structures in place that have no choice but to be exclusive, kind of like the lock on your door to keep unwanted people out of your home. Let's take an example of a university campus, which has various buildings, wings, and hallways. Some areas, such as the offices of the university officials, are placed away from the regular student traffic, from the daily chaos associated with a busy public space. It is nearly impossible to rub shoulders with the higher officials of that social structure. They are placed away from the common path, sometimes in offices behind a secretary who is positioned as a gatekeeper between the public and the officials. The only way to interact with them is to book an appointment through their gatekeepers, take a number, wait in the line-up, and be invited in. We cannot ignore the fact that very often, such barriers do not serve fairness, and their design creates things like systemic discrimination, which makes it harder for some people than others to access various social services and resources. A research of mine comes to mind, which I conducted to uncover the systemic barriers to Indigenous peoples' access to health care in Canada. This research revealed imbalances in the distribution of funding, which largely goes towards small and un-coordinated focus groups oriented towards health education, which the Indigenous community members themselves say are ineffective, while things like the expensive transportation for them to reach their medical appointments, from remote areas, is overlooked. The gatekeepers, such as single local representatives, are the ones receiving this funding from the government and then re-distributing it where they think it's needed, so they stand in the way of some people getting the right assistance. There are many examples of systemic imbalances that serve as borders between people, and between people and resources.

Architecture affects all kinds of social relationships. Researcher Festinger, and colleagues, investigated how people formed friendships in a new housing complex. They found that physical distance is different from **functional distance**. Someone who is physically more distant but functionally closer may become your friend faster than someone who is physically closer but functionally distant; or in other words, harder to just randomly run into. Their study, mentioned in a *Wikipedia* article, found that for example, "in a two-storey apartment building, people living on the lower floor next to a stairway are functionally closer to upper-floor residents than are others living on the same lower floor. The lower-floor residents near the stairs are more likely than their lower-floor neighbours to befriend those living on the upper floor."[40] So, people may live close but rarely see each other because of the design of the building, or the neighbourhood. As insignificant as they may sound, various spatial boundaries create and reinforce psychological boundaries. Piece by piece, they contribute to the construction of your daily life, and shape your interactions with other people. We will talk more about this concept further in the chapter about romantic relationships.

On a positive note, you possess the freedom and power to choose how you respond to the barriers that exist in your private space, and how they affect your interactions within it. We must also remember that it is possible to penetrate the spaces that may appear blocked off to you, and that can be done through many ways, which will mostly require things like your diplomatic skills, networked connections, persistence, professionalism, or even simple kindness. People can at times resort to more aggressive or violent ways, which is not something typically respectable. Sometimes it's just enough to knock, and it shall be opened unto you. Or as my grandma often told me, "If they throw you out the door, go back through the window." Now, she didn't mean to be forceful, but just to dust yourself off and try again after you've been denied something that you need to accomplish. As you've likely seen in children's stories, there are often trolls guarding the treasure, and they're not always as scary as they may appear; they just ask you to put in some effort into persuading them to let you in. Simply having great communication skills will open many doors, and allow you to walk through many walls, something you will become better at after you're done with this book! Now rush over to the next chapter to find out how you not only learn from your social environment, but also how your deeper self operates within it.

CHAPTER 3

SELF IN THE WORLD

"From mirror after mirror, no vanity's displayed: I'm looking for the face I had before the world was made."

– W.B. Yeats

3

Not Just Diplomats, but Also Actors

Have you ever wanted to be an actress or actor? Well, what's interesting is that you are one, whether you like it or not. You are not just perceiving the world around you and acting out of that perception, but you are also manipulating the perception of other people. We are all actors because we continuously put effort into managing how we appear to others. I can already see all the "real ones" thinking, "I'm not fake; what you see is what you get with me," or, "I am my own person!" But the truth is that you are indeed manipulating how other people receive you, more often than you think.

Consider this super basic example: If you ever had messy hair when you're at home, but styled your hair before you went to meet your friends at a restaurant, you have just engaged in *impression management*. How? A famous social researcher, Erving Goffmann, has connected the concept of theatre performance to our everyday social life, and came up with the *dramaturgical perspective* as a lens through which we can better understand this phenomenon of people acting differently around others than when no one is watching. He saw this world as a stage, and humans as actors whose behaviours change on and off stage. People usually want to be seen in a positive light, or have things in mind they want to achieve, so it's almost inevitable that in any social interaction, there is usually some degree of performance involved. He wrote about his **self-presentation theory** in detail, in his book, *The Presentation of Self in Everyday Life.* This was the first book to describe face-to-face interaction as a sociological study.[41]

People constantly move from ***front stage*** to ***back stage*** as they manage the way they present themselves in various situations. You are standing on your front stage when dealing with the outside world, and back stage when you are in private, protected from the view of others. Front stage is where you try to control the impression that others will receive about you. Back stage is for planning and rehearsing your script, preparing your outfit, relaxing, or taking some alone time, although there may be times when you may be joined by someone else who got a back stage pass. When you want people to see you as a well-maintained and attractive person, you will likely show up with styled hair, or a strategically selected wardrobe, in order to convey that particular message to your audience. When you know that you will be staying at home all day, it is unlikely that you will style your hair, or put on your best outfit.

It's not just about looks, but also about behaviour, manners, choice of words, body language, and much more. When a child wants to go to their friend's house, or eat that third cupcake, they will likely use their cutest voice when asking their parents to allow them. The acting can come in as a leverage to get something, or to avoid getting undesired reactions from others. A couple gets into a major argument in the car (the back stage) while on their way to a friend's birthday celebration at a restaurant. As the curtain goes up, when they walk into the restaurant, they will likely put on nice smiles like nothing happened, in order to save themselves from embarrassment or gossip, or from ruining the mood of the event. That's an example of two people engaging in a mutual agreement to manage their performance as a team.

Goffmann also observed the tendency for people to save face. *Saving face* means that people will often cover for each other's social failures in order to preserve reputation, and spare some embarrassment. Here, that couple has an agreement to not let others see them fight, so they know to stop as they reach the "front stage" position. Saving face also happens without such an agreement. There is an interesting customer behaviour that often happens at the makeup counters, where beauty advisors perform makeup applications. You may assume that someone who works at the makeup counter is a skilled makeup artist, but that is not always the case. It often happens that the client is not happy with the way their makeup turned out, but will not say anything to the employee because they don't want them to feel bad or be embarrassed. I could always tell how someone feels about their service, by their behaviour when paying. When an advisor didn't make them happy, the client would often exhibit this specific nervous smile, and answer in short words rather than full sentences as they do when they're happy, because at the makeup or hair salons, women just can't stop talking when they're feeling content! Yes, there is this strange natural response within many of us that seeks to protect others from disappointment or embarrassment, even if it means being disappointed ourselves. I'm sure you can think of many examples of saving someone's face, or when someone saved yours! If you have a story, I'm curious to hear it. Leave me a comment on my website or under any of my Instagram posts.

The Chameleon Self

There is an old Japanese proverb that says that each person has three faces: one that you show to the world, one that you show to your close ones, and the third face you don't show to anyone. As you move from one interaction to the next, or one context to the next, you manage your behaviour. Most often, it doesn't even take much thought. If you happen to be at a business seminar, you automatically become serious and attentive because it is a context that expects users to adapt to its purpose, which is learning. If you decide to join the other attendees for a drink at the restaurant, after the seminar, you will likely become more relaxed and chatty. In the meantime, you most likely didn't think consciously about that switch in your demeanour; you just simply flowed along with the setting.

Temporarily acting the part is not problematic; it is something that has been part of human daily life for ages. Various scenarios require various types of conduct. Acting with class in a public setting should be a standard for everyone. It will typically score higher social points and help you uphold your inner balance. It will also show respect to others with whom you share this world. Various settings require specific conducts of behaviour, so you must adapt in order to move with the flow of the space and not against it. When you forget to turn off the sound on your phone when at a meeting or presentation, and your phone's cute ringtone starts blasting across the quiet room, and as you nervously dig into your bag to find that beast and shut it off, know that the other people's autopilots are already taking notes, and it can affect how they approach you later. They may not want to take you seriously during networking time, because they may see you as not responsible enough to do business with if you can't remember something as simple as turning off your phone before a meeting. It may seem as something so insignificant—and often it can be an inaccurate judgement—as I'm sure someone like Elon Musk has made such mistakes in his career, which don't have an effect on his image, but it's something to keep in mind, especially if you're desiring to advance in your status or you're just starting out in a career.

There may be situations that can cause you to disguise your true self too much; for example, when you're always nice to someone who has been making it a point that they have an issue with you, but you decide to just take their abuse because you don't want to cause an argument. Some people tend to elude confrontation, and would rather let things go or pretend everything is fine, even for a long time. But it is often necessary to unleash some of your defence energies, and let them know that you find their attitude hurtful. You must strive to master your inner chameleon so that you don't lose yourself in the process when it leads you to suppress your true feelings. I remember, when I moved to Canada, I quickly realized that the elementary school I ended up in had no intention, as a whole, to accept me for who I was. I found out the hard way that my high-end European fashion outfits, with a rock'n'roll flavour, weren't cool enough for this school. I spent all my savings on them to make sure that I went to my new country in style, only to end up being bullied for being different, or for being myself. Not to mention that my lack of English put me in a special class along with the disabled kids, and to be honest, there I could freely breathe.

Like most people, you may assume that others will like you for who you are, and you just have to "be yourself." How often do you come across the popular slogans convincing you to just be yourself? As if life wasn't confusing enough, there are situations where this very popular encouragement is actually not always so helpful. There are many situations where it's better that your spontaneous and bare self takes a seat in the back as you let your professional or classy version of yourself take the stage. Most people are nervous when going to an event such as a job interview, because that's something that doesn't happen very often, and it requires a higher degree of self-monitoring. If you have practiced ahead of this interview, you are much more likely to be less nervous and do well. You can even go as far as maybe asking someone neutral, like a mentor or a coach, to practice with you and honestly point out your flaws, such as correct your choice of vocabulary, body language, or unnecessary habits. It's best to become aware of such things sooner than later. Are you one of the many people who say the word "like" way too often? Such automatic words take over the focus of what you're "like, try-ing to, like, say," and it can easily break the attunement with your audience. What about unconscious body habits, such as swinging your leg back and forth when sitting in a chair, twid-dling your fingers, or biting your nails. Those can also be dis-tracting to your listener, aside from making you seem less self-assured. Something I personally have to watch is to not be too forward, or too casual, when speaking with a potential future boss or business partner. Being too friendly, too talk-ative, or too quiet and laid back from the start, can send an unbalanced energy to the other person, and they may think that you're not serious enough.

In a more negative scenario, people who have negative inten-tions can get the impression that you're too nice, and they will be able to take advantage of you. Kindness or friendli-ness is often taken for weakness, so be aware who you award it to, and how much. That is one of the things I am personally working on. I approach everyone in a friendly manner by de-fault, but sometimes it can put me in a more vulnerable posi-tion as it gets perceived as an open door. Being aware of that has made me consciously pull myself back during interactions with others that are unfamiliar, and recalibrate my self-monitoring if they haven't given me a clear, positive, energetic indication.

I hope it's becoming a little clearer how managing your impression isn't necessarily equal to being fake. You must be wise in how you use it in this game of life, which requires you not only to stay afloat but also to win. This topic dawned on me when a friend of mine once called me in distress. She said she had met some good looking guy at the park while walking her dogs, and when they sat down on the bench and engaged in a long discussion (of course he was sooooo sweet, and so charming), she felt compelled to tell him her entire life story: where she's from, where she lives, what she does for a living. Eventually, he began persuading her to come up to his apartment, and he became a bit forceful. She ended up running off in a panic. When I asked why she had told him so much about herself, she said that she's just an honest person, so as he was asking her questions, she was caught off guard and didn't know how to lie on the spot, and just replied in a straightforward manner. She was just being herself: a friendly, bubbly person who just moved to a big city, eager to make new friends.

Being raised with the focus on acting in a socially desired manner often makes people question whether it's okay to break a social norm. In this case, that norm was not wanting to appear as a liar, as most of our parents taught us it is wrong. They are right; it is wrong—but parents often fail to also tell us about the situations when it's necessary to do so. She failed to manage herself for her own good; she pulled back the curtain and let a stranger behind the scenes without even checking for a pass. In non-threatening situations, it's also beneficial to be skilled in getting out of telling the truth, or giving too much personal information without necessarily lying. When employees call in sick, they still anxiously rant to their manager about why they are unable to show up, despite the law not requiring them to do so due to privacy reasons. Your manager doesn't have to know whether you had stomach problems or relationship problems—all you are required to say is that you are unable to attend for personal reasons. That's it.

To be clear, this is not a manifesto against being yourself, nor is it against transforming yourself to suit the situation, because both of those extremes represent the core deliberation of this book. The most benefit comes from mastering your environment while maintaining good intentions for all involved. Hopefully, after reading it, you will become better at allocating yourself somewhere on this scale as it fits your unique life situations. In that regard, we must bring out one of the many conflicting clichés being thrown at us from representatives of the popular culture, as they shout to be yourself, just as much as they shout for us to be somebody. What?! Can these societal gurus make up their minds? Be like your father, be like your sister, be like your ancestors, be like an angel (and sometimes be a little devil), be like the person on the screen, or on the throne, but make sure to be who you truly are, and always strive to be a better version of yourself—just don't forget who you truly are!

I was provoked to think about the meaning of this popular goal to be "somebody" by an extraordinary professor, David Penner, from McMaster University. Especially as a person who already has more than one college diploma and a university degree, I was faced with a new concept to process. His profound teachings have created many explosions in my mind throughout my adventure in his courses. We are often told to be ourselves, and also to be somebody, and to get success. In one lecture, he presented a completely unique perspective from what we were used to hearing. He said that "if you don't think about success, you can call that success, free from the measure of others, free of what you are to have accomplished." He noted that it may sound strange coming from a professor, who students may consider successful because he has a stable job, which is the common goal of most students. But he made us think: What is success to us—each and every person? Maybe he caused some students to re-evaluate where they were heading in their lives. Are they just satisfying the fear of failure their parents had imposed on them? Fulfilling their family's dream of being able to tell others "my son/daughter is a doctor/lawyer?" The students had to think about whether they were there out of personal passion for what they were doing and where they were heading. There is this huge pressure being put on the young person to be successful, and the measure of success is presented in television shows, music videos, and examples of material wealth.

We must shine some light on the type of young people who tend to feel like they aren't made for the typical lifestyles and careers suggested by the general public. They are the ones who are constantly told to grow up. They are the ones who are often great at something like drawing, designing, writing poetry, or playing instruments, and wear funky clothes that reflect their artistic nature. Unfortunately, what often happens to them, as well as to youth in general, is that they find it challenging to market their talent to the world, and are forced to get a job doing something that is not aligned with them. Probably the biggest shock in many people's lives is when the "kid lifestyle" suddenly ends, and real life begins. That is the most vulnerable time in a person's life, when they have to put down their toys and suddenly start paying bills and buying necessities. Our first job is usually where many of us have most likely learned that being ourselves doesn't always fit the situation, and we had to adapt our conduct to serve the needs of the business. At what point do you decide to stick to your unique style and push towards the ability to be able to make a living, without having to conform to the societal expectations of you? Or, at what point do you decide that maybe you're not able to do that, and that it's time to try to develop a new "you" in order to move ahead in life.

As you mature out of childhood, the adult world quickly teaches you Goffman's dramaturgical perspective: that you must put on a different face in different places, and with different people. Trying to fit into the expectations of adult life makes people drift away from the one true face they came into this world with. Spiritual teachers will often advise people who are disconnected from their purpose, to think about what they were passionate about as a child, and what they wanted to become when they grew up. That is supposed to give you an idea of your life's purpose. The sad truth is that most people fall into the demands of the daily hustle, and move away from the frequency of **self-actualization**, the realization of their talents. But there are also many examples of young people who follow their inner calling, straight through the barrier of that decisive life stage, and balance their talent with business skills so that both can be in harmony.

Goffman was not playing (pun intended), as he accurately described this strange phenomenon of us being actors on the stage of life. Impression was important to people back in the old days as well. It seems like those who had cunning ways of impressing others, often got way ahead of many humble folks. Take the fictional story of *Aladdin*, for example. Despite it being just a story, its moral does apply to real life. Aladdin made the genie transform him into a prince so that he could impress the king, and therefore be able to marry the princess. After the princess found out that Prince Ali was actually Aladdin in disguise, she actually preferred that fact, though maybe not as much as her father did. What about Cinderella? She was living a hard life but was able to transform into a princess to be able to meet the prince; but then she had to run off by midnight because that transformation was to wear off. The prince still ends up marrying her after the whole ordeal.

Will there ever be a time when the naked truth governs everything, when we don't have to pretend anything anymore? I like to remain positively hopeful, as I already am noticing more and more illusions bursting into pieces on the world stage. But for now, you must still manoeuvre through this social production studio. Sometimes, to get the results you want, you have to adapt like a chameleon to a situation or the company you're in, and pick your battles, or face the greater chance of not getting the benefits you set out to acquire. In some cases, the change can be elevating and become a catalyst for you to discover other parts of yourself that you didn't even know existed, and possibly even force you to move away from some outdated parts of yourself that could have been weighing you down. Whichever image you choose to try out, always remember to keep in your heart that one true face of the child within you, because you were born perfect.

In Their View

Okay, I must check on you at this point—you're still here reading this, right??? Okay, awesome! I do realize that this information can be a bit of a shock to your ***self-concept***, which is the beliefs you have about yourself, the knowledge of your personality, and the image you hold of yourself, which makes you separate from other people. Before I was exposed to all of these psychological truths about my fellow humans and myself, my image of myself was full of confidence, and at the same time I didn't know why I kept making the same mistakes. I also thought that I could easily read other people quite well, but after going through the study of psychology, I realized how overblown I had made my belief in that skill. Even when I was correct, I still would choose the wrong behaviours, which came from my lack of understanding of my cognitive processes that were stronger than my confidence or skill.

What helped me snap back to positivity was recognizing the huge benefits that come with the growing pains of this psychological transformation. It was time to level up! This was the best thing I had ever done for myself, as it cleared the way for an abundance of positive things that rushed into my life afterwards. I started meeting totally different people, coming across exciting opportunities, and winning more often. Being through this shock myself, I assure you that this discomfort, which you may feel after finding out things that you may not have been ready for, is only temporary. It's all well worth it. You will surely restore your inner balance when you get away from error, so you can flow more smoothly through the stream of life.

If you are like many others, you may sometimes think about how you may appear to other people. Back in 1902, Charles Cooley developed a theory called "**the looking-glass self,**" which he wrote about in *Human Nature and Social Order.*[42] This theory explains how your self-concept may become dependent on your interpretation of other people's views of you. How you think they see you is how you may see yourself. Other people serve as a mirror, reflecting yourself back at you, as you try to make sense of their reactions towards you. You may internalize such interpretations into your own self-concept, and then act on that potentially faulty information. Keep in mind that how you think they see you can be wrong, or you may be exaggerating it. An example from my own family comes to mind. My mother came to Canada from Poland with a Master's degree. But because her conversational English wasn't perfect, and she didn't have Canadian experience, which most jobs required, she thought that her only job options were among various general labour jobs, but she wasn't successful in getting those either. This lack of response made her even more disappointed in herself. She thought that these interviewers didn't like her, and that she was no good for even basic positions, but maybe they were trying to do her a favour. Finally, one of the interviewers told her that she was actually over-qualified for that type of job. I guess that was kind of a good twist of events that cleared her smudgy reflection in the looking glass.

It can get tricky because various individuals actually have a unique view of you, based on their interactions with you, or based on their own biases. For example, your friends may describe you as outgoing, but your grandparents may describe you as shy. Both may be totally correct because you display a different part of your self-image to different people, as they see you in different contexts and situations, which connects to what Goffman's dramaturgical concept describes. This means that people's views of you are rarely complete. Each person sees you playing a role on that specific stage within your shared reality. When you try to imagine how the particular person sees you, you may select to internalize that incomplete picture. You may select either the more pleasing views or the more negative ones, and go somewhere else with that internalization and expect the same. For example, if a "crush" from high school didn't return the affection of their admirer, they may have been so affected by that rejection, that they took the belief of unworthiness with them into the future.

There are situations where you may think that someone likes you, only to later find out that they were just playing a good front-stage performance for some reason. If that happens to you, don't feel bad. Celebrities, successful entrepreneurs, or anyone who has something of value that others may want to access, often go through this type of dynamic. Imagine winning the lottery. How many people would suddenly want to be your friend? As the popular saying goes, you find out who your true friends are in hard times.

Coming to terms with negative thoughts related to feelings of rejection is very important in order to take the weight off your spirit. Remember that to rise up, you must throw unnecessary baggage out the door. This reminds me of a recent example: My family member had been driving a co-worker to work every day for five years because they lived close by, and the other didn't drive a car. Recently, she told her co-worker that she would no longer be able to drive her, for personal reasons. Now this co-worker doesn't even say hello to her anymore at work. Through five years of continued interaction, effort put into leaving earlier for an already early morning shift, and daily, shared conversations during the ride, it must feel like a huge waste. Now this co-worker views her in a negative light because her goal was no longer attainable. What if she spreads this attitude to others without, of course, providing the real basis for her opinion? These illusions, performances, and hidden goals are sometimes not even recognized by the perpetrator themselves; they may not even recognize that they're acting irrationally, but it can surely cause unnecessary stress or drama. When dealing with such an unfair response, you need to work up an ability to detach yourself from the situation—mentally, emotionally, and energetically. Try to treat it as a necessary lesson, which upgrades your inner radar, and makes you more confident in your ability to sense when something doesn't feel right with other people, and retreat kindly from such an exchange as soon as possible.

When You and You Just Don't Agree

Let's now talk more about balance: that thing that you hear yoga instructors talk about. We will focus on psychological balance, although keep in mind that psychological, physical, and spiritual parts are all connected. The fact that humans tend to seek happiness makes them naturally resist instability. There are exceptions as always, and I do personally know people who thrive in various degrees of mental or material chaos, and instability can become part of their lifestyle. Normally, people do like to have peace of mind, and comfort of stability, to the point that they will even pay more for it. It's part of your mental processes to seek *cognitive consistency*, as well as try to maintain it. Consistency puts chaos to rest, permanently or just temporarily. The term *cognitive* refers to something that occurs in the mind, and *cognitions* are your attitudes and beliefs about anything. *Consistency* is when things agree together, are compatible, or mix well with each other.

The challenge with cognitive consistency is that it's very easy to throw it off balance, especially in today's world, which is full of pushy information sources constantly competing for your support. Our human need to feel special doesn't help here either. The tension that is created by the clash between a couple of your cognitions, or between cognitions and behaviour, is called *cognitive dissonance*. In less academic terms, it's pretty much something like hypocrisy or excuse making.

A famous researcher, Leon Festinger, first investigated this concept when doing ethnographic research for his book, *When Prophecy Fails.*[43] **Ethnographic research** is probably the coolest research method because it requires the researcher to become part of the community that is being studied, sometimes having to infiltrate that group while going undercover, which is what Festinger and his colleagues did. The group that sparked his interest was a religious group led by a housewife from Chicago, who made public her experiments with spiritual energy channelling. She then claimed her revelation that a great flood was coming to destroy Earth on a specific date, but if believers were faithful, they would be flown to safety in a spaceship. She was able to convince members of various backgrounds, education levels, and economic statuses to give up possessions to submit to this "cult" and spread this news. Festinger and his colleagues were present with this group on their special "end times" date, as they waited all night for this spaceship to save them from the great flood. When it didn't happen, the leader panicked, and on the spot channelled another message from out there, somewhere, which stated that the planet would be spared, thanks to their very own great work. You absolutely have to check out this story in full, because it's mind blowing.

Imagine if a captain, steering a ship to a specific destination, suddenly realized that he messed up the directions, and he refused to admit that he was wrong. Where would that ship end up? To get to your destination you must follow a path of truth even when it's paved with rocks. It's not that easy to simply admit being wrong, and many people have a very hard time with it. Admitting that you were wrong can come with consequences, or simply be a blow to your ego. Jeffrey Daugherty, a YouTube personality with a mission to help people un-indoctrinate themselves out of faulty beliefs, simply says that if you're not willing to be wrong, you won't give yourself a chance to be right! It sounds so easy and yet so many people haven't been able to come to terms with it. Some sort of expected punishment may be one of the reasons causing this. I assume that if we all agreed to normalize being wrong, the tension associated with that realization would lose its power before it reaches cognitive dissonance. That could possibly be the solution to unnecessary conflicts, and open the way for progress. If you ever end up in a stock market chat scenario, you will quickly notice that there will be many people there who are unwilling to talk about the downside potential of the stock they currently feel passionate about. That makes them vulnerable to losses because of this strong desire to be right about their stock pick. Because they are so forceful about their conviction they cause other people to follow.

There are many things you may not know, and not knowing is a naturally valid excuse for resulting behaviour. But the popular issue is that once you know the truth, though you still really want something that is wrong to be true, you will be inclined to find many excuses to convince yourself and others of this illusion. In an article for the *Everyday Health* website, psychiatrist Alauna Curry explains that "in a perfect world, you'd have a solid belief system that determines how you act (not the other way around), and your beliefs and actions would be clearly aligned. Cognitive dissonance creates inconsistency that can lead to mental anguish. So in order to return to that place of harmony, you've got a choice: You can change your beliefs, change your actions, or change how you viewed your actions."[44] Prolonged mental tension can be very destructive. Since your body is designed to reduce harm by restoring consistency, it will push you towards the **reduction of dissonance**.

Reduction of this annoying dissonance will likely happen in one of three ways. One way is that some people will change their beliefs. Members who were more invested in the cult, such as the leaders, tried to resolve this uncomfortable situation by replacing or adding beliefs, which could allow them to continue their performance. In their case, that process was probably conscious, but people do this on an unconscious level as well. As predicted by the researchers, more commitment means greater dissonance arousal. Secondly, a person can also change their behaviour, which would be the best option. The less involved group members were more likely to be honest with themselves and admit that they had fooled themselves. It's easier for the less involved to just cut their losses and move on. The third way a person can reduce this dissonance thing, is by reducing the importance of the factor in question. Some members could say, "Oh well, I like the people here; I got used to coming to these meetings, so I'll just stick around and see what happens." They have reduced the importance of the shady situation that just went on.

Which resolution to dissonance gets selected depends on many factors, such as the level of investment into this thing that's being defended, social ties, desire for belongingness, reputation, and so much more. People have to make a decision in order to restore the mental anguish they are feeling. Waking up to the realization that you, a smart individual, have believed some outrageous things, can be embarrassing even to your own self. It's kind of like when a person believes their romantic partner, who is clearly cheating when they say they're not. In a song called "Talking in His Sleep," Toni Braxton[45] describes the feeling of shame, guilt, and fatigue of that mental anguish caused by finding out that your partner has been involved with someone else, but not wanting to confront it. Unfortunately, in this desire to escape from discomfort, people often resort to a fake balance. Toni later sings that maybe she's overreacting, and that is an example of the mind suggesting an excuse so that it doesn't have to deal with the hard truth, at least not just yet. It may suggest things such as "it's just his/her friend from childhood; they're like family to each other; they're not on a romantic level." Your autopilot just wants to resolve this imbalance, at least temporarily, but is not concerned whether it's a sustainable way of doing so for your well-being in the long term. Fake balance, brought on by choosing a "replacement belief," will sometimes be enough to pacify the person who is suffering from dissonance, for a bit longer, without them having to completely face the hard work required by admitting the truth to themselves or others just yet, and making major changes.

Cup Fulfilled

Humans are driven by the desire to be recognized as valuable. We tend to attach meaning to things, as we attach meanings to our lives. A rock on which Bob Marley often meditated, is not just a rock; it's a rock on which Bob Marley sat and meditated. It has gained a special meaning because of where it ended up. People have meaning, even if we don't know them; and it seems that it's especially those who have a giant sense of purpose, who have their name carried throughout generations and countries. To some people, Bob Marley has a spiritual meaning; to others, he's more artistic, or culturally sentimental. There is a common belief that everyone has a special purpose to achieve or fulfill in their life, and must strive towards this goal.

What's really interesting, and troubling at the same time, is that according to a statistic presented in an *Inc. Magazine* article, 92% of people never reach that set place.[46] Why such a high number? We will talk more about the concept of happiness, or the feeling of life fulfillment, in the last chapter, but since we're on the topic of its enemy, the evil cognitive dissonance, we might as well see how they connect. Cognitive dissonance can arise between the belief that you should have a purpose—a reason for living, that grand goal to achieve, a dedication to something significant—and the contrasting worry that this purpose thing is unclear or just not going very well. I am certain that most people aren't even sure if they know what that purpose is. It can be a feeling of being lost in the world, even though that person may seem to have it all. Life direction is a very common concern that comes up in psychological coaching, as well as in psychic consultations. That's not to say that this topic comes up by that person's initiative; typically, it kind of knocks on the door in the middle of the consultation, which was initially meant to be about their troubling love life, or work issues.

People like to often put that topic off to sometime in the future—when they think they will be ready to get to it, when everything else perfectly lines itself up, and all of life's problems become taken care of—and then they will decide to think about what it really was that they were meant to achieve in this life. Though life likes to keep up the pace that gets established, things never really stop; something always keeps happening. Every day goes by the same way, and purpose remains a mystery, or at best is mistaken for something else. There is an older Polish song that just came to my mind. In the chorus, the singer, Maryla Rodowicz, sang about this desire to just get onto a random train, not care about anything, and just let the train take you wherever you are meant to end up. Getting up daily and just doing the basic routines, without much purpose or direction, is kind of like getting into a random train each morning you wake up, and saying; "Take me wherever, as long as it's a round trip." Lack of that feeling of being useful to some greater or special cause, lack of direction, and no end goal other than the simple expiration of the mortal body, is the cause of great mental anguish, and can often be behind the feelings of general swings of unhappiness, or feelings of something being missing. Many will unfortunately look in the wrong places: toxic relationships, destructive jobs, addictions. A good example is the many people who retire from work after many years, and feel a sudden sense of emptiness because their routine becomes disrupted and they feel like they're no longer useful, productive, or needed.

Finding a special purpose seems to bring joy to one's life. There are many studies that show it; all you have to do is do an online search for the topic of life purpose, and you will get a flood of articles convincing you that this is definitely a necessity of life. But if the above statistic is true that almost all people on Earth are not likely to actually achieve it, that could suggest that almost all of the people on Earth are living a lifetime of cognitive dissonance about living out their purpose, when they're actually mistaken, or some just simply pay it no mind. What can happen is that people assuming that they have this special purpose or goals to reach, may stress themselves out by thinking about it, and can try to resolve this dissonance by coming up with some satisfactory answer to eliminate this question. This answer can be something that aligns not with the person as an individual, but with what they have internalized from the social norms prevalent around them. Many women, for example, especially in cultures that value women's roles within the home, often say that their life's purpose is caring for their family. If you ask men, their answers often reflect their lives outside of the home, such as their business, status aspirations, or hobbies. But can your major life purpose involve something that humans do naturally anyway, such as procreate? Do people just come up with a random purpose that seems right according to societal norms they learned, only to pacify their cognitive dissonance about not knowing what that real purpose actually is? Or if they know what it is, maybe they're blocked by their circumstances and it could be nearly impossible to achieve it, so they just find some resolution that matches, and voila? Or—this is the tough question—do we even have a special purpose at all, or are we just merely existing to survive, live, and die, day by day, simply put?

When we hear about this topic of purpose, it often is connected to a career, something related to making money and survival. To many people, however, it's also about fulfilling some inner calling, like saving animals or children from harm. Becoming a police officer or an addictions counsellor can be a realization of someone's purpose of helping others, and it is not exactly something that provides great material or status gains, but it is a job that can be dangerous. In the case of police officers, it's not a job that most people signed up for because they felt the strong desire to be widely hated or feared. There is definitely a strong sense of purpose present there. The search for a fulfilling way of life is often on the minds of many people. This issue has gained popularity in modern times, although this idea of special purpose, or "something more," has been pondered by the many Alice's in Wonderland or Pinocchio's of this world, since the early civilizations. More recently, since the start of the industrialization period of our society, especially in the Western world, many people were moved away from artisanry and into employment because there was a demand for production after the war. Most people in society used to simply be a farmer, a shoemaker, a carver, or a painter, and sometimes a soldier, a doctor, or an astronomer, and their sons followed. Unfortunately, back in the day, women were mostly mothers, homemakers, or nurses. There wasn't as much of this guessing game about what you will be when you grow up. Most had some task assigned, either by themselves, their parents, or by life (unless of course they were an Alice or a Pinocchio, who desired to change their stacked deck and set off to wander the world).

In the Western world, the Industrial Revolution started offering opportunities to work in factories, where the labour was divided into repetitive tasks, while diminishing creative control. The creativity and freedom of being a shoemaker and creating the shoe from start to finish, was replaced by structured monotony of the production line system, where now they were in charge of just one part of the shoe, over and over again. That was a time of major changes in the world, and major changes to many people's minds, being not sure if it was for the better. The mass-produced merchandise, which common people could now afford, was there to restore their happiness.

Recently, with the growth of the internet, so many new ways of making money have emerged, and slowly people started becoming more and more entrepreneurial again. This has caused a divide between those who break out of their scheduled work life and are creative enough to make something of their own, and those who remain in waged jobs. The latter often find themselves questioning whether they should also do something entrepreneurial, and as they question their abilities, the dreaded dissonance arises.

Steady employment is a great thing for many people, although it's getting its share of disinterest from many young people who have been inspired by the talk of the few self-made millionaires of our modern society, or those who pretend to be ones on social media advertisements, in which they command you to sign up to their "get-rich-quick" scheme. Though the famous "nine to five" can often be very lucrative and fulfilling. I've personally felt like I should be a detective. Unfortunately, I didn't go that route, but if I had, that would have been an interesting job to dedicate my purpose to, especially if I could help save children from harm. Many common jobs, or those so-called 9–5s that multi-level marketers and success gurus cringe at, do actually make people happy. I found a very interesting statistic, which accounts for a major reason why people remain at such jobs. Besides things like job security and benefits, a major factor that keeps people working for someone else is a good working environment. Survey results presented in a *MarketWatch* website article show that "7 in 10 professionals refused to work at a top company if it meant having to endure a bad office environment."[47] If we look at an example of the cosmetics sector, which I'm quite familiar with, the customer service employees make near minimum national wage, plus maybe some basic benefits. Despite that, they often stay there for years because they love interacting with people every day, receiving free products, getting creative with makeup, and being able to chill out when they come home, not having to worry about their work spilling over into their private time.

Now, there is also an ugly side of this topic, and that is when people try to justify dissonance regarding their career life. From my experience in the life-coaching industry, one of the biggest challenges for many working people is detaching themselves from unfulfilling jobs, going for a promotion opportunity, or jumping into something that brings them more joy. One successful fitness trainer, Ives Morrisson,[48] is glad he took such a daring jump when he left his office position within an established financial institution in order to become a full-time trainer, and he hasn't looked back since. He says he wouldn't have been able to give his full attention to building his own business if he kept holding on to his office job. His job was making him tired, and it just didn't suit his energetic nature. The desire to help people become healthier, drives his success rates, and it appears to be his purpose that he boldly followed.

This kind of jump often comes with uncertainty and disruption to an already established order. Quite possibly, that's where that 92% of people are stuck, as they have chosen a job or a career based on many factors other than what their deepest life purpose dictates, and are afraid to leave it behind as they fear the unknown that lies ahead. In such situations where they're not happy, or they feel like they're missing something in their career life, cognitive dissonance thrives like a parasite. Remaining in an unfulfilling position can actually be quite destructive to your overall well-being, and it doesn't necessarily have to be physically unhealthy. An inspiring psychologist, Dr. Steve Taylor, who like myself combines psychology with spirituality as they are profoundly connected, states that human beings crave purpose, and suffer serious psychological difficulties when they don't have it.[49] Purpose can play a major role in extreme cases, such as being a victim of an accident or sickness. Many doctors would agree that people who have a strong sense of purpose find it easier to survive. Purpose, or we can even call it will or drive, is found to be a fundamental component of your overall wellness, and it can ignite lots of powerful energy, propelling you to do things you never thought would be possible. Purpose can be that thing that makes sure you are okay after the jump.

Cup Overfloweth

As you descend deeper into this book of simple but not so simple life knowledge, I hope you are not feeling too over-whelmed with the process of stripping away the layers woven by your environment throughout the years. If it feels a bit strange, it is only because you were used to these layers; they made up who you are for so long that you began to see them as part of the real you, just as if the clothes you're wearing today would attach to your body, and you just keep putting on more clothes over top. If you don't do an inventory of these layers, you may not be aware of which ones are benefi-cial and which ones are just dead weight. It is very normal to feel discomfort when you are making any changes to that which you're so used to. But for you to move forward, those changes must be made right away, even in an abrupt manner, like tearing off an old Band-Aid.

This reminds me of a story from when my daughter was a baby. She was in love with the soother, and she got so used to it that she would not go to sleep without it. When she def-initely outgrew it, we tried hard to make her forget it exists. These attempts created maximum stress with minimum re-sults. Finally we threw it out the window as she watched, and we said that a birdy caught it and took it to another baby who needed it. It's not good to lie to children, but in this case, the benefit outweighed the cost. Sometimes to get to the next level, you must cut off the very thing that binds you, from the object of addiction; in this case, it was a soother gone irreversibly, but it could very well be that last cigarette, an abusive partner, or some practice that doesn't serve you, which you still keep around while knowing very well that it's got to go.

Don't get me wrong; you are not to become an empty slate. The things you have learned throughout your life are much needed, and you are not getting rid of them entirely. You are just replacing or removing the things that are faulty, outdated, useless, incorrect, or damaging, and things that elicit a state of confusion within you. Additionally, you probably want to ease your path towards increased efficiency in your life, by not allotting as much power to the unbalanced or unhelpful aspects of yourself. In turn, you will begin to give more power to those aspects that are helpful to you in your maintenance of a smooth flow, internally and externally; as within, so without.

CHAPTER 4

THE FRIENDS AND FAMILY DEAL

"Grown-ups never understand anything by themselves, and it is tiresome for children to be always and forever explaining things to them."

– Antoine de Saint-Exupéry, *The Little Prince*

4

Team Fam

Balance really proves its significance, as well as complexity, within the realm of *family*. So many personal and societal effects are based on our family matters. These effects range on a scale from positive to negative. Family gives us all the foundation for our lives, so none of us are exempt from its influence. Maintaining healthy and balanced dynamics within a family should be of high importance, but it's probably one of the most difficult things to achieve. Challenges for family members can come up when the dynamic of the family overpowers the sovereign spirit of each individual. On the other hand, similar or even greater challenges can turn up when the family reach is inadequate or destructive. To a large extent, the institution of family is responsible for our health, wealth, relationships, personality, and beliefs, and those surely are not islands of their own; they do in fact contribute to the creation of wider societal outcomes.

The benefits of having a somewhat complete and somewhat positive family structure in one's life are quite considerable. The European Union has recently recognized the value of assisting families in their burdens of maintaining positive outcomes. Despite a decline of 7.3 % in the number of children aged less than 18, between 2000 and 2017, their expenditure on family and children benefits were increased by 40.6 %.[50] That's because the world is changing fast, and the major changes are hitting home. According to the National Centre for Biotechnology Information, in America, the rate of *marriage* for women in 1960 was 77 per 10,000, but this had decreased to 37 per 10,000 by 2008.[51] That is a decrease in marriages by almost half! In India, as a comparison, the changes are happening in the structure of a typical family, as people are moving away from *joined families*, which include other family members such as grandparents, and into *nuclear families*, those which include just parents and children. Such societal changes are due to various micro and macro level factors, and they may vary in some ways throughout contexts. There has been an increase in *divorce* all around the world, with the most in the Western countries, with America leading the way, or Portugal leading the European division, along with Luxembourg, Spain, and France, according to the *Statista* website.[52]

Divorce is a powerful factor shaping the future competence in all areas of a child's life, as it manifests itself according to "different strengths and weaknesses, different personalities and temperaments, and varying degrees of social, emotional, and economic resources, as well as differing family situations prior to divorce,"[53] says pediatrician Jane Anderson in her article about the effects of divorce on children's health. Ronald

Simons, and colleagues, have examined the deeper effects of family breakups on children, and they found that children of divorce may be at higher risk for adjustment problems than children living in nuclear families."[54] Their research revealed one very eye-opening fact: that especially boys have the toughest time dealing with the effects of separating from their father. This aligns with the message that many African-American rights advocates, here in North America, have been trying to get across, attempting to reverse the devastating effects of the deep issues in the systemic leadership existing for so many years, which sent many males to prison. The researchers also write that "parental divorce increased a boy's chances of becoming depressed regardless of quality of parenting or level of parental conflict. This finding suggests that the effect of family structure on the internalizing problems of boys is not mediated by family processes. Perhaps even optimal post-divorce circumstances are not sufficient to compensate for the sadness experienced by boys because of the departure of their father from the home."

The negative effects of single-parent homes, or even cohabiting and re-married parents, are substantial, no doubt about it! But as conscious thinkers, we must not spiral down with negative emotions and forget to check for any positive effects to things that sound so negative, like the word "divorce" does. Men can suffer due to a bad marriage, because of emotional abuse or financial burdens. They are not as likely to express their feelings, and it can manifest as addictions and health issues due to stress. Women are often subject to physical abuse in the home, and restraints on personal freedoms; and they continue to do the majority of daily housework, which can cause stress and contribute to negative mental health outcomes. In her research about single life, Dr. Bella Depaulo lists reasons why divorce can be beneficial for women, such as that it lowers rates of suicide, lowers incidence of reported domestic violence, and it's linked to less instances of women being murdered by their spouses.[55]

Let's look more broadly for a bit. I guarantee that the original meaning of the word "family" will surprise you, as it surprised me! The word comes from Latin language, and it translates from "famulus," meaning "servant." Looking into word origins can really paint the historical trajectory in your mind, without even doing much historical research! It can reveal so much depth of the particular human experiences building on each other through time. The concept of "family" is considered to be a major institution of society. Why is the family considered to be an institution, when we think of institutions as being schools, hospitals, prisons, or banks? The book *Exploring Social Issues* states that "although there is variation from society to society, the family generally has the primary responsibility for the tasks that are crucial to survival, including reproduction, socialization, production, and consumption of goods and services, and emotional support."[56]

As an institution in society, family also serves as an agent of ***informal social control***, defined in *Wikipedia* as "the reactions of individuals and groups that bring about conformity to norms and laws, including peer and community pressure, bystander intervention in a crime, and collective responses such as citizen patrol groups." This control exists within families, and enforces behaviour of its members through their reaction to violations of family norms or social norms, internalized from the society they live in, or the culture they're part of. For example, if a society generally assumes that it is wrong for a person to have sex before marriage, date someone from a different religion, or smoke cannabis, then the parents, uncles, and grandmas will likely make attempts to judge or punish the dissenter to some degree.

Family members tend to automatically assume a guardian role over the other members, whether they're younger or older. It is a good thing, to a certain degree, because a good familial influence is central to shaping good character traits, or providing advice and care. Familial support also plays a role in the maintenance of mental health, such as prevention of suicides. Although control is not something that humans take lightly, whether consciously or unconsciously, control often elicits resistance, or can make way for various mental health issues such as anxiety. Humans are natural freedom lovers, and control can surely stand in the way of the natural unfolding of the individual's personal life path. Imbalanced control over another person is a factor that can spoil family communication and disrupt family ties.

In small towns just about anywhere, it's nearly impossible to do something in secret without the whole place finding out about it. Until about 12 years of age, I grew up in a small town called Olesnica, in Poland, where it was hard to hide anything, so gossip was very common. Here, this informal social control played out as a benefit, because it provided a great place to raise a family, and it still scores quite high in that department. This awarded much safety to children, giving them the chance to trek around town on their own without much fear. Childcare was easier in many cases (depending on the design of buildings within the neighbourhoods) because neighbours would often watch each other's kids while they played together, either outdoors or inside each other's homes. That close-knit connection between families was providing a watchful eye over all children. If one neighbour's kid was smoking a cigarette behind the garages, the other parents who saw it would go to their parents and tell them. Society makes family what it is, and family makes society; it's a cyclic relationship. Understanding how the concept of family connects to society is key to having a more valuable perspective on the world's social issues, and will help you deal with your own or other people's family matters.

One of my past anthropology professors, Celia Rothenberg, wrote a very interesting book, especially for those of you who are intrigued by topics of spirituality and psychology. It's called *The Spirits of Palestine*.[57] Celia spent time doing ethnographic research in the Palestinian Muslim village of Artas, located among the four mountains in the Israeli-occupied West Bank. Her work is a wonderfully presented example of a very collectivist lifestyle and the experiences of young people living within it. It's a place where many residents remain for generations, and everyone in the community knows each other.

The unstable political situation and the strong traditions combined, create very intricate personal lifestyle situations, which Celia was interested in hearing about from the young women and (less often) men whom she interviewed. The inability to move freely, and the limited economic possibilities, seemed to clash with the fact that if someone actually moved away, they ended up missing their family and community so much that it made it hard to function in the new place. Mobility is limited there due to the political restrictions and cultural beliefs, mostly regarding women's roles. The young women who often go to another town to marry into a new family, are forced to suddenly adapt to a new environment and a new family, while not being able to freely visit their home as they wish. Such limited possibilities had a negative psychological effect on many of them, which manifested in a very unique way. Especially if you like to learn about spirituality or religions, I recommend reading this book to find out what's so unique about the findings.

The Western countries are known to have more ***individualistic*** norms that emphasize personal development, and those with more ***collectivist*** norms include Asia, Latin America, Africa, and some parts of Europe, where the vibe of collective cohesion dominates. Family remains a largely debatable concept, because its definition keeps changing throughout time and place. If we look back to the ancient Romans or Greeks, the elderly group consisted of people in their 40s or 50s, because the average life span was just that, if not less, largely due to high infant mortality rates and a large population becoming soldiers and dying in battles. If you look at numerous Indigenous communities, they often lived in longhouses, which housed up to 20 families. The large family and close-knit community lifestyle is diminishing in many places in the world because of various factors, which mostly point to the effects of globalization, increasing industrialization, or promotion of independent lifestyle through pop culture. More and more women go into paid employment and don't stay home to take care of elderly relatives. Children move away or immigrate more than ever before, and leave parents behind in the home country. The construct of family is much differently understood in places like many big city centres, where large numbers of residences are occupied by single people or roommates. Would a roommate, with whom you share your daily experiences with, but who is not related or married to you, be considered family? Canadian law states that if a couple have lived together for at least one year in a conjugal relationship, they are considered to be in a common-law partnership. There may be so many factors at play, varying from country to country, culture to culture, family to family, which get to define these labels. See, it gets more complex than what our popular culture suggests.

If you ask people on the street what is the most important thing in their lives, most people will say it's their family. Understanding the socio-psychological processes at play in your world, and in the world around you, will help you achieve a more successful closeness with your family, or it can help you achieve a healthy distance, depending on what your personal situation requires. Being able to separate that which is YOU, from that which is your internalization of your family, or particular family members, can help you become more aware of your truest self. Through that, you will develop a greater understanding of your family members, and possibly even create, or strengthen, your bond together. You may start to see various family feuds from a different perspective, kind of like a family counsellor would. When counsellors examine things like life outcomes, addictions, phobias, and romantic relationship issues, they must consider family relations as an important factor. Family relations represent a large part of our lives, regardless of their extent, because even the person who lacks a family is likely impacted by that fact.

Parental Entanglement

Your parents have a completely different view of you than someone else, such as your friends, employers, or strangers. Clearly, this relationship is much more attached to you than any other, because of this binding biological connection, which turns into an emotional and psychological one as well. The earlier mentioned "looking-glass self" theory is very applicable here because the parental glasses tend to be coloured by that parent's own state of being. Most parents see their children in a positive view, and that's good because feeling valued is very important for the child's development. Problems arise when there is an imbalance in the way that parenting is performed, when parents see their children in an overly positive or overly negative view, and that view can be dependent not necessarily on the child but on the mental state of the parent. Children will likely then internalize that view of themselves. Unfortunately, in a family context, often the weight of these issues fall on the children.

One of the pioneers of psychology, and the founder of psychoanalysis, Sigmund Freud, challenged the concept of parental love, and described how the ways in which parents attach perfection to their children is reflective of them trying to live out their narcissistic fantasies of their own childhood. He was the first to study the concept of **narcissism**, which refers to the adoration a person has for themselves and their own image, but I cannot let this definition remain unfinished. It is crucial to add that it is important to see yourself in a positive light, and to love yourself. I would argue that the negative spectrum of narcissism starts where that adoration for yourself brings along spoiled energy, such as when jealousy, manipulative tendencies, lack of respect or credit given to others when they're due, or disregard for the suffering of others begins. This term comes from a Greek myth of *Narcissus,* who fell in love with his own reflection in the mirroring water, but not with a real person, and he died of sadness because his reflection didn't love him back. He was reborn as a white flower we now call by the same name. Next time you're dealing with a total narcissist, give them a bouquet of these as a hint. Narcissists are hungry for admiration, support, validation, and sense of entitlement, and they feed their self-esteem from such **narcissistic supply**, a concept introduced by Otto Fenichel, in 1938.[58] Narcissistic people become such because of the imbalances they themselves have endured during childhood, so the chain reaction is severe as it carries over from generation to generation.

There are specific qualities to watch for, which may represent the concept of a narcissistic parent. An online magazine, *The Insider*, presented an interview with people who later in life realized that they were raised by such a parent, and it lists a few traits to watch for. Those include things like being controlling and manipulative; so, for example, they tend to pit siblings against each other by favouring one, while scapegoating the other.[59] They often emotionally reject a child that reminds them of their own insecurities and flaws. The article suggests that as an adult, strong boundaries, detached contact, or no contact at all, are the best ways to deal with a relationship with narcissistic parents.

While mentioning boundaries, I think it's appropriate to add something I have observed in some of my friends' families, who actually have pleasant and supportive parents; but what happens is, when one parent dies, leaves, or gets sick, the other doesn't make much effort to remain independent. They can put plenty of expectations on the children to fulfill their emotional needs and keep them from being alone. They often don't want to sell the large family home and move to a smaller, more comfortable place that doesn't require constant work, which they call on the children to carry out for them. I can recall an example of when a friend of mine's father died and the mother remained alone. She refused to sell the big house because of the memories attached to it, and because she was just used to it. She could have bought a small bungalow or a condominium with no need for landscaping, fixing roofs, or shovelling the snow from a large lot. The children were obligated to help out with the work, while neglecting their own homes, along with their children and spouses, after working all day at their full-time jobs. That type of dynamic caused some friction in their marriages. The siblings also got into arguments about who was responsible to help out. Some have moved away, and the burden fell on one but not the other.

Do you think this parent is acting selfishly? Should this person make a decision to leave their emotional attachments behind and, for the sake of the family, get into a more comfortable place? There are many people who have lost their spouses at an older age, and still were able to find some new friendships or hobbies, and start a new chapter in their lives, but some fall into sadness and refuse to see a future. It is not to say that missing someone who spent years in your presence isn't justified, because it is an extremely tough life experience. But life has chosen to give more time to the remaining partner for a reason, and it can only benefit them to acknowledge this value. Not only in family relations, but also in politics and society, people often hold on to the past at the expense of others. Despite all of the challenges, caring for your parents or older family members is a top priority, and sometimes a situation can arise when you may have to take them into your home, which many people actually do. But when there are possibilities to resolve this in a way that can be close to a win-win for all involved, and maintain positive relations among family, then emotional reasons should not stand in the way.

Now back to narcissism. Most parents see their children as a representation of themselves on the front stage; therefore, challenging that representation can be difficult because the parent takes it as an attack on their own esteem. I can tell you my story from when I was bullied by the girls in my school when I first came to Canada. My mother repeatedly went to the school officials and begged them to do something, but they kept telling her that they hadn't seen these girls doing anything wrong, that they were great students, and that they would ask their parents to talk to them. The parents answered with outrage that it could not possibly be their sweethearts, because that's not how they were raised. The teachers sided with the parents and acted as if the bullies were their own children, possibly because of the attachment that formed throughout the years spent together; and at the same time, they didn't want to face a possibility that maybe they had failed to teach them some important things, like respect. I was the outsider, so I didn't seem to deserve a voice, especially if it challenged their idealized view of their own tight-knit collective, as they continued to "save face" for each other.

Grow up! So what does that really mean? Part of growing up and flourishing into a mentally and emotionally developed individual is recognizing when something other than your true self is influencing your decisions or ways of being. It is that recognition of yourself in the world. It is the knowing when you are being led by that which is not part of the true you. Therefore, I think that age is not a good measure of being grown up, or at least grown up in certain areas of life and not others. Being truly grown is rather the level of such recognition of your unique self, the one that is not of this world, though some may not fully reach this in their current lifetime.

One of the blocks that get in the way is worrying what others will think, as well as taking advice from the wrong people. Just because someone has a significant role in your life, it does not make them an expert in a particular area of life. Parents, or close family members, are usually at the top of the significant people list, so their views and beliefs, as well as feelings, often matter more than those of other people. So even their merely imagined presence can cause a person to avoid certain things, or behave in a way that would align with these people. Knowing that they would disapprove, be disappointed, or deliver some punishment, it can cause the child (or adult child) to feel sad, guilty, or fearful. Because this type of dynamic is present with us since birth, as we go back and forth with our parents or guardians regarding what is okay and not okay to do, it becomes somewhat natural and automatic.

Studies support this concept that other people's views and beliefs affect how you feel about yourself; they affect your behaviour and your thoughts, even when those people are nowhere near! There was a study done by psychologists Baldwin and Holmes, in which female university students were divided into two separate groups. Group 1 was told to simply imagine some of their peers in their mind, and group 2 was told to imagine their older relatives.[60] Next, the two groups were asked to help in another experiment. They were given a popular magazine and told to read a specific article. The article presented a story about a woman who had a sexually themed dream about a man who she was physically attracted to. At the end, all participants received a survey to fill out. The results of that survey showed that those who were told to imagine their peers, before reading the article, had rated it higher than the women from the second group, who were told to imagine their older relatives. The "older relatives" group gave the article much lower ratings! This means that merely imagining your older family members, or maybe even family members in general, unconsciously affects your attitudes towards some things; in this case, it affected people's sexuality. When constantly having your family on your mind, it can affect your other areas of thought, and change your standards of thought. The randomized participants of the study were repressing their liking towards sexual topics after being primed with thoughts about older relatives; and those who were primed with thoughts of peers, likely they thought of someone they were attracted to, and that caused their opinion to shift into a positive appraisal. In that case, if the difference in people's opinions can come from the type of priming the particular mind has received, then how can we ever know when we are being ourselves or when we're being influenced by something else?

The Commercial Family

Popular brands are a large influencing factor in social inter-actions. Aside from the inevitable enjoyment of the produc-tion quality or the creative value that popular brands often provide (let's face it, you often do get what you pay for), it is also through brands that people attempt to convey some mes-sage to others.

The popularity of the cheap "knock-off" (copycat) products is also noteworthy here because it exposes the deeper matter of contention hidden within those who are not exactly inter-ested in the superior quality of the branded product, but who just want that brand to speak on their behalf in the social world. They are the ones who seek to be seen as someone who is not an outsider to the group they are trying to appeal to, or as someone worthy of respect, while brandishing their affiliation with the particular "crew" that defines itself by their choice of brands. Most people want to be seen as being on the side of the majority, to receive favourable treatment. A choice of style can be perceived as having some form of a protective factor, a subconscious silent appeal for sympathy that sends out a message of "don't come after me, I'm one of you." It fits one of David G. Myers' 5 factors of attraction: the tendency to give better ratings to those who are more similar to us.[61] Brands become a common identifier; in this case, one that links to a majority, and serves as a sign of belonging to a group that has power in numbers. It leaves a bigger chance to come across an ally. For example, who would you think is part of a bigger "tribe"—someone who is wearing a *Nike* t-shirt, or someone who is wearing a *Harley Davidson* t-shirt? It is clear that the person with the popular mainstream brand, that many various demographics deal with daily, will not spark any tension. A person with the *Harley* shirt may be taken as a symbol of a unique, smaller group, which can cause a sense of unpredictability in those who don't deal much with that particular culture. This reminds me of my friends in Poland, a husband and wife with young children, who are naturally unique and tend to stand out from the typical family stereotype. Because they live in a building where everyone minds everyone else's business, they often mention trying to blend in because the neighbours can be very judgemental.

The adults are guilty of creating a world increasingly entrenched with big corporate interests for the young ones to learn from and incorporate themselves into, a world where they often will be evaluated on the brand of clothing or the make of car they select. Brands are a huge part of the lives of young people, and they in turn influence the brand choices of their parents. Youth are quicker at picking up on, as well as creating, new trends, and their opinions seem to get the attention of adults in reference to what is cool and uncool. Parents often respect their teen child's brand recommendations. One example comes to my mind, which may not have been widely noticed: When I was in high school, many "cool" girls were putting lots of gel into their hair to the point where it looked wet, in order to make it stay straight. A few years later, the flat-iron, or hair straightener, became the hottest (both physically and metaphorically) hair tool that suddenly ended up on every teenage girl's Christmas gift list. The next thing we see is hair salons smoothing their middle-aged female clients' finished "dos" with a straightener, rather than with a curling iron like they used to. It became trendy. What's even more interesting when things like this happen, a new brand comes out of nowhere and beats the veterans who often are somewhat asleep by the comfortable push of their existing structure. Here, the consumer hair appliance giant, *Conair*, took a back seat behind the cool kids table, because *Chi,* the new jock, arrived and swept all of the following into their corner by having women of various ages dropping nearly $200 apiece, instead of $39.99 for *Conair* curling irons that were available everywhere. Now, some years later, *Dyson* blows competition out of the water with their advanced hairstyling appliances, with a mind-blowing price tag of roughly $500. It easily sold out in most of its Canadian retail locations the second Christmas in a row, leaving the overconfident, procrastinating dads and husbands scrambling for this hot-list item.

This situation also knocked on the door of many electronics brands when *Apple* came around, or car brands when *Tesla* brought forth their fun-filled and future-forward electric cars. Young social media influencers have definitely played a role in making these products trendy. Just look through Instagram and you will see people posting pictures with *MacBook* laptops sitting on a cute desk with a nice coffee cup beside it. The sleek design of the laptop, as well as its higher price, makes it a centrepiece in the representation of a youthful motivation and drive towards success, on its way to replace that which cannot keep up the pace.

It's valuable for mainstream product advertisers to target young people and use them in marketing material. Did you know that the term "Tween" itself has a marketing origin? The marketers know that kids have the capacity to drive purchases. In some places like Quebec, Canada, it is against the law to advertise to kids 13 and younger, although the companies tend to break this rule because it's still worth it for them to pay the penalty for violating the law. Children are found to be brand-aware from around 2 or 3 years old. After all, they do hear things like "pass me the *Kleenex*," "do we have any more *Windex*," and "meet me at *Starbucks*." They also see and hear hundreds of advertisements per day.

McMaster University's Dr. Sarah Clancy studied the impact of pop culture and dress styles on the development of children's identity. She interviewed many adolescent girls in her research about the types of marketing trends directed at children, as well as their effects. She asked them to simply describe their favourite outfits, to see what comes up. Most of the participants had predominantly mentioned brand names over and over, saying things like "I usually wear my *Nike's* to school."[62] Many of the kids in this study were downward from the middle class. Brands appeared to be very important to them, and cheaper versions of the popular brands are often seen by children in a negative light, leading to stigmatization of kids who don't have such things (knockoff products won't get a pass with kids, by the way). They learn to differentiate between brands at just 3 years old! The wrong brand as a gift can spoil the mood, big time. If grandma accidentally gets "Susie," not "Barbie," for the grandchild's birthday, she has no idea what's coming! Kids have their own social capital to attain in their little-big worlds. The children whose clothes pass the inspection of their peers tend to have a higher chance to enter more admired social cliques in their school. Kids and teens, somewhere, somehow, pick up these social judgments that lead them to compare who's got the better brand, and who's got the no-name brand. No name, no game!

Money Doesn't Grow on Trees

It is true that the financial situation of many families out there is not easy to be cheerful about, but getting into the habit of turning the negative language into a ***positive affirmation***, meaning an optimistic message, will likely have long-term benefits for children, as well as whole families. Focusing on positivity is almost always a better option than fuelling negativity. There is a common assumption in society, which I often see in comments on social media, or in real life, that children do not get enough financial learning among all the other things they are taught in schools. They don't get to learn this from the pop culture icons who they often look up to, as they only subject them to suggestions of overconsumption, or some shady ways of making money. On the home front, if you listen to how most families talk about money matters, you will likely hear lots of fear-based communication regarding financial strains, hardships, the need to save, and an uncertain future.

Fear-arousing communication is a method of persuasion by using scary examples, often used in advertising to influence people to stop speeding, or buy an alarm system for their home. Parents often use this method when persuading the child to adapt specific beliefs or behaviours. That is most likely how they were taught by their parents. Teaching children about various dangers is crucial. Though, there is a difference between raising awareness, and negative talk. It seems so natural for adults to continuously warn their children of possible negative outcomes, that it becomes this template for communication. It starts from "you'll fall," "you'll get sick," and then moves to "thanks to me, you have a roof over your head," or "better hold on to that job." Changing the patterns of speech directed at children, and also adults at themselves, is something very tough to achieve, especially if many people don't even realize the extent of harm they are causing with the words that so randomly come out of their mouths daily. In his interview with Dr. Oz, the prominent psychology scholar Jordan Peterson raised an important point that is crucial for all parents to understand in their efforts to protect children from child bullies or adult predators. Jordan talked about the fact that such predators look for those children who won't put up a fight, who will withdraw and not make it clear to the bully that there will be consequences. He states that "if you're teaching your child to be terrified of strangers, that's really not a very good strategy. You want kids who are confident and who will make a noise when someone messes about with them, and that characterological strength has to be built in"[63] Arousing fear or strangers in the child does not build the child's character to act rationally in the face of danger, but rather it may cause them to forever be too timid and closed off to making new connections which they will need to crate healthy new relationships or be successful in networking which can propel them further into success, something we will discuss more in the next section.

"MONEY DOESN'T GROW ON TREES"
ADVENTURES OF YOUNG BILLIE IONAPIE

It is true that there are stressors and challenges, such as increasing bill payments or relationship issues, that often pollute the dream of smooth adult life for many young parents, diminishing their capacity to remain conscious of positivity as they progress through the obstacle course. Positive thinking and speaking can easily become forgotten amongst the sleepless nights and tiring days. What could a financially struggling parent say to their child when they can't afford to buy the toy they want so badly right now? With some creative effort, they could affirm the child that they are working on ways to get more money in order to be able to buy the toy soon. If statements like "we're poor" or "Mommy doesn't have any money" are said to a child regularly, there is a high probability that this child will carry this mindset into their lived reality by expecting poverty, and possibly assuming they are not capable of achieving good things, so they may not even bother trying.

It is a fact that children repeat the status of their parents—why? Could it be that they encode the approaches to money from their parents? Some members of the stock market community already show their children how to think in terms of finance, like Richard De Sousa, from *Rich TV Live*, who talks to his young children about the stock market drama and trends, and teaches them the meanings of some stock specific vocabulary. The kids often see him dealing with CEOs or other investors on his YouTube show, and pick up on the information, which will shape their minds for the future. That type of attitude gets the child comfortable talking about money, as well as getting them to think creatively about how to attain it.

There is an easy solution, and it really is grade one material for parents and guardians everywhere: You just have to remember to turn negatively framed statements into positive ones, before they settle into the child's unconscious mind. (There are studies that show benefits of positive talk, which I will talk more about in the next couple of sections.) How would you do it with the statement, "If you don't put on this hat, you will get sick?" You can turn it into: "If you put on this hat, you will be able to go to the playground more often." It would be more beneficial to say to the child: "If you do your best in school and pick a career you will enjoy, it will provide you with all that you need to be well." Does that mean, for example, that Richard shouldn't tell his daughter about the losses, the depressed moments he experienced, or the shady dealings that go on in the business world with an often-dark character? No, it doesn't; in fact, it is important to find a way to raise awareness about various negative situations that can be encountered on our paths, but it doesn't have to be done in a doom-and-gloom kind of way, and it must be balanced out with continuous positive encouragement and useful instruction. But many parents often use **downward social comparisons** and give their kids examples of low-waged jobs of alleged unsatisfactory positions, as they point to the janitor in the school, or the cleaning person at the shopping centre. I'm sure that pretty much everyone has heard as a child, that if they don't do well in school, they will be cleaning toilets for a living.

Very often, parents make incorrect statements to their children, which does them a disservice because, when the children find out the truth, or their logic tells them to doubt the validity of what the parent said, it leads to some distrust. It can undermine the intelligence of the parent who is meant to be a mentor to them. The child may later challenge their parents with information they found on the internet, like proof of people who didn't go to school but didn't end up in low-paying employment either. There are many successful people for whom school was as foreign as another planet, such as billionaire Sir Richard Branson (by the way, hopefully not foreign for much longer, since he's been aiming to fly out to space). Well-known people in history, such as George Washington and Abraham Lincoln, did not graduate from college. Examples of well-educated people who have experienced poverty are also abundant, and the world famous Serbian engineer and physicist, Nicola Tesla, was one of them.

Despite all of that being true, we must not get carried away, because statistics are actually on the side of education, at least in America; but I would argue that this is also true for most of the world. American adults with less than a high school education are more than twice as likely to be unhappy with their lives, as those with a bachelor's degree or higher.[64] Canadian statistics, from 2015, show that education really matters, especially for women. Women with a bachelor's degree had 58% higher earnings than the women who only had a high school diploma, and 41% higher earnings than those with a college diploma.[65]

Many children choose their post-secondary program out of fear of poverty, because they keep hearing about the challenges they may face while looking for jobs. There are always people saying something negative about the economy, even when the economy may actually be okay, or possibly may not really be a sole reason for that person's financial hardship. There are plenty of people who thrive in bad economies. This fear of poverty can have real consequences because it can steer the young person into choosing a profession that will not satisfy their soul, and can misalign them with their true calling, which may exist elsewhere. By the time they graduate, they tend to realize that this field may have become oversaturated, or they just don't like what it involves. *The Independent* writes that "one in three (students) told researchers that knowing what they now know about their university, they would have chosen a different course."[66] This confirms what I have heard from many post-graduates. That was also me after high school, when various life events, along with my own faulty judgement, caused me to go on to somehow end up with a few college diplomas that I didn't exactly find useful! Years later, after gaining experience in manoeuvring within the strange adult reality, I decided to go back and do what I was really meant to do. I love studying psychology and other social science fields, so the five years of extremely exhausting work, doing research, writing lengthy papers, taking hard exams, and doing presentations, ended up being an enlightening experience because I was interested in the material I was dealing with, although I noticed it wasn't the case for everyone.

It's best to have conversations about education and career options with children early on, and try to entice their minds into exploring various possibilities, so they are not in shock when high school ends and they are rushed to pick a program. Family has a huge influence on the future of their children, as most children tend to reproduce the social status or social class of their parents. They also reproduce parents' educational attainment. According to the *Statistics Canada* website, education of children highly correlates to the education of their parents.[67] The correlation is the strongest where at least one parent completed university; their children are more likely to graduate from university, and it remains strong even in situations where the financial status of such educated parents is on the lower end of the scale.

Canadian musical artist Drake, seems to be a good example of someone who benefited from having parents who knew the value of providing a success conducive environment. They seemed to have encouraged his natural talents, and provided a motivating environment that posited a certain standard to live up to. According to *Wikipedia*, his parents divorced at a young age, and despite having issues of their own, they both shared a love for music—his father was a musician and encouraged their son to remain focused on his talents.[68] Drake is quoted in *Yahoo News*, explaining that he didn't actually grow up wealthy. His mother rented part of a house in a wealthy neighbourhood because she was willing to live far beyond her means in order for her family to be in a good environment.[69] Energetically speaking, this encouraging positive energy must have been powerful enough to catapult Drake beyond the Canadian border, and into the millions of hearts around the world, which was, and still remains, a statistically rare miracle.

You may be thinking that many parents, teachers, and guardians most likely won't put in all of that effort to affirm positivity to their kids. People are too busy, stressed, or depressed, and some just aren't on that level of thought and just go with the flow when it comes to the psychology of their kids. And that is all true, but if the seed is planted, even in a few minds, the ripple effect created will be significant enough to benefit the greater good to some degree, and as the saying goes, brick by brick and you have a house. Even a drug-addicted parent telling their children of the importance of not ever getting into such a thing themselves, is a big thing, and a step in the right direction. Just trying opens the way for progress. Limiting the negative "power words," such as death, hospital, sickness, poverty, hunger, pain, etc., is most crucial, and will have a great effect on the mind of the child. We will go deeper into the magical energy of speech, later on in the book, so make sure you stick around!

The Currency of Social Capital

Most of us don't have rich families. For the majority of people on this planet, a wealthy family is often something just seen on television. As mentioned in the previous chapter, people often reproduce the social status of their family. This happens because of many factors, and one of them is the family's social circle.

Drake's mother made sure to place her family in a wealthy area because she most likely knew the value of **social capital**. Social capital is a concept that measures your personal network of people, and their capacity to benefit your life in some way. Living in such a wealthy area has its benefits. Let's give the previous title a little twist: Money *can* grow on trees— that is if you obtain a relationship with the right people who can help you reach the branches. Some people can possess a ladder, which you could borrow; others may already be up in the branches, and might give you a hand to pull you up to their level, or more likely to some level along the way. For example, politicians don't just win or lose an election because of the quality of their skills or other admirable traits. A great deal of leverage comes from the people who are willing to endorse them, or donate to their campaign.

Just look at the popular examples of many politicians. Justin Trudeau and his father, Pierre, have both been prime ministers of Canada, similar to the presidency of George Bush and his son, in the US. Justin has won himself a second round in the 2019 elections, so it is possible that people saw something in him that they thought was worthy of their vote. Pierre was a prime minister before the 1980s; Justin's position came many years later. With a significant inflow of new immigrants to Canada since then, along with many younger voters being unfamiliar with his father's rulership, it gives some weight to the defence of his own qualities attracting the votes; although the social capital his family has already gained with their status, in the higher spheres of society, must have certainly added a good amount of leverage. The familiar sound of the last name alone can skew people's opinions towards the favourable end, because familiarity feels more comfortable, a tendency which we will further unpack in the next chapter.

If we look at American politics, some top politicians have been in charge of society for over 20 years, and according to the *oldest.org* website, most members of Congress are nearly senior citizens.[70] In Canada, it may be even more extreme. At the time of the writing of this book, out of 82 current senators, only 14 are below 60 years of age.[71] Undermining the importance of experience in such responsible positions, it just shows how much something like social capital matters in places of power. Being within the same context for many years, often in the same areas, states, provinces, or regions, keeps people within the same social circles or networks. Through time, you get to know others well, maintain relationships, perform all kinds of dealings with them back and forth, as well as share private moments together at each other's kids' weddings or charitable events. What can come out of such interpersonal dynamics is the prioritization of each other's interests before the interests of the public they are to serve. Getting into politics is a tough task for those just starting out, because if you are not part of that crowd already, you will have to break all kinds of ceilings, and perfect timing may be your biggest hope.

The art of communication is something that allows for **upward social mobility**, which is that increase in social status awarded by your achievements, wealth, or family connections, and sometimes even connections to higher social circles. Upward social mobility often includes a move up that tax bracket tree. There are many people whose family connections can provide a quantum leap for their endeavours, although there are many exceptions, like those who don't really employ their opportunity for some reason. Take for example Rob Kardashian, who seems to be a bit detached from his famous family members. It often happens that there will be such individuals who don't fit into what everyone expects them to. There is generally sad news about Rob in the media, like back in 2014, when he was quoted in a *Page Six* online magazine article, saying, *"It's crazy how this whole year, my whole relationship was only negative; all I did was gain f–king 40 pounds and lose so much money,"*[72] referring to his failed relationship, which left him emotionally hurt. He seems to have been swayed away from building something for himself with the help of his seemingly supportive family, swayed by the temptation of emotional fulfillment leading him off his path. Someone like Ivanka Trump seemed to have the skills to utilize her family status, from running clothing businesses to becoming a presidential advisor to her father. Another example is Stella McCartney, daughter of Paul and Linda McCartney. She has taken her family position to higher levels by pursuing education and career in fashion design, and additionally becoming a powerful voice for animal rights. There's more to this game than just the name; lots still depends on the active maximization of this potential, and great communication skills, which allows for successful interactions when the famous family members are not around.

Those who don't have family in high places should not give up. Everyone has their own unique path, and maybe you are required to do your best with what you have. Becoming more artful in communication creates leverage so you can sometimes skip some steps, and rise higher with less effort. You will need to seek out the right people on your path in order to elevate yourself higher and further in various aspects of your life. The famous actor Sylvester Stallone has a story that really resonates as an inspiring example to those who think there is some lack that is standing in the way of getting out there and getting hold of those who can elevate you. Sylvester has a speech issue and facial injury that resulted from an accident at the time of his birth. But that didn't stop him from pursuing his purpose of becoming successful in the film industry. An article by *biography.com* says that "he created a screenplay about a rough-and-tumble thug who struggles for a chance to make it as a professional boxer. According to several reports, Stallone refused to sell the script unless he was allowed to star in it. Despite having a pregnant wife and little money in the bank, he held out until he found two producers, Irwin Winkler and Robert Chartoff, willing to let him play the lead."[73] He was not afraid to go out and negotiate with industry leaders, and didn't allow his visible flaw of the very area of his body that is responsible for the delivery of communication, which is powerfully symbolic on every level.

Social capital also provides families with benefits other than just the material. It can be emotional support, such as providing advice in challenging times, or physical support when you need someone to water your plants and check on your home when you're on vacation. All of that is positively correlated to overall health and well-being. Italian National Statistical Institute conducted a large survey, to analyze the relation between friendship ties and life satisfaction. The survey participants included thousands of Italians living as heterosexual couples. The results showed "that friendship, in terms of intensity (measured by the frequency with which individuals see their friends) and quality (measured by the satisfaction with friendship relationships), is positively associated to life satisfaction."[74] The article states that "a faithful frequency of contact with friends, together with positive satisfaction with friendship relationships, connects individuals to a range of extra benefits, including a higher sense of belongingness, better health, and more overall support." It's also important to note that "low-quality relations and/or the lack of positive interaction may elicit anxiety." There are some situations, like the earlier mentioned case of the young Palestinians interviewed by Celia Rothenberg, where they were not happy with their close-knit family and community life that was overflowing with support. The women were taken care of, weren't expected to go to work, and had family members, neighbours, and friends all around them. But it wasn't what they seemed to desire. They craved to have more control over their own lives, some privacy—they dreamed of careers and worldly experiences—and all of that support felt restricting.

There is an overwhelming amount of research proving that close community connections, regardless of social status, are beneficial for the quality of family life, but there has to be a voluntary and balanced physical connection involved for the best results. Unfortunately, on the other hand, here in the Western world, the fear inducing security culture, increased demonization of strangers, or immigration as people spread across the world, is causing close-knit networks to become smaller and smaller. Neighbours often don't know other neighbours at all, unlike my old neighbourhood in Poland, where I could have easily named all of the people in my building, which car they drove, and where they worked. We didn't need artificial intelligence—the older neighbours who would sit on a bench outside all day knew it all. The widespread connection to the internet-based social life is visibly taking over some of our person-to-person connections, which actually tend to be stronger than those based mostly online. You likely won't be calling your internet buddies or your Instagram followers to come to your birthday party or your wedding, or to water your plants when you go on vacation, but you will be looking in your contact list for those with which you have personal contact on the physical level. Remember, even one of the least human of fictional characters, the Tin Man from *The Wizard of Oz*, needed the person-to-person connections, which helped him discover himself and find happiness. So, since we're still human, let's be open to human things and not be afraid to talk to each other on the street, and say "good morning" to a total stranger passing by. You have no idea how far that energy can carry!

Bad Seeds

We often wonder how some people can become aggressive or mischievous towards others or even themselves. Where does it come from? Parents are often blamed for unleashing bad seeds into the world. Is it all the parents' faults for not raising their kids properly if the kids turn out aggressive or deviant? I often look at the comments under social media posts that show news of youth related crime, and I most often see people writing things such as "where are the parents," and "how did the parents allow this?"

Who or what is to blame has become an old debate, but it's important to look beyond just blaming a single source, like the family. Responsibility for the increasing youth gang activity and crimes has also been placed in the hands of those who arrive last to this scenario: the "public parents," the police officers. Deeper causes are often missing in these conversations because then it would point to sources such as the education system, the entertainment industry, and other societal entities who have some power in socialization of children and distorting the life of parents. Such agents of socialization are interconnected in their effects on the life outcomes of youth, and separating them in order to simplify the blame is doing this cause a disservice. *The Guardian* article presents a relevant example of this, as it recalls Kamala Harris "defending her decision to criminally prosecute parents for their children's truancy."[75] The article argues that "truancy occurs disproportionately among children whose parents are poor and less-educated, and among children who don't feel safe at school, who have to work or support their families, who have mental and physical health issues, and who are in unstable living situations."

It is, again, easier for the mind to just pick something to fixate itself on, in order to simply resolve discomfort without doing a deep dive into all the parts that come together to create the reality at hand. Most people also like to distance themselves from any blame, responsibility, or failure. Their mind often demands an easy explanation and an easy solution to complicated issues while maintaining a sense of safety. That's why the practice of **scapegoating** has been utilized throughout history in all kinds of situations, from an individual level all the way to the societal. It is a tendency to pick an entity of attention to pin all the blame on, and beat it like a piñata, with accusations, in order to quickly resolve one's own mental anguish or achieve some goal. Putting blame on an external factor is an extreme way of diverting attention from being in the wrong, or doing wrong. It happens to be a political tendency to accuse an opponent of one's own wrongdoings, re-directing the attention of the audience by way of crating hype.

Now let's discuss the topic of troubled children from the angle of genetics and generations. Children can turn out to have different kinds of **temperaments**: Some are more outgoing, some less, some are aggressive, and some are calm. According to the American Psychological Association, temperament refers to someone's personality, including such characteristics as energy level, emotional responsiveness, demeanour, mood, response tempo, behavioural inhibition, and willingness to explore.[76] Are people with an aggressive temperament born "bad?" And if they are, will that continue into their adult lives?

To answer these questions, it is necessary to recognize how the biological/genetic factors, combined with socialization into the environment, which includes parenting, come together to shape the temperament of the individual. Scientists from the University of Barcelona recently identified forty genes in humans and mice that can lead to a risk of aggressive behaviours. The article describing this study for *Science Daily* states that "the origins of the violent behaviour are multifactorial and respond to the interaction of several factors—biological, cultural, social, etc.—which can modify the expression of the human behaviour."[77] American Academy of Child and Adolescent Psychiatry more specifically lists these main ingredients, which can make up a recipe for violent behaviour: previous aggressive or violent behaviour, being the victim of physical abuse and/or sexual abuse, exposure to violence in the home and/or community, being the victim of bullying, genetic (family heredity) factors, exposure to violence in the media, use of drugs and/or alcohol, presence of firearms in the home, brain injury, or the combination of stressful family socioeconomic factors, like poverty, severe deprivation, marital breakup, single parenting, unemployment, or loss of support from extended family.[78] These facts are begging everyone to realize that all children are the responsibility of the society, not just the parents. We all vote every day with our attention; what each of us supports and validates grows, and then starts making itself at home in our society. If you continue to give attention to forms of entertainment that glorify things like drug use, guns, and prostitution, through acceptance, it will permeate the wider society and easily make its way to children's sensitive environments, and shape their ideas of "normal."

Typically, it happens that specific traits, like aggressive behaviour or shyness, do remain quite stable throughout the life course. If someone was outgoing as a child, they would likely be outgoing as an adult. (Keep in mind that these things are often mediated by additional life factors.) There was a longitudinal study conducted in New York by Thomas and Chess, who followed 140 people, from infancy to adulthood, both difficult and easy babies. The goal was to find out if early temperament is related in any way to later outcomes in that person's life. At the end of this study, researchers found that about 60–70% of the difficult babies continued to have behavioural issues when entering school. This was the case for only 20% of the easy babies.[79] Longitudinal studies really deserve praise! I find it just amazing how much patience and commitment it takes to continue the same research through the course of many years. The tricky part for the researchers is to keep in touch with the original participants, who may have moved away or opted out for some reason.

There is a positive to all of this because when there is a will, there is a way! Psychological studies should be utilized more often in designing optimal strategies for reducing problem behaviour in early childhood, which would positively impact many children's futures, as they themselves impact their communities and the world. Something like imbalanced ***temperament***, which can be brought into the current life while simply hiding in the person's genetic structure, can actually be corrected with appropriate psychological intervention (and not necessarily one that involves chemical substances). Studies suggest that parents or caregivers have the power to correct a great amount of the child's negative temperament by making sure that they respond calmly when the child is acting up, and remain consistent in their responses, as well as acknowledge when the child behaves in a positive way. Unfortunately, what often happens is described in **Coercion Theory,** by Gerald Patterson: "a process of mutual reinforcement during which caregivers inadvertently reinforce children's difficult behaviours, which in turn elicits caregiver negativity, and so on." Smith, Patterson, and colleagues have examined the reciprocal influences between observed coercive interactions between children and caregivers, oppositional and aggressive behaviour, and they state that "the emergence and persistence of conduct problems during early childhood is a robust predictor of behaviour problems in school and of future maladaptation."[80]

Troublesome kids tend to be much more sensitive to their environment, and they feel environmental stimulants more intensely; therefore, they react in a more intense manner. Parents most often will respond to that intensity with increased stress, and stress keeps getting reproduced in a vicious cycle. The aggressive response of the parents gets internalized by the child, creating the foundation for their overall development—kind of like in the **attachment theory**, which shows that the ways in which parents respond makes a big difference in shaping the child for future relationships in adulthood. This proves that love is the solution that can put out the fire of aggression. When overactive children are continuously met with understanding and calmness, when they are assured that their hypersensitivity to the surrounding world is comforted and not punished, they seem to slowly internalize the positive vibrations and not the negative ones. They have no choice but to learn from the examples in their environment, and if it's positive, they will soak it up, just as they can soak up negative influences.

No matter if you're dealing with rascal children or rascal adults, staying calm will help you maintain control of the situation. Masters of reality have cultivated an ability to manipulate their environment by managing their responses to it. It is also their duty to use this skill to benefit the greater good. You are a master in the making, as all are who walk this Earth. We were given certain traits, but we were also given free will and, with that, the power to reshape, restore, and reprogram some of our undesirable and imbalanced aspects. It just takes willingness to put in some work, and we could really use each other's help in the process!

CHAPTER 5

AFFAIRS OF THE HEART

*"Perfume heralds a woman's arrival,
and prolongs her departure."*

– Coco Chanel

Back to the Basics

There are many theories that explore the existence of human beings, but one that is still widely brought up, not just within psychology, is the *evolutionary perspective.* This perspective looks deep into the origins of our existence. It zooms into the depth of our time here on Earth, and sees the underlying motivations of human behaviour as natural genetic progression towards survival, in an ever-changing environment. Why are we talking about evolution in a chapter about romantic relationships? Because, since as long as we can trace, the design of our human biology has been behind this mysterious "pull" we experience, attracting us to other people. It is important to note that it is separate from the energetic pull we may experience on a spiritual level when we meet a potential soulmate; although the lines here are quite blurred, and debates about this topic could go on forever.

Romantic relationships are automatically associated with the act of sex, which aside from being a fun pastime, and having mental health benefits, it is a necessary factor in procreation and the survival of our lineage, and of the human collective as a whole. Throughout this book, we will mostly focus on straight relationships, but many concepts may also be familiar to other sexual orientations. Sex is something that often comes with some type of physical attraction; it can be based on looks, or even on things like status, intelligence, or some talent (just think of the old rock stars and the young women begging to go back stage and even have their body parts signed by them). Since I got on the topic of male rock stars, they do have a very masculine aura around them, which is something many women feel a pull towards, resulting from that evolutionary desire for being close to someone strong. In the most basic understanding, evolutionary perspective suggests that the types of things humans tend to be attracted to are related to this pre-programmed desire for continuation. Dr. Russell Eisenman explains it well, stating that "many or most of the findings refer to things that are unconscious: The person does not consciously know it. For example, if you were to ask people why they did something, they would not necessarily say 'to have children' or 'to spread my genes into future generations,' even though these may be the underlying motivations. Thus, we need to use the concept of 'the unconscious' more often, since much of what the theory deals with is not part of conscious awareness."[81] So even our romantic choices are happening on the unconscious level, with a genetically imprinted filter telling us that we like someone because of how valuable they will be to our well-being, and potentially to our future children, even if someone is not planning to have any.

All the way back in the 1800s, a famous naturalist, Charles Darwin, whose work became the foundation of evolutionary studies, presented the scientific ***theory of evolution*** by natural selection. In his famous book from 1859, *On the Origin of Species by Means of Natural Selection*, he talks about ***natural selection***, the principle that decides who gets to survive the earthly struggle for resources.[82] Or, as Darwin preferred to call it, "the struggle for existence." Natural selection is based on the idea that only the strong survive. This idea was behind a popular song, "Survival of the Fittest," by New York rap icons, Prodigy and Havoc[83] (who I had the pleasure to personally meet while they were in Poland). The song is known for having the top rap lyrics of all time, and it says "until my death, my goal's to stay alive, survival of the fit, only the strong survive." Did Prodigy read Darwin, or did he just realize this through his participation in the societal contexts around him? He did stay alive for 43 years while living in one of the harshest neighbourhoods, until sickle-cell anemia took him into hospital care, where he actually was taken from this world though an apparent accidental choking, which was legally challenged by his family.

Darwin mentions a very profound example in his book, highlighting the certain interdependence and interconnectedness of living species. He gives an example of a plant, the mistletoe, which is intricately dependent on the services of other species. It doesn't have roots; it hangs onto tree branches from which it absorbs the necessary nourishment, and its seeds need to be eaten and then pooped out by specific birds, and that's how it gets "transported" to where it can try to successfully attach to a new suitable host. Some of the mistletoe species require the action of special insects, whose job is to deliver the pollen from the male plant to the female plant, as they are of opposite sexes, and the female plant is the one to produce the white berries. That is one hell of a trajectory towards survival.

The evolutionary perspective recognizes the human desire to procreate and survive as a major aspect of human life, and tries to explain how it plays into our interpersonal relationships. There has to be something to this psychology, as I remember long ago, in my own family, we only had one boy cousin, and the pressure was put on him to have a son, or else our last name will cease to exist. Humans tend to have a fear of dying, and most definitely have a fear of dying out as a family, as a nation, as a species, and so on. So what does that have to do with human attraction? We are dependent on each other, just like that plant is dependent on the bees, trees, birds, and other divine beings. Most humans are driven by this genetic impulse, which is dictating to their subconscious, the need for not only survival but also preservation. For some families, preservation and continuation of family legacy has been a major focus. Sometimes it can even be extreme, like the royal families of the world—they surely strive for their name to live on.

The reflection of the evolutionary theory is reflected in the wider society. Ladies, especially single ones, you may have realized that men can quite often appear to be attracted to more than one woman at a time, and it may appear that most men are more sexually open than women are. Gentlemen, you may have also noticed that many women desire the safety of a commitment from a man who is capable of providing resources. If you did, then an overwhelming amount of studies are with you on this. It is a fact that males are the major consumers of pornography and sexual services, and it seems to be driven by this unconscious need for gaining a favourable response from more than one female. By no means am I bringing this up to put men in a negative view—that is the type of emotional and dualistic response I speak against—but I do believe it is important for men to make sure they enable a greater understanding of their own intricate human nature, as well as their personal inner emotional mosaic, which will help them consciously correct some imbalances that may be quite destructive to their quality of life. Jason Carroll writes, in an article from 2018, that "as much as one-half of women in romantic relationships disapprove of pornography to some degree, and that nearly one-third of engaged and married women view pornography as a form of marital infidelity. These findings are particularly noteworthy, given that it appears that in early couple formation, many women may have little understanding of how much their male counterparts are viewing pornography."[84] Try to find a male strip club anywhere—now that's a challenge!

Of course, there are exceptions, and this, as anything else, is mediated by other factors. There are surely plenty of women out there, who want lots of children, or who don't want any at all, who enjoy interacting romantically with numerous men, even sometimes while in a relationship, and ones who like much younger men, or ones who like to dominate. And there are many men out there who do not want to have children at all, or who are happy with the one same partner forever—although the evolutionary approach to human attraction is hard to deny, if we look at the big picture. Studies continuously show that most men tend to be more attracted to women who resemble an ideal candidate to have children with, and that most women tend to seek out men who appear to be capable providers, and protectors of their potential family.

A study, by Buss and colleagues, asked more than 9000 adults, from 37 countries, about the characteristics they value in a marriage partner. Most men expressed their focus towards physical attractiveness, while most women leaned towards traits such as ambition, industriousness, and earning capacity. They also found interesting changes when looking at the cultural evolution of these values over a 57-year span. Both men and women increased the importance placed on physical attractiveness of a potential mate, as well as an increase in the importance of financial prospects, especially in males.[85] That means that in the time from the 1930s to the 1990s, something started changing in the minds of the general public, and both males and females slowly began to place more value on outer qualities.

We live in a world where not everyone who arrives here gets to carry on, and we can even think back to supposed civilizations that no longer exist, such as the Mayan, as well as possibly even the Atlantean or Lemurian civilizations, which have been investigated for centuries by many intrigued researchers of these mysterious lands. It seems that beings who have the most effective ways of collaborating with their environment, and adapting to its changing nature, are able to stay here the longest as a group, lineage, family, race, species, and so on. Personally, I'm not sure how important it is for me to carry on my genes throughout the world—once I detach from this life, it seems like that issue may not matter anymore. I see this body as a vehicle for the spirit. The spirit likely continues on somewhere, but the body, as a naturally decaying mechanism, is meant to be given up, along with the rest of the material and maybe even non-material things we hold onto in this physical reality.

Whether it's genetic programming, or effects of socialization, or a mix of both, it is a fact that from an adolescent age, humans become guided by the unconscious need to secure a partner for the future. With all the evidence, it is impossible to avoid looking through the scientific lens to try to explain why relationships between men and women have always been known to be an extremely complex equation!

Cords to Your Past

Unlike the evolutionary theory, which explains relationships by looking way back in time, **attachment theory** explains how you approach your relationships by following the connections leading back to your own childhood. This developmental psychology theory looks at the type of attachment you had to your parents when you were a baby. So, however your parents treated you back then, has most likely shaped your approach to your romantic partners in adult life. Your past can contribute to feelings of either insecurity or confidence; it can also decide whether you will have a hard time forming or maintaining various interpersonal relationships. To a certain degree, and in some areas more than in others, your past can cause you to unconsciously expect people to treat you in a similar way as how you were treated as a child by your caretakers.

Childhood problems and relationship problems co-occur very often. Keep in mind, it is not the case that all people who have relationship or social conduct issues, automatically have mental health disorders; although Alan Sroufe and colleagues write in their article, about attachment and psychopathology, that "relationship problems play a key role in both determining that there is a problem warranting diagnosis, and in determining the specific classification."[86] **Pathology** refers to any deviation from a healthy norm, and it's the study of disease. The researchers remind us that while these connections are existent, the cause is complicated and "rarely can one say that a certain pattern of parenting (or a certain relationship experience) directly led to a pathological outcome in a linear manner, yet it is certain that relationship experiences often are a crucial context for the emergence, waxing, and waning of pathology."[87] There are various mediating factors between the cause and effect, which play different roles in shaping the state of the individual. In some cases, mental disorders can even arise as a result of the particular relationship itself; for example, if it was abusive, then it can become a root of mental health disorders for the person who is affected while not having a connection to childhood.

It was John Bowlby who first came up with the concept of attachment when he wrote a pamphlet about the orphaned children of World War 2. Later, researchers Mary Ainsworth and colleagues expanded on his work by conducting experiments in which they studied bonds between infants (between 12 and 18 months old) and their caregivers, mostly the mother, and how those early bonds impact their relationships later on.[88] The study involved leaving the infant alone in a room for a moment, and then observing their behaviour when the mother returned. They also had a stranger enter the room to see how the baby would respond to someone they didn't know, in the presence of their mother. These responses were put together to describe specific **attachment styles,** which to some degree apply to many people.

The most easy-going attachment style is the **secure attachment**, one that may be a rare gem, to an extent. Secure people typically had caregivers who provided them with feelings of trust and attentiveness, and displayed positive emotions. They were basically raised by other secure people; they didn't have to worry whether they would be abandoned for too long, frightened, irritated, or have their wants and needs be ignored. Secure people are quicker to lose interest if someone isn't meeting their needs, because they are not desperate to hold on to someone by all means. Their future romantic partners may translate their non-clingy nature as carelessness, if they themselves are on the needy side of the attachment spectrum. Secure people are not necessarily cold; they do know how to show affection, but may do it in a way that doesn't sabotage the balance of their own well-being.

The **insecure/anxious ambivalent** style stems from having caregivers who can be quite inconsistent, overbearing, or unpredictable in their reactions towards the child, which makes them anxious because they never know what to expect. Later in life, they will desperately want to be close to someone, but may become confused about how much love they actually want. This type can go to both extremes and downplay their interest for someone, or at other times behave desperate for them. Desperation also prevents people from being selective in their choices of partners. With the rise of the internet, such people may complain about feeling lonelier than others, and therefore may tighten their grip on the person they feel good with. They may also fall victim to relationship scams much more easily, because this need for being loved can blind them to any red flags.

Insecure/anxious avoidant attachment develops when the child's caregiver is more distant, neglectful, overbearing, or are for some reason a source of threat. Sroufe and colleagues explain that "in the face of chronic rebuff, infants may learn to cut off expression of attachment behaviours."[89] They may learn to give up asking for affection or help, because they expect to be rejected anyway. This teaches them to distance themselves psychologically from the need for close relationships in the future, partly because they want to avoid disappointment, and partly because being warm and fuzzy may subconsciously annoy them a bit. Avoidant types can grow up to avoid anything that their unconscious mind recognizes as attachment. They can have a harder time being close and intimate with other people, especially for the long term.

It is mind blowing how much childhood experiences shape the unfolding of adult life. If you have been wondering what drives various behaviours in relationships, you may want to see if any of these attachment styles apply to you, or to the person you're thinking of. Also, you can become your own best psychologist by trying to take a good inventory of your own behaviours and feelings as they relate to romantic partners. Take note of any imbalanced experiences from your childhood, imprinted deep within, that may be causing you trouble. Know that you are strong enough to not just overcome them, but also to rise above them—but first, do not be afraid to acknowledge their existence. If you're not sure how to recognize what is blocking you, it's a good idea to contact a skilled energy practitioner, such as a tarot reader or astrologer, and they will be able to help you spark your inner guidance system to recognize these inner blocks. If your situation is more extreme, then a good psychologist may also be beneficial.

In the profound words of Carl Yung, "once the unconscious becomes conscious, it will direct your life and you will call it fate." If you allow the deeply rooted unpleasant factors to remain hidden within you, they will have the power to steer you into the wrong situations, as you wonder if you just have bad luck or what. When you uncover all those unbalanced emotions that have imprinted themselves into your operating system, you will start seeing increased positivity entering your life on a shiny horse, or maybe even on a unicorn if you wish. Once you fully know yourself, you can truly love yourself, and then you can be a better vibrational match for stable, fulfilling, and drama-free relationships.

Likelihood of Liking

What motivates you to like or love a person? As the number of single people, and those who are not satisfied in their relationships, increases, many are wondering where they have gone wrong. So many theories and factors apply to this in-

Affairs of the Heart

tricate equation, and still, when it happens, it just literally happens, like out of the blue. Is it up to how your mother treated you as a baby? Freud surely says so! Is it your genes, zooming your attention towards a qualified candidate for reproduction? Darwin would agree! Is it socialization into a culture that directs you towards a person that your family would approve of, or that friends would be jealous of? Or is it an invisible energetic magnetism that synchronistically puts you and your special someone on the same floor tile, at the same time, only to look into each other's eyes and realize that this is the one? Attraction is like a special program designed by your personal fitness trainer: Custom built to suit each client's personal situation, it is the right mix of specific ingredients, movements, and timing—only that this trainer seems to be some invisible force that directs things. Below, let's look at some of the other ingredients found by the study of social psychology.

Those who challenge the evolutionary perspective, often take on a sociological approach to attraction, and argue that men have been conditioned to mostly focus on the physical attractiveness of a potential romantic partner because it has been imposed on them by powerful societal influences, like the entertainment industry or product marketers. They may also claim that women are conditioned to be drawn to images that represent men in suits, or with six packs. Or Brad Pitt! There is a tiny little detail that must be mentioned to give some context to this conversation: The majority of those at the very top, and in ownership of the popular media companies, are men.[90] It may not be a coincidence that during the rise of television and magazines, people started to place more weight on physical attractiveness as an important quality in a mate. It's not hard to notice the overwhelming amounts of sexualized portrayals of women in the media. Many music videos are notorious for featuring near-naked women, or commercials and advertisements presenting digitally perfected female examples of sexual desire. Is pop culture conditioning men to focus primarily on the physical attractiveness of women? Or did men focus on physical qualities of women since the beginning of time, and pop-culture has just intensified that tendency by feeding men with more of what they seemed to be into? What do you think? Sounds like it's both, doesn't it?

Under the right conditions, spatial closeness is also something that can make way for emotional closeness. We already discussed the effects of architecture on our relationships, and how the studies by Festinger proved that people who are regularly using the type of spaces that allow them to see each other more often, or rub shoulders with, have a bigger chance to become emotionally closer. The ***propinquity effect*** is a powerful determinant of interpersonal attraction, which describes the effect of ***proximity*** and ***similarity***, physical or psychological. It's quite obvious that people who come in contact with each other more often, have a higher chance to become friends or lovers. It is kind of a no-brainer. Statistics support the propinquity effect. The *Statista* website reports, in 1995, that most heterosexual couples met through friends, which puts them quite close, because friend networks are often not temporary. Bars and restaurants are popular matchmaking locations, and people often frequent bars that are close to home, where they meet others who also live close enough, which removes the obstacle of distance. Other places include work and school, and less often through family members.[91] I am bringing up the 1995 statistics for a reason. Why? Well, the rise of the internet and online dating portals developed after that time, which I wanted to exclude so that we could see how people behaved in person, without such influence.

It is much rarer for people to be involved in distance relationships, or make it work out with people from across the globe. Distance can make people drift apart. Many migrant workers can attest to that as they go to another country to work for a whole season, while leaving their significant others behind. My own dad was away from his family when he went to Canada, and it took a while before we could join him; that is the negative side of many immigration policies. So many couples are dealing with distance, but it's not something they find easy to do, despite the widely praised internet communication capabilities. Nothing replaces real physical contact. Many families fall apart simply because of that separation.

What the propinquity effect relies on is the concept of ***familiarity,*** which belongs to the study of psychology of influence and persuasion. *Psychology Today* writes that "if something is familiar, we have clearly survived exposure to it; and our brain, recognizing this, steers us towards it. Thus, one could say that we are hardwired to feel that the known devil is better than the unknown angel."[92] Most people are suckers for comfort, and familiarity also tends to feel more comfortable. You're more likely to get accustomed to something, or develop a liking for something, simply due to being exposed to it—that is called the ***mere exposure effect***. As in psychology, most things don't stay basic for too long. The mere exposure effect gets trickier when you realize that you don't have to actually interact with that object of exposure, to become familiar with it and start developing more affinity towards it. Could this be why they say that the devil you know is better than the one you don't?

Researchers, Moreland and Beach, tested ***mere exposure*** when studying the development of affinity among students. They organized a study in a university classroom, in the middle of the semester. Participants included a few female students who were unfamiliar to the regular students of that class. Their job was to attend the in-person class sessions, and they were forbidden from interacting with anyone in the classroom, not even with the professor. They were seated in the front row so that they could be easily seen by the rest of the class as they moved around. The study controlled the number of class sessions attended by the particular participant, which was from 15 sessions to zero. At the end of the semester, the actual students were shown slides with pictures of each of the participants, and they were asked to confidentially rate the personality of each person on the slide (that is still without knowing anything about them). The pictures of the women participants who attended the class more often, were rated much more positively than the pictures of those who attended less.[93] It means that there is a high probability that just seeing someone around more often will make you automatically increase your liking towards them. I can't help but think about political elections: The more visible the candidate is, the more votes they'll probably attract.

Like attracts like—but wait; don't opposites attract? Both *similarity* and *complementarity* are included in the list of things that attract people to others. You may find that you like it when you have things in common with the people who surround you, and you may also enjoy when people around you compliment you in some ways. A person who is outgoing and likes to be out in public may want a partner who also enjoys being out of the house, which will help to avoid clashes of interest further down the road. But if someone is terrible with finances, although they can cook well, and they happen to get with a person who can't cook but who is great with finding extra sources of income, then this type of relationship formation would require some logic and conscious assessment of similar goals and complementary characteristics, which combine to create a highly functional relationship.

Something More

Humans are magnetic; they are full of energetic forces that constantly attract or repel. Even in physics, electrons with opposite magnetic fields pair up with each other, and whether they pair up is dependent on the strength of their individual magnetic force. Energy cannot be overlooked while thinking about the topic of human attraction, because it is an undeniable part of human life. People often tell stories of nearly unbelievable coincidences that have led them to meet someone special.

The topic of soulmates is a debatable one; it's very hard to say whether everyone has, or is meant to have, that one person who is like their other half. I personally believe that every human spirit is perfectly complete on their own, but we may have a spiritual counterpart, either per lifetime or for eternity—kind of like twins, and each twin is a single perfect human, but they came to this world together, with many shared aspects. But who knows, I may soon change my view, with new information that presents itself on my perpetual quest towards higher knowledge.

Some of my experiences have led me to an idea that us humans are meant to learn specific lessons in our lifetime, and the people we meet and partner up with along the way are meant to assist us in learning these lessons. When a mission is done, or obsolete, a new person arrives to initiate a new journey of learning the next subject. There is probably more than one lesson going on simultaneously.

An astrologer and spiritual coach, Nico, from www.integrati-vemysticism.com,[94] has a similar view, which he expresses in one of his YouTube videos where he talks about the topic of soulmates. He believes that there are numerous types of soul groups, and we get attracted to members of our own group at different times in life, to take on certain work, and he says that when members of that group start to express higher vibrations of light, opportunities to connect through different types of experiences with other members of that group turn on. And that can be on any level, such as romantic, familial, business, or platonic.

There were situations where people entered my life only to teach me a new skill, or assist me in removing psychological blocks, whether they were better or worse. Important lessons can be taught through interactions with people, both pleasant and not so much. Sometimes energy can also repel people who are not meant to be together, or are meant to end a specific time frame together. It's usually obvious when the connection is not meant to continue, and it's usually accompanied by signs such as annoying situations that set you back in some way, a string of bad luck when together, or, of course, any red flags, such as increased distance or secrecy. Or, they distance themselves when spirit says it's time—peacefully, without a word, or sometimes through a fight—kind of like Shane in the famous old western movie scene by the same name,[95] which I actually found quite meaningful as someone who is an only child and has often arrived to and left places alone, feeling like I'm on some mission. Shane rides off on his horse into the valley, after an emotional goodbye scene with little Joey. Shane, the hero, left just as mysteriously as he showed up, after saving the family and the entire community from a serious threat. Joey's mother and Shane had a romantic connection, as if that was what guided Shane's random arrival there in the first place, despite being a complete stranger. He could have been her soul group connection, who came to carry out some mission to assist her, but they both understood that they weren't meant to be together at this time, because she had a family with her husband, who in fact respected Shane and even offered for him to stay and work with him. That was almost as a suggestive message that you don't mess with a man/woman on a mission. The way of the master is to know when to step back for the greater good, and allow the people that arrive in your life to assist, even if your emotions may perceive it as a negative thing at first.

Let's look at a popular royal example of Prince Harry and Princess Meghan, who have decided to leave the royal life behind while in search of a life of their own. In social-psychological consultations, I found it beneficial to utilize a very profound tool, such as the famous *tarot cards*, which allow for greater clarity of someone's situation. It often makes clients say that I "have hit the nail on the head." To have a little bit of fun, for the purpose of this chapter, I decided to pull a card for this royal couple, to explain the details behind their attraction. So, Meghan received the "world" card, which describes a personality developed through abundant life experience from being out and about, and someone who is confident, wise, and positive; and because of those qualities, this person often ends up travelling the world. Harry received the "seven of cups" card, which describes someone who is living in a fantasy world, escaping reality to cope with hardships, and someone who is in the process of change.

These particular cards were pulled randomly from a deck of seventy-eight cards. I think they actually describe these individuals quite well. It sounds like they are on the opposite end of the social spectrum, possibly being complementary to each other. And I think it's obvious, just by observing them, that they do not seem to be similar—almost like from two different worlds, which they kind of are. One is outgoing and street smart, and comes from a regular upbringing. The other is a bit reserved because of his highly sheltered upbringing. He comes from a background of wealth and status, although we must not to confuse that with lack of suffering, as he has been through a lot, especially with losing his mother, Diana. Meghan has arrived to take him out of his fantasy world and give him a taste of the randomness of raw life. Maybe he just wasn't meant to devote his life to the restrictions placed upon him through his family ties, and if she didn't come into his life, he would have remained there unfulfilled. Since we're talking about energy, besides their micro-level life lessons, there may also be a higher purpose to why those two people have been magnetically pulled together. Maybe their purpose together is to provide a revolutionary catalyst of major change for the structure of the British society, or possibly even for the whole world.

Skeletons in the Closet

People like to be liked. It's something everyone has to keep in mind when interacting with others. Successful marketers surely keep this as a rule of thumb, as their job requires catering to the most powerful human desires. Your front stage self-presentation usually involves managing yourself in a manner you think will be well received by other people. Presenting yourself in a positive way seems like a natural thing to do, and it can be unconscious, like the voice of the salesperson transforming into nearly a child's tone when they ask you if you need help finding something. Especially on first dates, or in first interactions, it's almost expected for people to make sure they are as likeable as possible.

Social desirability bias is one of many response biases in psychological research, which gets in the way of accuracy. It happens when people want to be socially desirable, and will steer their behaviour in a way that will ensure that. Researcher Delroy Paulhus defines *response biases* as "any systematic tendency to answer questionnaire items on some basis that interferes with accurate self-reports. Examples are tendencies to choose the desirable response or the most moderate response, or to agree with statements independent of their content."[96] You may wonder why I am talking about questionnaires. It's not like you will be bringing a questionnaire to a date! I mention this information because these psychological tendencies also apply to the interpersonal interactions in your everyday life. To be seen as socially desirable or just simply liked, most people engage in *selective self-presentation*. The information one shares about themselves may be enhanced or fully untrue. They can also purposefully withhold information that could elicit a negative impression.

There are individual differences in how a person presents oneself positively, and emphasis can be channelled into two different areas: *agency* and *communion*. Paulhus defines *agency* as "the meta-concept associated with self-advancement in social hierarchies." The person may talk about their status being higher, or about making more money, who they know, and where they've been. This reminds me of a friend I used to have, who hung out with a wealthy individual, and he often bragged about the things that his wealthy friend had, as if they were his own. In reality, this friend of mine had a hard time managing his finances himself, so he was using his successful friend as a mask. Paulhus defines *communion* as "the partner concept associated with maintenance of positive relationships."[97] This may be someone's presentation of their friendly self, through a projection of generosity, helpfulness, or loyalty.

The types of biases people exhibit while answering questionnaires will come up in various life situations, like on a first date. All of the stress and excitement in that kind of situation makes it so easy to set aside your conscious filters, and actually believe that what is being presented by the other person is the reality. Social desirability is a major reason that makes **questionnaires** and polls less valid, especially if they're not completely anonymous; although even anonymous questionnaires may not be fully reflective of people's true thoughts. People can actually be lying to themselves without even realizing it. Paulhus and Reid describe self-deception as "the tendency to give favourably biased but honestly held self-descriptions."[98] Many people don't want to admit some things, even to themselves, so they will not admit it elsewhere. This could be due to **cognitive dissonance**, or things like **societal norms**. When it comes to a topic like the frequency of sexual activity, studies often show that women tend to underreport the amount, and the men overreport. In their research article, Christine Kelly and colleagues write that "social desirability bias is particularly problematic in studies involving sexual behaviour, as respondents may deliberately answer questions inaccurately, either by underreporting stigmatized activities or by overreporting normative ones, if their actual behaviour would be considered socially unacceptable."[99] Some things end up being stigmatized in various cultures and societies. They are established by way of attitude-shaping agents such as advertising, mass media, or religious values, which are powerful enough to dictate what is praised and what is looked down upon. A popular belief that has been in existence for a long time, is that it's not socially desirable for women to have a sex life, or talk about it; so women tend to shy away from admitting the frequency of their sexual encounters, not wanting to be called a "slut." The term "slut" is used to slander women for the same behaviour that gets men called a "player." Society tends to spare men from that burden. By the way, did you know that the Nordic Goddess named *Freya*,[100] who represented love, beauty, sex, and war, was known for having many lovers among the gods and elves? There are many mythical as well as real examples of women having multiple men, in the past and now, such as Draupadi, a central character in Indian history, who was married to five brothers.

It is important, however, to maintain a level of respectability, and to make sure that women, as well as men, understand the value of committing themselves to a quality candidate with whom it is possible to join forces and build a "kingdom." It is also crucial to keep in mind how much unfair labelling harms relationships, and individuals on all sides. When men are praised for their sexual frequency (and let's face it, there is nothing wrong with sexual frequency, as long as it's consensual), and women are condemned for the same thing, there will be many more feelings getting hurt, and wrong choices being made. It may interfere in the emotional health when it elicits feelings of guilt within women. Not just in the West, but in most cultures, it is socially desirable for men to brag about their sexual voyages. Single men like to talk about their single life now, and married men like to talk about how popular they were with the ladies before marriage... and then they like to mention how they met their perfect one, but they still want to brag about those prior. This common trend causes most men to over-estimate rather than downplay their sexual encounters, as studies continuously confirm. Many men even seem to prefer to exemplify a single man's image online. Through their study of comparing online presentation of men and women, researchers Magnusen and Dundes have found that men don't mention their relationship partners in their posts, or on their social media page, as much as women mention on theirs.[101]

The realm of online dating has become a favourite hangout for *social desirability bias*, where most people try to show themselves in the most desirable way they know how, selecting from a wide range of options on the scale of lies, enabled by the lie-blurring ability of a digital screen. I'm sure you have experienced someone presenting themselves in ways which, at some point, you realized weren't true. But this practice of obscuring the truth often catches up with its culprit; and in more extreme situations, it can backfire. Besides being embarrassing, it wastes everyone's time and energy, which is valuable in our fast-paced society. It creates friction between two people because the truth will have to sneak in at some point. Also, for that person, explaining why they exaggerated their story can turn into quite an embarrassing verbal workout.

Pop-Culture, the Love Guru

In recent times, sexually explicit content moved from the magazines under the mattresses, to the digital screens within the palms of millions of hands around the world. With the increase in divorces, decreased popularity of marriage, and the increased exposure to sexually explicit material, concepts like commitment, romance, or love may be getting lost in dreams from the past.

The meaning of love or romance in our society, and how we relate it to relationships, has visibly followed the trends of popular culture. Our elders tell much different stories about love than most young people do today. Relationships, today, tend to be more fragile, as many people find themselves confused about what exactly love is. There has been a clear pattern of rising intensity and prevalence of sexual material in the entertainment industry, largely fuelled by sexual objectification of females. *Objectification* means treating a living being as an object, ignoring their intelligence, competence, or even emotions. Music has always been deeply inspired by topics of love, sexual attraction, and relationships. It also has attained this power to serve as a guide as to what men and women expect out of romantic interactions, and as a counsellor, to help the broken hearts feel supported. Artists are expected to express genuine experiences and emotions in their songs. Music is like an influential love guru of our society.

Open sexual discourse in pop music is a widely discussed topic, especially among the more mature generations, who say that the music of today has changed, just as our idea of love has changed with it. Especially in the last 20 years, there has been an explosion of explicit sexual content in "love" songs. The language of love has unquestionably changed. Popular love songs of the 50s contained sentimental vocabulary, praised the inner value of a person, and promoted generosity, with examples of giving someone your heart, as sung by Nat King Cole. Sex was something that everyone imagined in their own minds and kept behind closed doors. Such artists made listeners believe that just being in the company of the one special person was worthy of climbing over the highest mountain to get to them. Even a more modern musical sex symbol from 20 years ago, D'Angelo,[102] responsible for what became known as the sexiest music video around, has presented sexual energy in a way that was not counting on disrespecting women to captivate an audience. Even in the old R&B genre, which was very sexually charged, it lacked the in-your-face negative sexual overtones as present in popular music today.

The male and female artists express a very contrasting view of love and romance. Liz Phair, Halsey, and Dua Lipa all agree that they feel tired and lonely, which reflects the feelings of many young women today. They sing about the selfishness of men who see them as a toy. They don't refrain from blaming themselves for making bad choices, or being broken, and that is the message young girls are singing along to. In some cases, the women have taken a more aggressive stance, like Cardi B., who shows off her love of independence, attention, sexual explicitness, and the material things. Beyonce, with her dramatic sexual moves, has successfully used her own inevitable sexualization as an example of women's freedom of expression, strength, and domination; and if we didn't know that she has a husband, we could assume that she is quite angry at men.

The men, on the other hand, seem to be in a much better mood, as seen in the music videos or commercials. Yes, "seem," because dear gentlemen, this may seem like it's all serving you well, but once you look deeper, the reality gets darker. Your well-being can be at a disadvantage in the long run. Researchers Zubriggen and colleagues examined "whether exposure to mass media is related to self-objectification and objectification of one's partner, which in turn is hypothesized to be related to relationship and sexual satisfaction."[103] And it's inevitable that relationship and sexual satisfaction is good for our overall quality of life and well-being. The study revealed evidence for the negative effects of objectification within the relationships of young adults. Results showed the chain reaction of how "consuming objectifying media was associated with increased partner-objectification, which was related to decreased relationship satisfaction." Men who consumed objectifying media were found to be more likely to objectify their partner, and this in turn was related to their own sexual dissatisfaction. Among many studies with similar results, Gemma Saez and colleagues also found that "in men, a higher tendency to perpetrate objectifying behaviours, as well as chronically focus on their partner's appearance, is associated to a lower sexual satisfaction."[104] Maybe the rock stars from "The Rolling Stones" were consuming too much objectifying media, while spewing it back onto the masses through their famous song, "I Can't Get No Satisfaction." Told ya, words are spells... or wait, I didn't tell you yet! Those jewels are coming up in the last chapter! So stick around!

You know, it kind of makes me wonder, as men become more influenced by pop-culture to be superficial in their expression of love, romance, or sexuality, and the more they become unhappy with their level of sexual satisfaction, would that mean that deep within their core, men also have the same desires for emotionally nurturing closeness as women do? If we take off this layer of external influence, we may be moving further away from the evolutionary perspective. As the *Zubriggen* article mentions, "Objectification appears to have negative consequences for both the target and the perpetrator." Basically, the sexually explicit media content is harmful to the well-being of men, as well as women.

The modern male artists appear to be thriving in fulfillment and in love. They are in love with the shape of women, and the movement of their physical bodies, as Ed Sheeran proclaims. Some are even more in love with themselves, like Bruno Mars, who sees himself as a privilege to be around. Online magazine *Odyssey* writes that women are being treated like second-class citizens, while artists like Bruno profit from harmful stereotypes and "reinforce stereotypical gender roles on how exactly women are supposed to 'please' or cater to men."[105] Such messages permeate the minds of young boys, teaching them what the ideal woman should look like, and that all that matters is her body. This creates a society that is moving away from the genuine idea of love as it relates to companionship, generosity, and mutual fulfillment, the stuff that is often reminisced by our grandparents. Love is still out there somewhere. It is nice to see more love for nature and for animals today than ever before, and love for our families seems to be doing fine—although what will happen to families if love leaves the relationship department?

Humanity has always possessed a hidden sexual fire burning deep within its core—it's part of our divine design. The intensity and explicitness of it, and how much of it is shown to the world, is dependent on each individual's unique socialization, biological factors, norms and values, or psychological processes (like the one revealed by the earlier mentioned study, where the participants rated the sexual story after they were primed with thoughts about their older relatives or peers). Pop-culture is responsible for fanning the inner fire of human sexuality in the wrong direction, spreading it all over the social worlds of new generations, upon whom we hold high hopes for saving the world.

Music tends to accompany our inner development in the emotionally imbalanced stage of adolescence. Most music is consumed by youth, and most passionately too. The things kids don't want to talk to their guardians about, such as having a crush on someone at school, who may not have noticed, are comforted by songs that express similar feelings of desperation, confusion, or joy related to a special person. And I'm sure you may agree, whether you are in the entertainment industry or not, that entertainers are not known to be the most stable or successful in the love department. They often appear to jump from relationship to relationship, and their relationships are highly publicized, or even used to increase fame, in some extreme cases. Funny enough, many of those who are in successful relationships actually act as if they're not. For example, for so many years, I had no idea that Snoop Dogg had been married since the 90s. The image of a single man surrounded by numerous beautiful women, which he pushes onto the world, is not exactly aligned with the real image of his personal life; at least I'd assume this based on the fact that he is married, but not knowing how he actually gets down. I think it's safe to say, though, that his wife doesn't let him have "hoes" in different area codes... actually, wait, that was rapper Ludacris, who also has been in a steady relationship with his current wife, since 2009,[106] and the "area codes" song came out in 2011.

Influence doesn't have to involve conscious engagement; much of it goes straight to the unconscious level and grows there. It's not only affecting children through suggesting this extreme approach to love and romance, and that men are there to use women as objects, and women are there to be helpless, mad, or give into becoming a source of entertainment for men. Adults are easily influenced too, and as the studies reflect, sexual objectification can backfire and come back like a boomerang. It appears to be an infinitely hungry beast: The more you feed it, the more dissatisfied it becomes.

CHAPTER 6

CULTURED

"I succeeded by saying what everyone else is thinking."

– Joan Rivers

6

Dr. Humour

Think about the times you have laughed really hard. Did it involve other people? Most likely, it did. In fact, *Psychology Today* website states that you are over 30 times more likely to laugh in a social setting than laughing alone, to yourself[107] (which happens, and there is nothing wrong with that). Even when you are alone, and you laugh at something you saw on your phone, it counts as social, because it came from someone else, and you must have had something in common with the person who posted it to agree on the comedic value of it. It appears that humour has a strong presence within social interactions. Laughing is also found to make people feel good. But why does it feel good? Possibly, one of the reasons is that it satisfies some of the human needs for social connectedness, and sharing an agreement on a specific topic with someone else provides a confirmation of some level of closeness, and that can feel good.

In his sufficiently titled book, *Social: Why Our Brains Are Wired to Connect*, professor of biobehavioural sciences, *Matthew Lieberman,* presents his findings about how humans are not just motivated by their selfish motives, but within our drive for social connection, we have some motives to make others happy, which is partly why he says we are wired together.[108] You know those annoying laughing sounds that you hear on sitcoms? Do you know where that idea came from? It is probably one of the biggest psychological tools used by the media. An article in the *Association for Psychological Science* web journal says that this started when a "CBS sound engineer, Charley Douglass, hated dealing with the inappropriate laughter of live audiences; so, in 1950, he started recording his own laugh tracks. These early laugh tracks were intended to help people sitting at home feel like they were in a more social situation, such as sitting at a crowded theatre." According to the article, "studies have shown that people are more likely to laugh in response to a video clip with canned laughter than to one without a laugh track."[109]

Culture is a common factor in many social-psychological topics you come across throughout this book. You may have noticed that the things you find more funny are the things you are familiar with to some degree, that are part of your identity, your social roles, your status, age group, your beliefs, or things that represent the cultural norms of the group you're part of. When you find someone else who gets the joke you're laughing at, you both will feel some level of mutual connectedness or support. Shared themes establish a level of contact with strangers, ensuring us not just that there are others around us who also understand a particular inside joke, but that there are others around us who are on our side, if anything. The people you are in agreement with are more likely to assist you as compared to those who may not. Have you ever had a situation where you happened to express your true opinion of something out loud in public, and a random person who overheard you began to express their agreement? That happened to me recently, and it sparked such a great feeling. This was a feeling of being a real human, freely interacting with other random humans on the street, without fear, without reservation. Noel Carroll talks about this in his book about humour, when he mentions that "comic laughter in concert with like-minded and like-feeling revellers confirms, reinforces, and celebrates our membership in a community."[110] Laughing at the same jokes reminds people of things that unite them, things which the outsiders wouldn't understand. Carroll mentions the creation of an "us" vs "them" paradigm, through this act of sharing commonly popular thoughts. So that person and I were an "us," vs the rest of the people there who may not have agreed with us.

City Swag

While working on this book, many interesting things happened to inspire its contents. As I was enjoying some coffee here at a Coffee Culture restaurant (notice the word "culture"), I ran into one of Toronto's finest comedians, and popular social media personality, Brandon Walczak (@the6atsix on Instagram). He happened to walk into the place right when I was writing about the connection between culture and humour—something that he represents so well. Brandon has gained popularity because of his positively devious comedic talent. He makes his own very unique Instagram mini productions, where he parodies the nature of interactions between the urban youth of the Toronto region, which has developed a style and language of its own, and which is something that would seem foreign to outsiders. I have followed his posts for a while because the social researcher in me found his clever presentation of this social phenomenon very amusing. He is a master in presenting this culturally twisted parody.

Many young people of the Toronto region listen to urban music styles; many of them are from immigrant families, and the rise of Drake in the last decade has significantly changed the cultural landscape of this region. These factors, among many others, have resulted in the spontaneous creation of a specific Toronto subculture—not exactly named by any special name—that is recognized by the distinct vocabulary used, fashion choices, music choices, and so on. Small doses of this style of being, seem to be accepted, and can even add to your Toronto social capital, depending on the nature of your business or social group. A good example of this is the Toronto Raptors NBA team using the slang "We the North," and some people have questioned why there is a grammatical error: Shouldn't it say, "We're the North?" The answer is no, because it is an urban slang, and in this case not just Torontonian, but hip-hop inspired, and really should even say, "We da North," but that would be too extreme for mainstream marketing.

What Carroll describes in his book regarding comic laughter being a celebration of membership in a specific community, Brandon exemplifies in his Instagram and YouTube channels by way of his artistic portrayal of a specific culture, in a funny way that connects thousands of people through laughter. He not only makes people laugh at the things familiar to them, but also forces them to think about how they themselves behave in public settings, and how their behaviour may appear to others who are not familiar with this way of being. This forces people into an introspection about how closed off from the rest of the world they might be, while swimming in their own neighbourhood sauce and forgetting that there is a world outside to which all that they hold dear is actually quite insignificant. One of his videos goes even deeper into a sociological perspective, and cleverly portrays the blocks to success so often encountered by many of such sub culturally-entrenched young people, or people who are trying to turn their life around, when it is time to face the bureaucracy of the institutional and professional world.[111] Watch the video to see what I'm talking about. It is linked for you on this book's website.

Laugh Together, Cry Together

Culture and humour strengthen the link between members of specific cultures, but at the same time shut out those who "don't get it," which facilitates the "us" versus "them" paradigm that Carroll talks about. The stock market investing community on Twitter has cultivated a very distinct culture. The jokes made by investors about certain stocks, companies, and management officials, or even about each other, greatly contribute to the creation of that culture, and encompasses everything that sprouts out of participation in the concept of investing money. At the beginning, it appeared to me as if everyone was speaking another language, and I couldn't contribute anything to the conversations. I was googling what these people could have possibly meant, trying to make sense of the jokes. Later, when I learned charts, the ways of the market, and it's vocabulary, I was able to benefit from the goodness of that particular community's humour, and contribute to it. That's what it comes down to: Communities are sometimes formed organically, and sometimes they're manufactured, but they are something that humans seem to be drawn to, physically, spiritually, and emotionally.

Comedic and **tragic** visions are tools that help sculpt and uphold communities using their common values. Either one of these two polarities, the positive comedy and the negative tragedy, can be used to achieve the same outcomes. Comedy can be used to bring about feelings of togetherness, community, or belonging to a group, and so can tragedy. The investing community is a good example where comedy and tragedy appears regularly. Investors are brought together by the shared experiences of money loss, which is tragic, and the excitement of making money, which is almost comedic, because every time it happens, it brings joy to the participant. Jokes in that community are sometimes made out of the pain of material loss, foolish behaviours of newbies, or the annoyance due to impatience, and they can serve to uplift people who share similar experiences, which others, who haven't gone through them, just wouldn't understand.

It is clear that comedy and tragedy are effective in bringing people closer together, or at least in providing a feeling that it is doing so. In our increasingly individualistic society, it is becoming harder to have daily experiences of community, but shared humour can serve to create an illusion of connection when distance is involved.

You're So Funny

Those who are considered to be on the higher end of the funny scale, often happen to enjoy a greater VIP status in social settings. They tend to be the valued guests at social gatherings, and seem to make new friends easily. Most people aren't really funny, as we all can admit. And they shouldn't feel bad. There is lots that can be done to offset this concern,

and it is not even all that hard to achieve. Simply making people feel positive around you will bring you positive social results. Laughter is about feeling positive and connected to
others, or validated. You can try harder to be better at listening to others by asking more questions and allowing them to
speak, and offering words of encouragement, which will get
you positivity points with that person because they will be
impressed with how much care you have awarded them.
Don't try hard to be funny; let funny come out naturally. But
don't suppress it either. If people tell you that you're funny,
then believe them, and don't let your talent go to waste—you
were meant to share it. The world needs every bit of it.

In the first chapter, I really stressed the fact that in psychology, there is a rule that you cannot just assume you know
something based on your idea of it, or based on logic itself,
as you will likely end up being incorrect. Here is an example
of that. You would probably agree that most laughter happens when we hear or see something funny, right? Then you
would get this wrong on an exam. There is a cool study that
examines the science of laughter, presented on the *Psychology
Today* website, in which researchers observed and noted
1200 natural laughter episodes of random people in public
places. They found that most people are quite unknowledge-
able of the purpose of laughter. Actually, most people think
laughter is just a response to comedy. The study revealed that
only 10–20% of laughter is preceded by something like a
funny joke.[112] That means that about 80% or the majority of
times you laugh, it is not because you heard someone say

something really funny. People involved in a conversation, laugh even after someone says something simple like "it was nice meeting you!" It was also found that the speaker laughed about 50% more than their audience. Could this extra laughter in a conversation stem from my earlier idea about people wanting to appear nice, and the laughter may serve to add comfort to the interaction, or it could be triggered by things like nervousness, or maybe a desire for attention?

I'll tell you a personal story, because an ex-boyfriend of mine is a perfect example of this phenomenon. He has always been very physically attractive, but I can't say that he's a comedian by any means. I remember noticing this interesting behaviour from women when we were at social gatherings. Whether it was friends of mine, friends of his, or strangers, after he spoke, they would often respond by saying, "Oh, (name), you're so funny!" And the only funny thing was the fact that he didn't even say anything funny! What would normally follow would be this high pitched giggle, then a casual tap on his arm, as if that was to somehow solidify their gratitude for providing them with this mysterious amusement. This situation reminds me of a social-psychological concept of what is called the **halo effect**. It is a cognitive bias that makes your perception of one particular trait automatically spill all over other traits, and it usually involves the trait of attractiveness. Studies find that when people rate someone as attractive, they also give them the rating of being nice, trustworthy, or funny at the same time.[113] So here, my exboyfriend got away with being awarded social points for being funny, only because he was attractive. Even if he was saying something a little bit funny, the fact that he was attractive was energizing his funny rating to a higher level.

Next time you are in a group of people, observe when people laugh, what was said just before they laughed, and send me a comment on my website if you observe something interesting. We can maybe laugh together! After all, laughter is one of the few good things that are contagious!

Experts Agree You Should Keep Reading This Book

Many people assume that they know how to follow good judgement. Most of us are pretty confident that we will not fall for anything sketchy, or let others talk us into doing anything we don't believe in or agree with. But some of the biggest questions of human existence continue to be asked, like why do good people end up doing bad things, or why do smart people do stupid things?

Research into the theories of persuasion and influence continuously finds that most people (often it's about 60–80%) behave in a predictable way when they are under some form of pressure, or in an unclear social situation. For example, if you're parked in your car at the shopping centre parking lot, and a stranger in a nice suit and tie comes up and knocks on your window as if he wants to ask you something, the most likely reaction that can be expected is you rolling down your window. The predictability comes from feeling the urge to obey some societal norm, or act out of some inner schemas or biases that a person who is dressed like a professional can be trusted, and that it's polite to respond to someone who looks like they may have some position of authority. If that person was wearing a dark hooded sweatshirt and baggy jeans, you may have likely hit the gas and driven away. Predictability makes people vulnerable to being swayed or exploited in some way.

Cialdini defines **conformity** as "the act of changing one's behaviour to match the responses of others,"[114] matching up with group norms or politics. He admits that "researchers have tended to concentrate their efforts on examining social influence processes that are subtle, indirect, and nonconscious," possibly because compliance by using overt pressure tactics is an old way of convincing people of things. In recent years, conformity methods have taken on an invisible cloak. Many people conform to things because persuasion can make its way into your field of acceptance in a gradual and sometimes almost invisible manner.

You may find yourself caught between deciding to do what you think is best, or doing what may be the most acceptable to others. In the case of the **bystander effect**, people witnessing an emergency can become stunned by the ambiguity of a sudden situation, preventing them from acting in a fast manner. It is, after all, a valid concern for one's safety. The attacker could potentially hurt the good Samaritan; so, no matter what, always think before you put yourself in any danger.

Other than that, some people can feel inhibited towards performing actions that force them to suddenly take charge and step into the spotlight. It could be that they have been conditioned to seek the assistance or direction of someone with a greater position of **authority**. Leave it to the experts! Since even before your birth, the experts were in control of your situation—from x-rays, to birth, then vaccinations, check-up appointments, nutrition suggestions—not to mention the experts who were "experting" your body and spirit into the possession of a specific religious organization, claiming to take care of the evil that may otherwise overtake you. In many cultures, such as in North America, at least in recent years, it became a societal trend to leave specific things to the appropriate entity, division, jurisdiction, organ, agent, representative, practitioner... You get the point.

It is a great thing to just have all these people doing things for you, and all you have to do is pay them in one way or another. If you don't have to spend the whole day fixing the roof, it leaves you extra time to focus on growing your business or taking care of your health. Though, in this world full of experts, we must recognize how we have become increasingly reliant on others to do things for us, or assume that others have more knowledge, and we offer them our blind trust. With every cause comes an effect, such as the loss of creativity and initiative, possibly leading to the inability to take care of oneself, resorting to the mercy of strangers for increasingly basic things. It is important to discern which experts are valuable, because life without them is not really possible, and if it is possible, it's not going to be comfortable or even safe to some extent. Definitely hire an expert when the electricity malfunctions in your home; or when you need to lose weight, hire a trainer; or when feeling sick, do see a doctor. However, you should always listen to your intuition when dealing with one—if something about them feels off at any moment, it's likely off. Also, make an effort to learn basic things in your life, like where the oil goes in your car, and what type you need to buy. Do try to grow a vegetable; be curious about how basic things in your daily life actually work. It will train your mind to be on guard when experts fail, as they often can. After all, your life is in your hands first and foremost, and no one will care as much as you should.

Within a sudden social emergency, cognitive biases, like the **diffusion of responsibility,** show up. It's an automatic behaviour to look around and hope that other people are going to take charge first. When the fire alarm goes off in the shopping mall, people often look at other people to see if they are leaving or staying, and then they try to locate the security crew to see how they will act. People look to others for guidance because they may hold a low rating of their own abilities to do what's necessary in an unfamiliar situation, when suddenly faced with one. It can be consciously or even unconsciously. Most will try to automatically seek out someone who they perceive to be more qualified to make decisions or carry out actions. Many people are actually not that fast with decision making, and also many are shy. This also happens because people like to avoid taking responsibility for things, as we have learned when talking about the concept of actor-observer bias and attribution theory, which are about blaming external factors for their own mistakes. When there are others around, it's easier to assume that if anything, the responsibility is somehow divided between all who are present.

Looking to experts for guidance trains the mind to also more easily accept their authority. *Wikipedia* describes the concept of obedience as a form of **social influence** in which a person yields to explicit instructions or orders from authority figures. **Obedience** to experts and authority figures is also a social norm, which has been embedded within the sub conscious mind of most people, kind of thanks to our parents. Kids are repeatedly advised to listen to the elders, to always be polite to aunts and uncles (even if the kid senses some bad vibes, they're often ignored), to respect teachers, priests, and doctors, to listen to people on television, and definitely to never question invisible authority figures like Jesus, Muhammad, Abraham, Buddha, or Krishna, among others. I was lucky to come across a very funny and enlightening international film called *OMG*,[115] through one of my professors, Dr. Philipa Carter, whom I admired for her ability to present great truths in simple ways, seasoned with sarcasm and humour. In this film, the main character was driven to challenge the social norms of his community, and go after both the physical and invisible authority figures. He set out to sue God in court after an insurance company denied him payment for damages when his business was devastated by extreme weather, something that the insurance company classifies as an "act of God." I highly recommend this film. It presents the power of conformity to social norms, and the challenges of being an individual in a crowd, in a very funny and clever way, while providing many useful social and spiritual life lessons in the meantime.

It is important to give experts and other authority figures the level of respect they deserve, and to acknowledge their degree of wisdom and experience. You will likely benefit from consulting with an expert or better yet, a few, in whatever you're dealing with. What I want to mostly address is what many of our parents failed to convey to us, and that is to acknowledge the limits of that respect, and always do our own research into people, places, or organizations. This research must have some depth, so it has to consider things such as: What does that person want from me? Who's funding this message, person, place, or organization? Whose interests are linked to it, and how can they create bias? How will I benefit? Is this the right thing to do and serves the highest good? Obedience to experts and authority figures is charged up by the cultural influences that you come across throughout your life. They can be shouted or whispered in the popular media outlets, and passed from one generation to the next. When you put an authority figure on television, the effects will intensify because television is a platform that strictly limits who gets the inside pass, so it definitely adds substantial weight to the legitimacy of authority.

The status of someone like the famous Dr. Oz is an example of a media personality who became influential in many areas. I remember when I was in the cosmetics business, and many customers would ask about the skincare products or advice featured on that program. They tended to ignore the advice of the beauty advisors who had worked in the industry for years and were offering a tailored solution, specific for that person's needs, as they demanded the product that was advertised. Dr. Oz features an abundance of great and useful content, and he actually has a medical degree from a highly renowned university. But he has to pay the bills. Since his platform is a popular television show, it makes the information he provides susceptible to bias due to restrictions that come with the reliance on profits from advertisers. A professor of Georgetown University Department of Family Medicine has done a project to examine this show, and found that the hosts on the show frequently pushed products made by companies that advertise on the show.[116] Popular media content is increasingly influenced by economic ties, and all kinds of people are becoming authorities on various things, while influencing decisions of viewers. These agents are informally granted authority over numerous topics like skincare, medicine, fitness, psychology, and more. More and more entertainment shows are almost forcefully attempting to occupy the space of politics, and people will subconsciously attribute a person on the screen, such as a late night talk show host, to having expertise in whatever they are talking about, due to this ingrained assumption of the exclusivity of the screen.

When it comes to something like authority, the danger lies in the ***halo effect***, which we talked about earlier: the psychological tendency to attach qualities to a person who may not actually embody them. It can make you automatically think that if someone works at the bank, they are automatically trustworthy, sincere, or give good financial advice. Obedience to authority figures translates into respect, and respect can spill over to other related traits such as trustworthiness, legitimacy, knowledge, kindness, wisdom, or strength. Don't let the halo mesmerize you!

The Devil Made Me Do It

Society tends to award authority and expert figures with much control over the definition of situation, which means that those who have a higher status get to make decisions and define what is right or wrong for all involved. What tends to happen is, what I noticed after my experience in a university environment, people with money have authority over people with knowledge, and are awarded power. For example, topics that could be getting more research are not on focus because they may not attract much sponsorship. Marketers have utilized this automatic respect for not just authority itself, but our response to simply the symbolism linked to authority.

Images of people with white coats or sharp suits are used to advertise products, as it will match up to the concept of legitimacy and knowledge in the subconscious minds of those on the receiving end. The pharmaceutical commercials often show a model who is dressed to look like a doctor. Some advertisements will show symbols of various associations or groups who apparently support the product, giving the target audience a sense of security that some groups have put their name behind it. Next time you're in a department store, put on your social psychology goggles and take a look at the Clinique cosmetics counter. Their beauty advisors must wear the white coats at all times. They even get special pins to put on their coats to show off the experience level of the particular advisor. This company does happen to train their sales crew more than many other cosmetics companies, but professional nurses or dermatologists are likely not among them. The white coat gives off an aura of respect, expertise, and authority, and will affect how you process the information coming from the source that wears it. The company seeks to present an image of being the skincare authority among their competition, and the coats are meant to shape that perception in an often confused, overwhelmed, and sceptical beauty shopper.

The white coat has been at the centre of one of psychology's most famous studies ever done. This one was the one that messed me up the most and drove me to share it with the world. It is the shock experiment study by Stanley Milgram.[117] Run over to this book's website and find the link in the references section to watch it, because I can't possibly describe it as effectively as the video can. I think if everyone saw this, the world would be a much better place, because knowledge is power, and it would protect people from falling victim to negative or malicious influence, by making them prepared to be quicker in recognizing warning signs. This study was inspired by a very common concern that arose after World War 2 was over. People were left wondering to what extent regular people would follow orders of authority, and become persuaded to act against their beliefs, and even harm other people. Suddenly, you have huge numbers of regular people, killing other huge numbers of people, including men, women, and children, and no one stands up and says, "Guys, you don't think what we're asked to do is crazy?" Lots of research began into the topic of conformity and obedience to authority. Milgram's study found that as much as over 60% of participants followed orders despite their concerns of doing the wrong thing, and similar results turned up each time this study had been repeated, by him and others in the future.

Participants later couldn't believe that they allowed themselves to be influenced into proceeding this far with something that their inner spirit was urging them to stop. This realization actually left some participants disappointed with themselves. As hard as it was to come to terms with being so capable of being influenced to the point of causing harm, it was a very important lesson, which will help them avoid getting played in the future. As I mentioned in the beginning of this book, I used to think I was smart enough to know bad from good, until I saw the footage from studies like the Milgram shock experiment, which forces you to put yourself in the shoes of these participants, and to admit the truth to yourself that you may have followed these extreme instructions for some duration of time. It made me realize that anyone, no matter how smart, can fall victim to such influence when the right mix of factors come together in the right context, creating the perfect conditions for influence and compliance.

Socialization into a specific culture and its beliefs can influence decision making throughout our daily experiences, big or small. What are your thoughts after watching the Milgram study? Do you think you would have been able to recognize what was happening, and be one of the very few participants who actually quit?

CHAPTER 7

THE BOX

"He who has Science and has Art,
Religion, too, has he;
Who has not Science, has not Art,
Let him religious be!"

– Johann Wolfgang von Goethe

7

Elephant in the Room

S ometimes it's easy to get in this mood of not wanting to be around people. Sometimes I hear people say that they would prefer being around animals rather than people. Others say that they have an increasing urge to move to the countryside, closer to nature. I must admit that I think this way at times, not just because I have three super cool rescued animals at home and I'd like to have more, but because the older I get, the more I notice the very social conditions that made me feel the urgency to write this book. With the onset of distanced social interactions, brought on by the world health and political situation of 2020, it seems like this book was meant to come just in time to possibly prevent more cracks in the walls of our vulnerable connections.

Other humans can be a handful to deal with, often unconsciously, and it can sometimes feel that being alone in the world would be a relief. The irony is that as incompatible as humans can be, we have a built-in need for social interaction and closeness, and not just for an exchange of goods, but also for emotionally fulfilling interaction. Often, it happens that such need causes people to hold on to negative sources of interaction, because they prefer that to nothing at all. Being isolated from the social world, which provides social support, stimulation, and learning, has negative psychological implications. But balance is still key; it never stops. So whether you are more or less social, it is very important to know when your inner spirit calls on you to get out there and have some "people fun," or when you need to become a hermit for a while to give yourself a chance to meditate on your life's path, and deeply inhale the relaxing scent of some solitude.

We all belong to groups. Sometimes we sign up to them, or we happen to be classified under some. A group is when there are three or more people who interact together, and are connected by a shared goal, often influencing each other in some way. Groups are essential to societal well-being, and they can be a motivating factor in creating personal or social change, as it's not always easy to get things done alone. They can offer fun times, learning experiences, social support, and expansion of various talents, so benefits are endless. Most of the time, you choose to sign up to groups like sports teams, guided travel tours, fraternities, or various online clubs, but I think it's important to point out that we all belong to groups that we don't choose but are automatically signed up, such as family, nationality, or even zodiac sign. Also, interaction among members of a group doesn't have to be physical; it can be symbolic, where certain things like a flag, a religious figure, or a style of clothing can serve as a form of interaction among group members who may not even be aware of each other's existence. Such are the powers of a group.

As in any situation, it's crucial to be aware of the social-psychological processes that may be forming when various people link together. Think back to the ***mere exposure effect***, which proves that simply being around other people has some effects on you, and the study that showed that just thinking of an older family member, without being around them (and remember, family is a group too), has literally changed the opinions of the young women participants. I think it's safe to say that any group will have the power to affect the thoughts, feelings, and/or behaviours of its members; but of course, the strength of influence will be mediated by other factors, like the level of importance this particular membership holds in the person's life.

Perhaps the most well known of such group effects is the theory of ***groupthink***. Groupthink is this invisible haze that covers your true opinion or attitude when you're interacting with a group of people who you depend on, respect, or have some reason for solidarity with. People in a group will feel the need to maintain this solidarity for various reasons, and can feel hesitant to express their true thoughts, especially if they assume others will disagree. Or, it's easy to sometimes forget that there are people out there who just don't like any level of conflict, and don't like to stand out or be singled out, so they will probably just agree with something just to maintain peace of mind, and later they may just disappear without a word and deal with the issue in silence.

Earlier, we discussed the concept of **emotional dependency** in adults, and it actually shows up in groupthink. Dr. G. Jantz determined that one of the traits associated with dependent people is that "they have difficulty disagreeing with others, out of fear. Have you ever seen that tongue-in-cheek sign that says, 'Everyone is entitled to their own opinion, as long as it agrees with mine?' A dependent person has a variation on that sign: 'I am entitled to my own opinion, as long as it agrees with yours.' A dependent person does not feel worthy to express or have an opinion that differs from someone else they feel they need."[118]

Illusion of unanimity is a symptom of *groupthink* where silence means yes. In other words, it's the moment of "dude, I was thinking the same thing" realization, after you were complacent with something that you actually didn't vibe with at all, and you had no idea that in fact other people thought the same thing as you, and they also didn't speak up. Often, consensus is just an illusion. Other than this conscious inhibition of expression, each person's perspective is a unique kaleidoscope of ideas and thoughts. People often don't even know why they think what they think, and can change their opinions at any moment; therefore, the deeper we go, the more we may just realize that full agreement may be a rare thing if it's possible at all. People most likely never actually fully agree; there is always at least a sprinkle of some implicit differences, while agreement may be assumed on the surface. It's not something that you just ponder while attending your friend's birthday party or an industry-networking event, automatically thinking that people you're interacting with actually share the same views. And while your awareness levels get consumed by the energy of the conversation, the distraction of the setting, and the head nods of your listeners, you may simply not have the capacity to monitor that in such a moment.

I have linked a snippet of the *Curb Your Enthusiasm* sitcom,[119] where this **illusion of unanimity** is displayed for you in a clever and humourous manner. It may remind you of some dinners you went to, where something that the host served tasted terrible, but everyone agreed through their teeth that it was good, to avoid upsetting the host. Larry is probably the most groupthink resistant character I can think of (or even person, if that's how he is in real life). He has no filter in social settings. Here, he gets himself thrown out of a dinner party because he was honest and openly stated his issue with the quality of water that was served at the table; while everyone else quietly agreed with him, but they didn't want to admit it. Isn't it interesting how we're taught to be honest as a child, but in adult life, it seems like a poor social strategy? So, what would you do in this case—state your disagreement or shut up and drink up?

Groups have naturally formed "filtering algorithms," kind of like the internet ones that select the advertisements that show up on your screen, based on what it assumes you may be interested in. Many types of groups can have some common ground that preserves itself one way or another. Preservation seems to be an accepted way to keep groups alive, and members are prone to being isolated from views that are alternative to that common ground. Members of most groups out there must know that there is a high possibility of getting psychologically locked into a "group bubble." It can exist in a family context where the parents may be trying to preserve the family traditions or beliefs, and expect the same from their children. The children can hide their dissent due to the worry over upsetting their parents.

It often happens in religious groups, where members are directly or indirectly encouraged to block outside information that doesn't match the ideology of that religion. In his book, *Anthropology of Religion*, James Bielo mentions **bureaucratic authority**, one of Max Weber's distinctions of authority, which helps to explain the longevity and preservation of religion through institutionalization. He writes that "bureaucratic authority is oriented toward keeping the status quo, maintaining cultural conditions as they are, and reproducing the legitimacy of an institutional order." He then profoundly states that "in the bureaucracy, the office itself is more powerful than any individual who occupies it at any given time,"[120] because the leaders change, like for example, the Pope, but the seat remains unchanged and upholds the same structure through years, as well as the dogma that is embedded into the group must remain unchanged so that it doesn't create cracks in its walls. Whether it's institutionalized, large groups, or smaller groups such as the local moms' club, there is often someone who takes on the leadership role, appointed or just casually or naturally. It is almost inevitable that the group will develop some type of narrative within it, often based on whose ideas happen to be stronger or louder. Disagreement can then be taken as an attempt to overpower that leader, or a disruption to the perceived smooth flow towards the group's purpose, even when it actually could help the group survive better by pointing out mistakes.

The website *Your Dictionary* gives a highly likely example of this groupthink "bubble," which right away reminded me of my past experience while working for a (now bankrupt) large department store chain. This example talks about "a group of employees at a company with a product that is quickly becoming outdated, who are unwilling to consider new alternatives to advance in the industry. The employees may collectively live in a world where they can't understand why their product is not selling, and may refuse to acknowledge the economic reality that they cannot survive without advancing."[121] That's exactly what happened to my ex-employer, among other things. All levels of management projected a strange common theme of attachment to outdated ideas about the clientele, the products, and the trends, and made no effort to do their research, and anyone who came in with new ideas was purposefully discredited, because they posed a threat to their comfortable seat on a sinking ship.

When people feel free to be objective and speak from their actual point of view and experience, it can often have great benefits for that group, although it often comes out after the fact. The more quiet ones may hold the most valuable solutions that may be needed to make something work better, or prevent error, but group environments are usually too harsh for them to flourish. To understand the concept of productivity and why groups can't achieve synergy, Ivan Steiner coined the term ***process loss,*** which happens when group interaction flaws get in the way of the quality of problem solving,[122] and leads to things like loss of motivation due to reliance on one very extroverted member to dominate, even when they may not be the most competent in the issue at hand. The most competent member may be sitting silently, discouraged from speaking out. Process loss is inevitable when one person takes up all the vocal space and others just give up contributing elements of their expertise or concerns.

Breaking groupthink can save the group from making big mistakes. This can be prevented by allowing, encouraging, and even rewarding free expression for all members. Anonymous ways of communication could be utilized to allow wisdom to flow freely; after all, each person is a member of a group because they have some role to play, something to contribute, unless they're just there to be mere cheerleaders and followers of the leaders.

Birds of a Feather

Most people's minds have formed a specific schema representing the terms *discrimination* and *prejudice*, which pictures it as something that happens to specific demographics of people, in specific locations, often based in race or culture. But when you disassemble this concept further, it becomes more obvious that discrimination can apply to much more than our socialized mental constructions are most eager to suggest. It results from a complex psychological process that operates through our autopilot, perhaps rooted in things like that basic human instinct, the desire to survive, and to feel as good as possible in the meantime. Getting to the root of undesirable social dynamics, such as those exhibiting discrimination and prejudice, is key to successfully transmuting them. Unfortunately, our societies have not yet realized that the ways in which these things are largely approached is not working, simply because of that mere detail: The root causes are within our minds, that deep place where many prefer not to go.

Group membership most often comes with *categorization*, which ends up aiding the formation of *stereotypes*. *Social categorization* is meant to be useful to the smooth functioning of society, though our schemas tend to form in a way that makes us see categorization as a tool for judging people based on their appearance or lifestyle choices. Its purpose is to establish order, both within your mind and out in the public, because it is kind of important to distinguish a doctor from a receptionist, or a mail carrier from a salesperson. Dr. Charles Stangor explains in the book, *Principles of Social Psychology*, that "thinking about other people in terms of their social category memberships, is a functional way of dealing with the world—things are complicated, and we reduce complexity by relying on our stereotypes."[123] While shopping in clothing stores, I often get approached by other customers who eagerly ask me questions about the merchandise. I tend to wear black coloured clothing a lot, just like most sales associates do, and I may carry myself in a confident manner within stores because of my previous work experience, so the setting feels natural to me. Shoppers who are frustrated with not being able to find a sales associate to help them, and are distracted by the annoyance of holding a bunch of uncomfortable bags, possibly in a rush or tired from walking around the mall, see me wearing black while looking confident as I dig through the racks, and their autopilot makes a snap judgement of pairing me with a schema of a salesperson in their head.

You form a **heuristic stereotype** of a specific person or a thing, and you will later use this stereotype to make quicker judgements in daily interactions. The human mind is just not designed to ponder every detail all over again, each time we come across it. Stangor gives the simple example that "if you found yourself lost in a city, you might look for a police officer or a taxi driver to help you find your way. In this case, social categorization would probably be useful because a police officer or a taxi driver might be particularly likely to know the layout of the city streets.[124] You would be going off your already present stereotype of what a police officer or a taxi driver looks like, what they know, or how they are likely to behave, so that you can recognize this person and make the decision to approach them for a specific reason. This automatic categorization process exists to help our minds move us more efficiently through life among millions of various others.

Life naturally comes with some categories, such as an association to the country of birth, but people must love this category game so much that they cannot refrain from voluntarily labelling each other and themselves into all kinds of other limitless categories, such as flat-earthers, metalheads, or soccer moms. There has been a recent politicization of the name "Karen" here in North America, which is meant to force an inaccurate stereotype upon the wider society, stating that all women who exhibit specified negative traits and behaviours are somehow of this particular name. Though, as a result of categories, people naturally tend to favour those in their **in-**

group, and disfavour those who are categorized as part of their **outgroup**. It seems inevitable that **intergroup relations** often create all kinds of cranky creatures. Prejudice and discrimination are among them. Are you aware of the difference between prejudice and discrimination? **Prejudice** involves biased emotional responses and **attitudes** towards members of a different group than the one you are attached to. **Discrimination** refers to biased **behaviours** towards members of another group.

Reasons for prejudice and discrimination have been widely debated for a very long time, and most attention has been on the conflict over resources factor, but some research also began to point to the shortcomings of people's inner selves. There is an intrinsic desire for just simply feeling good. Social-psychologists, Tajfel and Turner, proposed the famous **social identity theory,** which explains how people find a sense of pride, worth, and self-esteem in belonging to a group or social category.[125] This helps us imagine our place in society, adding to a feeling of stability in the mind. The need for maintaining self-esteem is found to be at play here, and identifying with a better group raises the feeling of pride.

Tajfel and Turner wanted to test whether conflict over stuff like valuable resources or some form of material benefits is actually needed for ingroup favouritism to happen, and so they used the **minimal group paradigm** to test this in the lab. This method involved anonymous participants who didn't have any previous contact with each other, and the groups they were attached to were totally foreign to them. They were minimally connected in real life and in the lab because they didn't get to see the others; they were only told about them. They were instructed to rate two very similar art paintings. The researchers purposefully chose something as insignificant as just liking one painting over another, which didn't involve participants' pre-existent group memberships, so there wasn't any possibility of conflict over resources. The participant was told that they were divided into two groups based simply on their preference for painting number 1 or 2, and that's all they knew about each other. The entire time, they weren't in any physical contact either. In conclusion, results of this study showed that the participants still behaved in ways that favoured their ingroup and disadvantaged the outgroup! They also got to evaluate all participants, and what's really interesting is that they evaluated those in their ingroup higher, even when they were said to have worse performance than the opposite group members.

From what Tajfel and Turner found, it appears that people care about who they're being compared to, and they will make sure that what represents them is dressed up accordingly. Your *social identity* and *self-esteem* together lead you to evaluate people in your ingroups more positively than those in your outgroups. They write that "positive social identity is based to a large extent on favourable comparisons that can be made between the in-group and some relevant outgroups: The in-group must be perceived as positively differentiated or distinct from the relevant out-groups." Mere awareness of the presence of an outgroup, without much interaction or even its existence, can cause some discriminatory responses. Seems like our autopilot really wants to be better safe than sorry—so overprotective!

One for All, All for One

On the path of research, there is always more to discover. In this chapter, I wanted to show you how psychological research keeps building on itself, which will help you better understand things like those attention grabbing short articles that decorate many self-help online blogs or magazines. They often sensationalize one finding or issue, and easily take things out of context. Study findings can sometimes seem contradictory, leaving readers puzzled over which one is correct. As much as humans as a whole are still quite a mystery on so many levels, psychological studies are rarely finite. There is always more to unpack, repack, retest, and challenge, and the rocket of knowledge keeps flying up into infinity and beyond, discovering new meanings of life along the way.

Researchers Gaertner and Insko decided to test Tajfel's ***minimal group paradigm***, which we talked about in the previous section. They were guided by such questions as: "Is social categorization alone a sufficient antecedent of intergroup discrimination? Do category members discriminate in the MGP to maintain a positively distinct ***social identity***?"[126] They were trying to figure out if people discriminate only when they're put into categories because they want to be part of the better category. Or is there more to it?

Gaertner and Insko explain that "subsequent research and theory locate the source of discrimination that arises in the MGP in processes of *outcome dependence* rather than mere categorization. In the current research, we explore these outcome dependence perspectives and examine whether social categorization is sufficient for discrimination." The outcome dependent factors that spark discriminatory behaviour are *ingroup reciprocity* and *outgroup fear,* which reveal themselves as a result of digging deeper into the matter.

Ingroup reciprocity recognizes the fact that members of the same group tend to exchange favours with each other more often, and they know that adding resources to their own group will come circling back to them in some way. For example, there are often social campaigns telling us to shop for local rather than imported goods, that shopping local will help your local economy and the people close to you, therefore benefitting you in some way. Local businesses also buy from other local businesses, which keeps money in the community and raises the standard of your neighbourhood. Local shops decorate the streets you walk or drive through every day, and the older ones often provide memories of the past.

Outgroup fear is centred in the worry that outsiders will score what is, could, or should be yours, or your group's. This fear can be caused by a memory of some instance when some other group or group member behaved in a ***self-serving*** way, and took more stuff for themselves. In the mere expectation that someone else will take more than their fair share, valid or not, there is a tendency to try to prevent loss by scooping up more resources when there is a chance. When the sales staff gives out free samples in the cosmetics store, the expectation is to give "one per customer," but what often happens is that some people will take more than one, saying that they're taking it for their family member. I assume that such responses are mediated by things like how much the person values generosity, or their personal life experiences, such as child poverty, which may have taught them to boldly take advantage to survive. Interestingly, this phenomenon makes me think of my dog! He was adopted from a shelter as a behaviourally challenged pup with a past. Through his early life experience of possibly being deprived, he must have acquired an obsession with food. He will scoop up anything he can find around the house, even if it means stealing lettuce from the bunny who happened to be eating it on the floor, or drinking the cat's water even though he has his own water in his bowl. Maybe he just wants to make sure he has all the food he can find, just in case, even if he doesn't like it.

Who do you think is more likely to favour those in their ingroup, and discriminate against those in their outgroup— men or women? Yes, a difference has been found between them. Males discriminated more when they were put into a category, and less when they didn't have any attached category. It's possible that a sense of dominance, which gives way to discriminatory behaviour, can be triggered by being placed in "packs." Also, if a male has attached his **self-image** to that pack, that will motivate him to make sure it maintains a desired status. When a Toronto resident, who is a devoted Raptors fan, sees the team lose, he or she will likely take it personally to some degree, and may become eager to talk trash about the other teams or their fans. For a long time, many Torontonians felt a bit ashamed because their city's big-deal team wasn't really living up to expectations; but recently, things changed, and it visibly boosted the self-image of those who value this factor. If there were no distinct teams, there would be no reason for any hostility between those groups. Is that a good enough trade off, or not so much?

The studies also found that if a male believes that he is the one in charge of the resources, then that made him less discriminating against the other group, possibly because he felt un-threatened due to the added security and confidence provided by holding the power over the stuff, and not being dependent on others. It seems like it would be common sense to think that someone in the position of power, who is in charge of resources, would be more discriminatory and protective over it all, but the reality suggests otherwise (well, at least in the context of regular everyday people and not career opportunists). Men seem to ease up when they don't have to worry about relying on someone else to treat them fairly. Have you ever seen that guy at the club with the booth and the bottles? Knowing that he's in control of the alcohol, he is often inclined to invite people from all over the club to have drinks with him. On the other hand, as an example of some-one who's not in charge of resources, there was a person I knew who always grabbed two bottles of beer at parties, at once, when the host was offering them. He acted from an inner worry that by the time he'd be ready for another one, they would all be taken. This could be triggered by something that happened in his childhood, where maybe he had to com-pete with siblings, and his autopilot learned this response to protect him from continuously getting the short end of the stick. Or maybe he was an only child and wasn't conditioned to automatically think of others when something he likes or wants is in front of him. On top of that are the effects of that vulnerable feeling of not being the one in charge of something that has some greater importance. Interestingly enough, this person was quite generous with others whenever he brought his own case of beer, kind of aligning with the study findings.

Most of these studies are done in the lab, and often partici-pants are given a made-up scenario, such as being in charge of some funding, and they have to specify how they would distribute it to their own and to other groups. Later, the re-sponses are analyzed by the researchers. The participants are random, and most of the time don't know each other from before the study, so we must keep such factors in mind, be-cause maybe in real life scenarios it may be the case that some bond among group members may affect the level of dis-criminatory tendencies.

The finding that men discriminate less when they are "label-free" is something significant to consider when we think of our societies. It does score points against divisions and categorizations, suggesting that less categories equals less discrimination. There would be more expectation of benefitting from reciprocity, as similar others tend to help each other, and if there are no group labels to belong to and protect, and there is no one to compete with, well maybe then we would just compete on a more individual level. I have seen an interesting quote, stating that the only person you should compete with, is who you were yesterday. Though we must also remember that if there would be no specific categories, everyone would have to converge into sameness, and individual uniqueness would be in jeopardy. Isn't it interesting how—pretty much in every social-psychological dilemma that we have so far discussed—mastering balance on the scale of two opposite extremes is key?!

Oh, yes, I forgot to tell you about the women! Well, common sense fails here again. Women were actually found to be meaner than men! The researchers write that in their experiment, "categorized men discriminated only when dependent on others. Categorized women discriminated regardless of the structure of dependence."[127] It is commonly expected for women to be somewhat nicer and more caring than men, but the findings show something else, as women favoured ingroup members, and discriminated against outgroup members more, and they did it regardless of whether resources were involved, or without a need to be in control over the material stuff. (Let me just leave this right there.)

Friction

In his book, *Civilization and Its Discontents*, famous psychologist Sigmund Freud conveys that conflict is what naturally happens because there is a clash between individual desires and the expectations of society.[128] According to him, there is a tension stemming from the person's drive towards instinctive freedom in the face of the demand for conformity and repression of instincts, that has been built into most societies of this planet throughout time.

These days, anyone from a homeless person to a politician can have their voice heard through the internet, resulting in many entities trying to pull us to their side as they present various ideas and options. It's easy to get lost in the fast-changing structure of the place where we reside. I have seen someone leave a comment online written in all capital letters, and another well-meaning person commented back to stop yelling, but the other person had no idea what they were talking about. One of the new online norms is that you should not use all capital letters, because it means that you're angry. In reality, some people just do it to have their comment be more visible, or simply haven't really thought about why they pressed the all caps button, or they have bad vision and need all caps to see better—who knows? It can lead to unnecessary negative judgement and friction, simply from not being up to date with all these new social norms. This drive for freedom, that Freud was concerned with, can arise from frustration with all these rules, norms, and expectations that take away our mind's energy. This frustration is especially visible now with the current world events that have greatly polarized societies everywhere towards two opposing narratives. Like-minded people have always been drawn to each other, and dissatisfaction with unfair societal rules brings people together to form new groups that continue to push societies through time.

Groups have this specific power of a **melting pot**, blending the individuals with the group. Individuals are susceptible to internalizing group influences, and often come to feel like they're one with the group. If you criticize the group, its members often react as if you criticized them personally. A person from New York may not be following the New York Knicks basketball team too much, and may never go to their games, but if they go on vacation to Florida, and someone there says to them that Miami Heat is better, the New Yorker may feel personally offended to some degree, because the vulnerable feeling of being away from the comfort zone of one's own home town, or country, elevates a sense of pride attached to such personally salient things, which kicks in almost naturally. That person may not be able to name one player on the team, but may somewhat feel personally connected to it as a symbol of the same group they're "melted" in the pot with.

A very timely example of toxic group relations that spark friction is this spreading trend of the hostility produced by the opposing "left" and "right" political groups, in the USA, in Canada, and surely in many other places. The two political groups have somehow almost eliminated all the other groups through the dramatization of their polarizing antics, and therefore set an unwritten criteria of membership that is made up of specific beliefs they each want you to hypothetically sign under. If you happen to agree with one or more of the opposing group's beliefs, you risk facing resentment from the group you happen to side with. For social issues to be resolved in a fair manner, there should be a professional debate between agents who have different perspectives, and that must be met with compromise. Although, from what we see lately in the political context, the reduction to the two opposing "clubs" is turning into a battle that doesn't benefit the public, who somehow gets influenced into cheering it on. When we zoom out the focus, how can we not see how childish these adult games are, and that many adults actually never "grow up." I'm almost at a conclusion that if we were to replace politicians with actual children, the world would be in better shape.

The more adult-like humans try to be, the more they dive into childishness or irrationality. *The Guardian* published a very clever article about how emotions affect the decisions of voters. They write that "there can be no ideology that is superior on all issues and in all circumstances, except for the ideology of choosing the best policy for each issue separately and independently of political orientation. We need our politicians to make smart political decisions that are aligned with the public interest. Sometimes such a smart decision is liberal; at other times, conservative."[129] Picking a political side and not allowing for flexibility is like going to eat at a buffet restaurant where you're told that you can only choose food dishes from either the left or right side of a special menu list, and once you choose, you cannot touch the foods listed on the opposite side. Only when the full menu becomes available to all, we could finally just simply live, and not try to convince each other that somehow the way to balance is through divisions.

These divisions involve symbolism such as colour representation. Today, in Canada the Liberal party has used the colour red, and the Conservative party took on the blue. In current American politics red is associated with the Republicans and blue with Democrats, but did you know that this was not always the case? I'm sure you will be as surprised as I was to find out that "the assignation of red-as-Republican, blue-as-Democrat didn't become the standard until the last election of the third century in which America existed: the election of 2000."[130] As the Washington Times article further explains, it was the television networks such as NBC or CBS that would decide which colours they would use on their election map. It also notes that "we could just as easily use orange and green, but for the fact that red and blue offer much more contrast (and therefore are good for television)" and that "in our ever-so-polarized politics, referring to clusters of votes or states with a shorthand is awfully useful". Could it be that television networks have their fair contribution in creating a monster?

Red and blue are not only the wing colours of the so called political bird, but they also are the colours that somehow ended up representing two rivalling gangs in the USA as well as Canada. (This is one of the things that is similar about the two neighbouring countries: the "street" culture.) As the Thomas theorem proves, when you accept something as real it will have real consequences. It is important to recognize how powerful they can be in shaping the thoughts, feelings and behaviours of many people. A Toronto City News article writes that "gang killings over colours are an unfortunate reality south of the border and aren't very common in Canada, but rival criminal groups here have been known to take a life over trivial things."[131] These dangerous colour games apparently begun in London, England, back in the 1600s, with "each gang distinguishing its membership affiliation by using a different colored ribbon attached to their clothing.[132]

Among the many negative effects of inter-group hostility, bystanders get drawn into the chaos, as opposing groups can demand from them to take a stance and pick a side. But don't let them tell you what to think, and that you have to close yourself in a box. In some situations, sitting on the fence can save you from getting bit by angry dogs, or from having to join them in doing the biting. Maintaining a fresh and objective perspective is what allows for success through the ability to recognize that which others may be blinded to. There is an old Polish saying, that where two are fighting it's the third one that often gets to benefit.

Is the World Falling?

There are many assumptions about one of the biggest human concerns, which is the "evil" of the world. I'm sure you have often heard people say in conversations: "What is this world coming to?" There are often complaints that the new generation is worse than ever, and other doom and gloom about natural disasters, politics, or aliens. Do you think it is true that things are getting worse for the planet and humanity? If we just for a moment forget the sudden reckoning of the forever-famous year 2020, then going way back in time, the trend of world aggression has actually been decreasing. What if we have already been through the worst and learned our lessons—maybe now that level of awareness and the evolution of consciousness has moved us higher towards perfection—and we are possibly moving in the right direction? It's a complicated topic that keeps many optimists and pessimists frazzled.

My grandma is now 90 years old, and she likes to watch the daily news. As she is watching it, she says to me, "What is happening in this world?" It's something that many people just say automatically because it seems like there is more and more violence and aggression. I asked her what was in the news in the 80s, when I was born. It was the fall of communism in Poland, a country that has found itself to be the stake of the Eastern and Western opposing forces; and gladly, the USA called on Western allies and helped Poland out of the communist regime and Russian invasion. I was actually born right in the middle of martial law. When my mother was young, it was the Korean War. And how about when my grandma herself was young? That was the time of the Second World War, where her father was taken into the Nazi work camp, and moved her, her mother, and baby brother out of their home into some farm home, where they had to survive on their own with nothing. So has the world gotten more rotten, less rotten, or has it stayed the same? When asked, most people assume that the world is getting worse, when in fact it could have been getting better. Well, maybe up until 2020, but let's stay realistically optimistic for the future, with the understanding that we, you and me, have lots of power to create it.

There is an article on the *Forbes* website, which I have linked for you to check out, that summarizes all the things that are getting better in the world. The study, entitled *The Short History of Global Living Conditions and Why It Matters That We Know It*, by Max Roser, an economist at the University of Oxford, finds that on virtually all of the key dimensions of human material well-being—poverty, literacy, health, freedom, and education—the world is an extraordinarily better place than it was just a couple of centuries ago.[133] Do material improvements have any impact on diminishing violence among humans? Psychologist Steven Pinker of Harvard University argues in his book, *The Better Angels of Our Nature: Why Violence Has Declined*, that reduced deaths due to violence are due to the emergence of institutions like nation-states with strong central governments and trade networks, and wide-ranging communication increased interdependence among people.[134] Today, major worldly conflicts are often resolved with a greater degree of peace, unlike in the past. One good example from year 2020 are the "back-to-back peace treaties between Israel and a pair of Arab nations—the United Arab Emirates and Bahrain—signed at the White House," described in an *NBC News* article.[135] What's interesting about the shiny aura of peace, and the promise of prosperity, is that it becomes irresistible to the onlookers who will feel the FOMO (fear of missing out). When some groups are teaming up, other groups may not want to be left behind. The article states that "this breakthrough is likely to lead to more". As per the *White House* website, another peace agreement between Sudan and Israel has also been signed.[136]

There are many positive efforts being made, though it may not be obvious due to the prevalence of negatively framed information coming from many information sources. However, as discussed in the *Science Mag*, there are those who challenge Pinker's finding, and say that taking into account mathematics of population changes, it is actually more likely that violence in the world has pretty much remained the same as always.[137] These studies were mostly based in comparing the amount of people who died in battles throughout centuries, but we're not sure if that is measuring all around aggressive tendencies of humans, or if it is just measuring the power of one authority figure in influencing many people to go to battle, rather than random people just running around being violent. I'm also not sure if they considered the factor of technologies used in battle significantly improving since the old times, when soldiers would just run straight onto the swords of their opponents on horses, which is not the case these days. War can be waged on the psychology of the people, such as brainwashing and propaganda techniques used on the target population, not to mention biological warfare, which can be in the form of an unleashed disease.

What do you think from your personal observation and vibe? Is the world going in the direction of destruction, or is the world just being the world like it always has been, or is it somewhat painfully transforming into an even better world as more people unite and expose injustices. The internet has allowed all kind of individuals the ability to expose corruption, and people are waking up from their sleep with a renewed energy, more committed to fixing what has been broken.

Off the Handle

So what about individual aggression? The world is changing fast; societies are going through rapid transformations due to advancements in communication technologies, travel, globalization of big businesses, and modernization of living conditions. All these things result in the disruption of traditional lifestyles all over the world, and the pressures to keep up can leave many people feeling lost in the process.

Most people desire a stable and secure life for themselves and their close ones. When that is in some way constrained, when they find themselves unable to meet their needs for whatever reasons, it can spark the flames of frustration, leading to the explosion of aggression. This is called the ***frustration-aggression hypothesis,*** which states that aggression is a result of a frustration due to being blocked from attaining some goal, and "that frustration causes aggression, but when the source of the frustration cannot be challenged, the aggression gets displaced onto an innocent target."[138] However, many of the leading factors to aggression are often things outside of the persons control, such as adverse factors in their lived environment that they're dealing with, or their ancestors were dealing with, and it permeated the next generations. It is not easy to control the environment, or to change the government policies or the mindsets of other people, although there is power in knowing yourself, and knowing how humans in general tend to operate. The environmental factors that affect our cognitive and behavioural responses are the spark that ignite aggression, which can be calmed by understanding. The more masterful a person becomes, the more control they will have, and therefore make better decisions. Without this inner work, an uncontrollable spiral of negative events can occur. A person who lost a job due to cutbacks, and took their frustration out on their partner at home, which led to criminal charges, is in a position to continue to fall further and further from there. Then will come the debt from legal fees, and the loss of home, belongings, friends, reputation, and possibly even kids. With knowledge of social psychology, you will become more skillful in controlling how you act and respond, and will prevent yourself from sparking that fire. I must mention this though: I have met people who actually enjoy causing drama or ruckus, because it turns them on; it feeds their strange ego. Aggression among people is still there and always was, and it is important to understand it better, as it is a factor very high on the importance scale. It is about your safety and the safety of others, and they don't say knowledge is power for nothing—knowledge can be powerful enough to overcome aggression. Knowing what triggers people to be aggressive helps to avoid it, treat it, and prevent it.

There are biological factors that place some people at the higher end of the aggression scale, as we discussed in the chapter about the "bad seed" children, and how important it is to recognize the signs of overactive amygdala early in the child's life. *Amygdala* is the area of the brain associated with aggressive behaviour. A study published in *sciencemag.org* involved giving women participants a small dose of testosterone, and then testing their response to an angry face and happy face; I'm guessing in a video game format. They found that "amygdala activity after testosterone administration is bound to social ***threat*** approach."[139] So, basically, testosterone affects the amygdala activity that creates aggression, when dealing with something threatening. That response happens to help in dealing with threatening situations. You may have heard people say that too much testosterone is the cause of aggression in men. But not many bother continuing this statement further and noting that testosterone can be activated by many factors, such as stress of losing status, or scoring lower in a competition. Research by Carre and colleagues, from Brock University, has found that testosterone levels fluctuate with situational factors like threat, which we just talked about, and also things like ***loss of status***.[140] They made male participants play a video game with a fictional opponent, and the opponent was meant to steal points from the participant, which was meant to provoke them. It was later found that this participant's testosterone level was higher after the game than before he started. That would mean that testosterone alone is not as much of an issue as when it is triggered by some outer forces, and of course the intensity depends on other things. Their study demonstrated that "trait and state factors interact to influence aggressive behaviour, and thus, that these factors must be considered together when attempting to understand the mechanisms underlying aggressive behaviour."

What about women? Are they nicer, and calmer than men are in general? A study by Deaux and LaFrance has observed the behaviour of children, from various countries, playing, and they noted more pushing and hitting among boys. If we were to just take the results of such studies and run with them as we announce to the world that women are kinder than men, we would be only half-correct, and the misinformation could leave a negative impact once it became internalized by people who would push it further. Continuation into the topic reveals that women can also exhibit aggression or meanness, but it can present itself differently, and it can also be perceived differently by the observers or victims. Research by Coie and colleagues, and many others, finds that young girls are also aggressive but in ways that are more covert, like manipulating information with harmful intent towards others, such as spreading rumours.[141]

It is very hard to dispute the statistics that show a huge difference between the numbers of male versus female prisoners. The *Federal Bureau of Prisons* website states that 93% of people in the U.S. prisons are males, and only 7% females.[142] If we just go by this statistic, we will miss out on some very unexpected facts, such as the fact that aggression appears to exist in both women and men, but it is enacted through a different method. Factors such as the target of aggression also matter greatly. Men are found to direct their aggression at other men most often; things like bar fights are a very common thing, and alcohol is a huge factor here. When women are more likely to be physically aggressive, it is usually towards their male partner. What else is interesting is that this tends to more likely happen in the early stages of the relationship. One study, by Straus, examined rates of physical violence among university students in 16 countries; another study, by Archer, examined over 100 studies on this topic, and they all seemed to agree on this very interesting discovery: that women were more likely to be aggressive towards their male partner than the other way around. Let's take one example from the Straus study that is very local to me: In Hamilton, Canada, 13.5% of males perpetrated some kind of physical assault against their partner, compared to 24.5% of females.[143]

But there is a catch to this surprising finding, because when we separate the severe cases, it is revealed that males are more likely to perpetrate a severe injury. In the Hamilton reports, 5.4% of males perpetrated severe injury to their partner, and 2.6% of females did the same. Aggressive behaviour of males gets more attention in our society because visible damage is done by them, which is easier to report and charge criminally than trying to prove that someone suffered trauma or harm due to something like slander, manipulation, or being slapped. There was a case on the news recently where a young girl kept telling her boyfriend to kill himself, and he eventually did, so she was charged with his death. Think about yourself; if you lived in a building where you have two neighbours, and one assaulted their partner and the ambulance had to show up, the whole building now knows, because it's obvious and seems dangerous. Now, there is another neighbour, to the other side of you, who insults their partner every day and doesn't let them leave the home without their supervision, and they take all the money their partner makes. Neighbours don't really know what is really happening there. Which story is worse? Tough question, I know.

CHAPTER 8

LIKE A PRO

*"This industry is 90 percent business,
10 percent talent."*

– Armando Pérez (Pitbull)

8

Juggling Act

Work, work, and more work... Work is becoming more of a juggling act in our modern society. Trends are rapidly changing due to constantly advancing technological capabilities, and it seems to be aiding the increase in creative ways in which people are making money. It can be a great thing if work and life balance is maintained, but with increased work-from-home trends, work can become mixed throughout your daily experience—it can even make its way into your bed without you realizing.

A real estate agent can search through listings while waiting in the line-up at the grocery store, or a car dealer can order car parts while watching a movie with the kids on a Saturday evening. A YouTube podcaster is often staying up late doing research for the next show. The manager may be expecting that email report first thing in the morning on Monday, so there goes your peaceful Sunday. In the last couple of decades, ***work and family conflict***, or even work and personal life conflict, is becoming an increasing challenge for young people, especially those who are not attaining a stable income, one that allows them to leave work at work when it's time. My former professor, Paul Glavin, examined the prevalence, intensity, and determinants of multiple jobholding in his recent research. He suggests that this phenomenon is mostly due to problems of quality primary employment in the country. He writes that almost 20% of workers reported holding multiple jobs in 2019, and that rate is actually three times higher than Statistics Canada estimates.[144] This precarious lifestyle is an increasing burden on young people who would like to start a family of their own, but the challenge of securing enough stability to do it seems to be a major deterrent.

Change is a sure thing in this worldly reality. But it seems to be the case that humans don't adapt to worldly change as fast as we like to think. We are at least a couple generations behind due to the time it takes to get adjusted biologically to the changed environment. If you look at the generation of the elderly people today, they still have a hard time adjusting to the concept of computers and smartphones, even though these things have already been around for many years of their lives, in many cases nearly half. As we discussed earlier, if the epigenetic effect affects you based on what your grandparents did, or how they lived, that means that genetics are protecting you from what they assume you are going to encounter, based on past information they recorded during your grandparents' lives. So changes must take a couple of generations to really set in.

Human lifestyle has been changing from the very beginning, but because we tend to compare chunks of time by observing specific generations, it appears as if each group of people, such as your parents, grandparents, and so on, have a different reality to deal with as they go into adulthood. Maybe that is why it is so challenging to catch a break, especially if you don't have generational wealth to cushion your ride. In the Western countries, such as Canada or the USA, the generation of so-called "baby boomers," who were born around the 1950s, experienced a lot more employment stability than their children. In the last couple of decades, many larger companies have cut full-time positions, cut benefits, and started favouring more precarious positions because they appear less costly. Many factories use employment agencies to find workers who are called in for the busier times; and during slow times, the company doesn't have to lay off permanent workers, or be stuck with someone who turns out to be unsuitable. In its quest for modernity, ironically enough, our Western society seems to be going in a full circle—from entrepreneurial artisanry of the traditional societies, which was often carried out at home, then moving into structured employment due to the Industrial Revolution, separating home and work, and now back to blurring the work and home boundaries again. Let's see where we end up after the chaos of 2020 stabilizes, and battle fatigue sets in. It does look like the new revolution is more of a mental one, as physical demands are increasingly being fulfilled by robotics, and information is becoming a very valuable currency. Though, because information became available to almost anyone these days, it is becoming more controlled by a few players who may be trying to level everyone underneath them into an "equality" that is not exactly the type that equality advocates had in mind.

While the lifestyles of men and women are changing, like the switch from working the land to working the line, it seems that inner changes are not able to keep up. Our human genetic programming that shapes the human collective, and changes according to the conditions of our environment, seems to be chasing the environment rather than being in control of it, like the advanced beings that we like to think we are. Through the various advancements around the world, it is the case that people just cannot keep up with changes. As soon as it seems like everything is fine, and one can focus on growing their livelihood, something gets in the way of smooth sailing. For example, in India, the farmers have found themselves in a crisis. According to the *Open Democracy* website, their "government reported that 15,356 farmers in Maharashtra had committed suicide between 2013 and 2018. This means that seven farmers committed suicide every day for six years." They write that over 40% of Indians rely on agriculture for their livelihood.[145] Compare that to the United States where farmers make up 1.3% of the employed population, down from 70% in 1840, according to a *Business Insider* article.[146] The constant political conflicts, lack of resources, crop failures, societal changes, and influences of globalization are causing farmers much strife. The restrictions that rolled in with the storm of year 2020, have only made things worse, so abruptly erasing much of the advancement that took years of struggle to build up. The life of the individual suddenly becomes thrown into a situation where they must adapt and take on a new lifestyle, maybe even a few lifestyles at once, or else succumb to the storm.

Hustling Birds and Bees

The topic of **gender equality** often brings about all kinds of discussions within public and private contexts. There may be an abundance of reasons for continued friction around this popular topic in societies around the world, but before you get into a heated discussion, it is good to take a look at various layers uncovered by research, which may not be very obvious otherwise.

Most people hold multiple social roles at the same time; for example, being a father who is also a brother, son, coach, and employee is quite a normal thing—we all have many roles assigned or taken on in our lifetime. How people experience these roles is fluid across many dimensions, such as gender, cultural origin, and personal physical ability; and the amount and types of roles held can weigh, more or less, on the individual person's life outcomes.

In the last few decades, more women have been joining the workforce, which is something that's been a consistent subject of debates about equality between men and women in the distribution of the tasks and rewards, as well as the meanings of social roles. Married women, for the most part, have been glad to be able to contribute to the economy, build up their resources for retirement, and get out of the house, but the fact is that they come home to loads of daily housework to attend to, and children to look after. Pew Research Center writes that "among mothers who have ever worked, 39% say they have taken a significant amount of time off from work to care for a child or family member. This compares with only 24% of working fathers."[147]

Even if the workload is seemingly equal, and so are the material rewards, the way in which distress is internalized varies between men and women. It can be caused by a combination of biological as well as environmental factors. This difference of subconscious meanings that people attach to their social roles, needs to be respected in communication instances, as well as in creation of social policies. So before a husband or boyfriend says to his wife, "I do just as much work as you, if not more, so I don't know why you're mad?" he should consider the likely differences in the psychological makeup of men and women, and that will equip him with better tools for understanding where she's coming from. Research from the 90s, presented by Robin Simon in the *Journal of Health and Social Behaviour,* shows that juggling multiple roles has a worse effect on women's mental health than on men. This difference lies in the meaning that men and women attach to their roles, which causes the different levels of distress. The study shows that most of the women surveyed felt constantly needed, pulled in different directions, and confused. Nearly all of the women expressed guilt for being away from their children and neglecting their husbands.[148]

Men did not express these feelings of guilt or being pulled in many directions. Their thoughts about their clashing roles were that it's just the way life is; they saw it simply as their responsibility. Most of the men surveyed were connecting economic support with being a good father and husband, and about a quarter of the female participants believed that women should contribute economically. It is necessary to also understand where men are coming from. There cannot be equality without understanding. Men can be more vulnerable to things like psychological imbalances, stress, frustration, and aggression when they aren't creating adequate material results for themselves and their dependents, or when their efforts aren't appreciated. We must note that in the last couple of decades, men have taken more responsibility in household tasks, but women still do the majority of housework while being looked to as the primary caretakers of children, as found by Bianchi and colleagues in their book, *The Changing Rhythms of American Family*.[149]

A more recent survey by Pew Research Center, from 2012,[150] found that people really are confused over what they believe, and have a tendency to hold opposing views at the same time. Well, they didn't say that people are confused—I did—but the research said this: "The majority of Americans (79%) rejected the notion that women should return to their traditional role in society. Yet when they were asked what is best for young children, very few adults (16%) said that having a mother who works full time is the 'ideal situation.' Some 42% said that having a mother who works part time is ideal, and 33% said that what's best for young children is to have a mother who doesn't work at all." When you think about how opinions can change, shift, and vary, as they involve so many factors, like feelings, cultural norms, moods, personal situation or experience, and knowledge, it kind of makes me feel bad for politicians—just a little—because how can we create regulations that satisfy the needs of society when the society sends such a contradictory message? The author of that research, Kim Parker, writes that more employers now offer paid leaves and other family-friendly policies, "but while few Americans want to see a return to traditional roles of women at home and men in the workplace, one reality persists: Women most often are the ones who adjust their schedules and make compromises when the needs of children and other family members collide with work."

Similarly to the above findings, Paul Glavin and colleagues also demonstrated that even when men and women may both have equal amounts of stress and workload, they often differ in how they process their emotions. They used data from the National Survey of Working Americans to study the association between boundaryless work and feelings of guilt and distress. In this survey, they also noticed that men mostly saw combining work and family roles as something natural, while women reported more feelings of guilt. Women reported family roles as being more central to their identity, which is why they felt more guilt about their employment preventing them from fulfilling their family responsibilities.[151]

Most people are not aware of these distinct psychological processes, and many also still have a hard time seeing things from an alternate perspective. (Think back to the "mountain task" study mentioned earlier in the book.) After reading all of this, you are going to be much more automatically geared towards an accurate understanding of people's feelings when dealing with them, which will allow you to be the master of the flow, rather than a slave to the friction in any social setting, whether it's at work or at home.

The Leadership Ship

Leadership is an increasingly popular term in our fast-evolving society. It requires being artful in motivating others to follow. The rise of social media has really emphasized this age-old leader/follower concept in our social definitions, especially in business. But this term doesn't necessarily have to reside within the professional or business context. A skillful leader will likely maintain leveraged power across all kinds of social situations. Leadership involves *influence*, and it exemplifies itself in all kinds of daily encounters among groups or individuals, simply because we live among other people.

You have to deal with other people because that's just life. There will always be many little moments where you lead someone towards something, or someone else leads you. When a group of co-workers is going out for lunch, someone typically has more say than others in choosing the restaurant. Have you ever wondered what type of energy is contributing to the weight of that person's influence, considering that everyone holds a similar status to each other in that group? While researching the psychology aspects of various scams and tricks that are out there, I came across a pretty useful video-report by *CBC Marketplace, a* show about how to talk to cell phone companies. The guest of the show was a professional who helps people negotiate.[152] Participants who had unresolved issues with their phone bills were told to call the company live, and say exactly what he was telling them to. Most people are generally polite, and many get intimidated by others who are in positions of power, so they find it challenging to stand up for themselves when they feel cheated or wronged. When they actually try to gather up their courage and initiate this uncomfortable interaction, they find it even harder to keep their "leadership ship" afloat and balanced in the storm of emotions and thoughts; in other words, they fail to find a proper way to efficiently stand their ground.

The *Marketplace* video is an example of social psychology solutions in action. After watching it, notice what the leader did in order to stay afloat and not lose ground while talking to the operator, and notice how he led the other people to slowly break through the feeling of intimidation, levelling up their own dignity in this interaction. Just because someone holds something you want, or may be perceived as having higher status than you, don't be so quick to feel like you should forget about defending fairness. You must establish the energy you want to operate in, and establish the level of respect you want to receive. But the more skillful you become in communication, the better your results will become. The "Wolf of Wall Street," Jordan Belfort, became a Wall Street millionaire at the age of 26 because he was so skillful in negotiating that he was able to convince many people, including those who were on a much higher level than him, to invest money.[153]

Trust me, I have come a very long way in mastering the maintenance of balance in my daily person-to-person interactions. Still, every day, I have some sobering thoughts about how I could not have known this thing that just now dawned upon me. By automatically assuming that I have to be nice all the time, I was stepping further into vulnerability while giving others a position of leadership within our interaction. Something like excuse making, no matter how factual those excuses are, can automatically re-affirm your lower status and incite a feeling of authority in the other person. Instead, try to maintain a similar wavelength, in a respectful way, and be honest... to an extent. I remember going to an investor presentation where the CEO didn't make it for some airport related reasons, but his substitute didn't take too long apologizing to the audience, who mostly came there because of that CEO, and just moved on with the presentation like nothing happened. That's one of the wake-up moments I had to experience, to realize that maybe I need to revise my own attitudes in order to benefit my business.

These interactions can be confusing; how can you tell whether you have been too much of an asshole, or too passive? How can you tell if you need to be nicer, let things go, or be more pushy or ridgid? Feel the situation; don't just get stuck in the thoughts. Feeling the situation will channel in to you the right response, but if you are in your head trying to come up with what to say next, you will not hear what your intuition is trying to tell you. When you take charge of your own mind, emotions, and behaviour, then you can take charge of leading others. Next time you're in a confusing spot, think back to your "ship"—is it rocking? You will feel the waves intensifying in your interaction, and you will feel when you're about to get rocked. You will sense the tension in others fluctuating, and you will have the chance to prove your masterful ability to curb it when needed, and drive up the energy when it's low. You will be able to know exactly when someone could use a laugh, and when someone needs a moment of silence and solidarity. Always use your gut feeling as a notification system telling you to start making your way towards balance. Balance here means striving towards a positive outcome for both sides and all involved. If you can master ensuring win-win situations, you will cultivate great results all around and be rewarded with greater admiration or respect. Then you will be a natural leader.

Leading Ways

In business, things must match up like a puzzle, or else friction or imbalance is inevitable sooner or later. Various studies into leadership have revealed a blueprint of people's specific leadership styles, and mostly have not found a strong connection between good leadership skills and personal characteristics. Quality leaders do tend to be more extroverted, achievement driven, or even tall, as Stewart McCann's analysis of great presidential qualities has found.[154] The motivational towers of our popular culture like to shout more about the stronger traits that leaders should possess, but it is important to also consider matching the candidate's **leadership style** with the needs of the particular position. Knowing what you know now, after reading about the power of the situational factors earlier in this book, you should get yourself into the habit of always considering the context, the type of setting or culture that you're working with. Also, if you know what type of leader qualities your boss or business partner tends to lean towards, you will be able to approach them in a more efficient way, and leverage your differences while avoiding conflict.

One of the leadership styles specified in the study of social psychology is **transactional leadership**. Elliot Aronson and colleagues have written about this in their book, where they define transactional leaders as ones who set clear, short-term goals, and reward people who meet them.[155] Such leaders are good at fulfilling the current needs of the organization, and keeping things running smoothly. The second style is ***transformational leadership,*** which describes people who get a bit more positive attention, and most research focuses on them, although it doesn't mean that one is better than the other. Aronson's book defines them as leaders who inspire followers to focus on common, long-term goals. Can you think of examples in your previous business, or education, or daily life experience, where you came across a person who fits either description? What kind of a leadership style do you think you would be, if you were in that position?

If you ever were in a position of any form of leadership, whether at work or at a summer camp, and you had a bad experience with it, which made you resent such future responsibility, think about whether that position suited your leadership style. I have a friend who for many years has worked for a popular cosmetic company, located inside a department store. She often was told that she should take the manager position because they saw how dedicated and skillful she was, and her energy attracted long-term clients. She was afraid of doing so for the longest time because she didn't think she could be a cold, task-oriented manager, which seemed to be a trend. Management in the retail sector often give more weight to short-term results because they know that they may not last too long in the position; they often either move up, get moved, or get let go. But the employees often remain, especially the more mature in age, who tend to treat their jobs as a permanent thing; therefore, they like to base their behaviours on what is good for the long run, and they can clash with the management who just wants to have quick results to deliver on the conference call this Monday. Finally, something in the Universe pushed my friend to finally take the management position that opened up right in front of her nose, again, because every manager there would last only a few months. She ended up doing well because her transformational style, which focuses on the long-term, lasting results by cultivating relationships with clients, and which somehow keeps them coming back for years, actually suits that particular business that is based on person-to-person contact, as well as keeping the peace among the co-workers. In another location of the same chain, there was a manager who was only task-oriented and was quite cold-hearted; and long story short, she destroyed the whole department because she showed absolutely no concern for anyone's feelings, and was uninspiring in the ways she presented her expectations. Some people quit, some cried, and some just ignored her abrupt attitude because they knew that was just the way she was. In reality, she was physically harmless... but psychologically draining. She had a great gift of being a very fast worker who moved with the speed of light, and had a hard time understanding why others weren't keeping up with her speed. I surely hope management everywhere gets to read this book—in this fragile economy, companies cannot afford to have imbalance in the wheels that are to drive their businesses forward.

Which style is better—***transactional*** or ***transformational***? Well, it depends on the situation, but in an ideal world, the right mix of both styles is needed. Would it hurt for a transactional leader to realize that maybe they need to work on being a bit more personable or inspiring? Or maybe a transformational-type leader needs to polish up on how to scale productivity, or maintain order. A ***meta-analysis*** study, done by researchers Judge and Piccolo, which is a study in which researchers compare many existing studies on the same topic, has confirmed that the most effective leader is one who applies both styles.[156] I would give that award to Kim Rivers, the CEO of Trulieve Cannabis Corp, one of the very few women in the business, whom I spoke with personally. Her company was on my radar the moment it was listed on the stock exchange, simply because of my intuition, which she later proved to have been on point, with her success rate, which in my opinion is largely due to her ability to balance both leadership types. Elon Musk, of Tesla Motors, in my view is a perfect transformational leader; he's known for his often-discredited long-term vision, his inspiring and sometimes outrageous ideas, as well as his positivity, which attracts the love of numerous followers. He is one of the few company leaders out there who has armies of investors throwing loads of their money into their stock, mostly because they are investing in him, the CEO. Not many companies can say that. His educational attainment is in the field of economics and physics, which represents his mathematical attention to detail, and his mindful ideals come from the ability to look at the big picture beyond limits. I have watched his company's stock go from $200 per share, in 2017, to over $2000, in 2020, which is extraordinary. Despite all of the market drama and negative analyst predictions, Elon's masterful balancing of both worlds—the material and the spiritual—continues to carry him to the moon.

Just Right

Your ***self-presentation*** on the ***front stage*** is what gets you the social desirability points in the social world. ***Social desirability***, as we already discussed earlier, is a tendency to respond to questions in a way that will make others think well of you. The front stage experiences can come with some level of ***social anxiety*** for many people, and that should always be kept in mind—even the coolest cats can tell you that even they feel like they can be socially awkward at times. ***Social anxiety*** happens when a person has a desire to impress others to some degree, but for whatever reason, they lack the ***self-efficacy***, which is the confidence in their own capabilities.

Stage fright can overcome a person in regular daily interactions, such as when you're walking into your new job and worry about how the current employees will react, and you already know they will discuss you. Although they probably mean well, people can get protective over their mini environments that took effort to establish and get used to, and they most likely don't want their order to get messed up. When you are meeting with new people, you naturally want to light up your personal stage with the nicest light, but in the midst of fun and excitement, it's easy for your emotions to complicate your smooth performance. People will ask you questions about yourself, like the inescapable one: "What do you do for a living?" Or, "What do you like to do for fun?" It is likely that you, as well as many people, will add a bit of sparkle to that answer. For people with higher levels of social anxiety, it's actually beneficial to put some effort into doing that, within reason, rather than undervalue yourself, or not mention enough interesting or desirable things about yourself, which can be interpreted as self-doubt. If people sense that you are not confident enough in yourself, they may wonder why they should be confident in you.

Where do you draw the line? This may relate to what we already talked about, which is making yourself sound better to reduce **cognitive dissonance**; but the line must be drawn between the concept of strategic self-enhancement and bold cover-up of unsatisfactory aspects of your life. Making yourself appear desirable is not only okay, but it is also necessary when you are happy with who you are and where you are in life, and when you know you are following your purpose, and that others can benefit from knowing what you have learned. Improvement is naturally expected on a path of purposeful life, and in order to collect the benefits presented along this path, you must tailor your self-presentation to be impeccable. When you find yourself in social settings, in person or online, which are meant to bring you some extrinsic benefits, you must keep emotions in full check. If you tend to be more outgoing at social gatherings, it is important to watch when the boasting warning light starts flashing within you. Stay mindful when the conversation is going well and your comfort level increases, especially after having some drinks. That is the moment when it is easy to get carried away and hand the microphone to your "autopilot," and that most often brews trouble.

Especially when you're in new social settings, keep in mind to somewhat tease people by maintaining a certain balance in the conversation. Give your conversation participants just enough interesting and slightly boastful information about yourself, so that they're curious to hear more. Keep it simple; if you are like me, and you like a million things, just pick a couple to discuss with new people, so that you don't confuse them or appear to be "a jack of all trades, master of none." Trust me, it took me a very long time to become conscious of this in my own life, and I still catch myself slipping. Every salesperson can tell you that you can easily talk yourself out of a sale; and in the same way, you can talk yourself out of a valuable connection. When talking with a person you just met, after you say your point, remember to ask them some simple questions right away; and it's best to make it an open-ended question that will stimulate their mind, such as, "Tell me what your favourite experience is, from this event so far," or, "What is the greatest thing you've learned while working on your project?" People want to talk more than they want to listen, and they are expecting you to care about them as well. So ask them how they feel or what they think, rather than taking their silence as an invite to keep rambling on, which can cause an imbalance that will be felt.

One of my mentors, Raymond Aaron, teaches in his Communication Training workshop that the person or people you are talking to only care about themselves! This argument makes the audience a bit irritated with him at first, but later, when they get the whole point he is making, they quickly set aside the dissonant ego, and realize how beneficial it is to keep that in mind. Raymond talks about this in relation to communication because this realization has made him a much more effective speaker and teacher. When he speaks to a crowd, he makes sure that he always appears as if he is talking to just one person and not a bunch of people, because the subconscious mind can filter info that may appear as if it's not directly related to you, which is this automatic inclination for people to care about themselves first. If you are doing a speech, and you start by saying, "How is "everyone" doing tonight?" then "John," in row two, will not feel like the word "everyone" is speaking to him, despite the logic of knowing consciously that of course he is included in that generalization, although the unconscious is running its own program in the background. If you instead say, "How are you doing tonight?" then each person's autopilot will catch it as relevant because it feels more directly aimed. You are you; you are not everyone. If you are a team leader, you must try to keep this in mind when you are communicating to more than one person, and then watch how people pay more attention to what you're saying.

Raymond also presents this idea through this clarifying example: Imagine you came to his teaching event with your friend, and he had these beautiful, 24-karat gold-plated, rare $200 bills to give out to everyone who bought a ticket—but there was a mistake in the amount ordered, and YOU don't get one! Will you be joining others in their happy dance, or will you be pissed off that you didn't get one? And who cares that your best friend is beside you, basking in the sparkle of that shiny bill. It's not likely that they will offer you theirs, and it may not be fair to expect them to—you probably would feel bad taking it from them anyway. Most likely, you will feel negative emotions and not be happy for your friend, or for anyone in there for that matter, because—guess what—you care mostly about yourself, and others care mostly about themselves, and maybe their loved ones; it depends.

Balancing Alpha

Alpha: the first and brightest star in the constellation, the first letter of the Greek alphabet, the dominant player in the game. Alpha doesn't necessarily have to be a masculine aspect, as domineering traits can be found in female characters too, but it is something that has been attributed mostly to males. When discussing the dynamics of networking and communications in the professional world, we are forced to give attention to the topic that just keeps on coming up over and over, and it is the low level of female presence at the top of the professional stratification ladder.

Statistics keep showing a lack of women in high positions across many sectors. Pew Research reports that in 2017, 5.4% of companies in the S&P 500 (an index of 500 biggest publicly traded companies) had women CEOs, up from 2.8% in 2007.[157] It's both a positive and negative thing at the same time... positive because female participation in high places is growing, but negative because... well, just look at these percentages; they're so tiny that it's like getting a pay raise at your local general labour job (you just don't notice the difference after getting something like 0.25 cents per hour raise every year). These facts are so ambiguous that they make a good example of why this female economic empowerment debate is still going strong on the worldwide forum.

I must make it very clear that bringing up this social imbalance is not intended to be an attack on the traits representing masculinity, by any means. There are many reasons why males tend to occupy the most powerful positions. Leaving reasons aside, it's more important to focus on effective solutions for the good of all involved. More and more women are taking on higher professional roles, and both sexes must make a conscious effort to understand their own, as well as the other's, mental and emotional processes in order to protect the well-being of the organization, as well as its players for whom work is a major chunk of life. Improvements in communication will assist in reducing stress at work and at home.

Differences cannot be purposefully ignored in order to elicit equality, but differences, or unique qualities, should be utilized as they naturally flow. You cannot use inequality to achieve fairness. Society and its leaders must start this action from the roots, not the leaves. If women aren't signing up to become car mechanics, should the government put extra effort to encourage women to do so, if it's met with lack of interest? These are important factors to consider, because sometimes we try to force water to flow upstream.

I am often troubled when I see a list of some companies' boards of directors, and I see seven men and one woman. That tells me that there is an imbalance happening in the company, and something like **group polarization theory** of crowd behaviour is a potential risk to its operations. In the paper, "The Law of Group Polarization," Cass Sunstein states that "in a striking empirical regularity, deliberation tends to move groups, and the individuals who compose them, toward a more extreme point in the direction indicated by their own predeliberation judgments."[158] In other words, if you and a few co-workers meet together to discuss the organization of a work charity event, the group is likely going to get all fired up to do something very elaborate as you discuss it; but after the meeting, when the energy deflates, most members will realize that you need to scale back much of the plans you came up with. Sunstein looks at the macro-level implications of this phenomenon, and he writes that "it helps to explain extremism, 'radicalization,' cultural shifts, and the behaviour of political parties and religious organizations; it is closely connected to current concerns about the consequences of the Internet; it also helps account for feuds, ethnic antagonism, and tribalism." It is a fact that most societal leaders are men, most radical rebel groups are made up of men, and there is no one there that could balance out these energies and provide a reality check.

Women's familial responsibilities tend to be a major concern of employers who associate it with jeopardization of productivity, but reality seems to point away from that concern. Women actually can really hold it down when it comes to handling their business in the midst of family duties. One of my professors, Marisa C. Young, and colleagues, have compared male and female lawyers in their study, and analyzed how both genders spend their time in various work and home tasks. They found that women-professionals devote more time to housework and childcare than men, and yet research shows they generally devote just as much effort and time to work as their male peers.[159] How do they manage that? Well, it does come at the expense of their leisure time.

So why is it that women find it harder to advance to higher positions or get the right acknowledgement? In the professional context, men naturally gravitate to other men, and exchange favours with other men, and since they occupy most of the high positions, the cycle just keeps going. What I have noticed in my personal experience is that the men who were able to provide me with a helping hand, didn't do so, because they felt uncomfortable engaging with me as a young woman, especially if they were married. There was a really crazy thing that happened to me a while ago. I was at an event presented by a valuable coach, who was a married man, and I won a prize, which was a personal coaching session for free. This person has high-level connections, and coaching with him is pricey. So when I got up from my seat to claim my prize after my ticket was drawn, he looked at me and said, under the guise of humour, "I have to draw again because my wife doesn't approve of me being alone with other young and attractive women." I'm glad this happened in front of the whole audience, so that maybe some people had the epiphany about what it really looks like for women on their way through the "glass ceiling." I lost out on a valuable connection, which could have led to other valuable connections, simply because of me being me—a woman. For example, the *catalyst.org* website notes that among entry-level employees, men are more likely than women to have managers and senior leaders act as sponsors, serving as advocates, providing advancement advice, and identifying opportunities.[160]

In his book, *What Men Don't Tell Women About Business: Opening Up the Heavily Guarded Alpha Male Playbook*, consultant and CEO, Christopher Flett, writes the harsh truth about how men tend to think about women at work, and reveals everything women need to know to understand, communicate, and compete with men in business.[161] This information can also be helpful to young people who are going into their first employment, and possibly some men who deviate from that alpha vibration. I'll be honest; as much as I am aware of the benefits of playing the game of success, by working with its trend and not against it, on the contrary, I am hesitant to advocate for telling women that they have to manoeuvre their behaviour or their appearance. I believe women should be spared from yet another burden placed upon them. Then again, if we were to stay within the realm of reality, I also want women to power up, become more in touch with their emotions, stay on top of revising what works and what doesn't, and be effective in improving their status, which in turn can improve their well-being.

If women have to use this information to their benefit right now, before the world changes to accommodate fairness, then all the power to them. The information Christopher provides will shock most women, but he makes a point that he used to be on the high end of the alpha scale, but as he realized that it wasn't an ideal way to be (it's all about balance), he became an advocate to educate women. He identifies some habits that women exhibit in the professional world that stall their progress by projecting a vibe of weakness. Men trust strength and confidence in business, and stray from any signs of weakness. According to the author, weakness is shown by doing things like bringing baked goods to work, nodding and smiling too much to keep a conversation going, waiting to be called upon to speak, focusing on social aspects and maintaining friendships over business benefits, and many other things that show the nurturing nature in a group setting.

I recently had a meeting with a successful real estate agent, Zuzana Misik,[162] who is a confident, intelligent, gorgeous woman, born in Slovakia, Eastern Europe. She immigrated to Canada as a child, where at a young age, she followed her passion for real estate. We discussed this exact topic of dealing with professional men of high status. I've been curious how she manages her self-presentation on the front stage of the luxury real estate world. Despite the fact that a large percentage of real estate agents are actually women, the best deals, investors, buyers, builders, and other worthy connections are found among wealthy men who are very hard to break through to. What Zuzana described as her methods for dealing with professional men, has completely confirmed what Christopher Flett advised in his book, and she didn't even know about the book! In her passion to not just be equal to men, but to rise above that equality paradigm and be the fullest representation of her own power and status as a clever, professional, and daring business woman, she was able to build such a confident aura that it speaks for her when she enters the room. But it wasn't always like this—that construction process of self-confidence that doesn't break under pressure did not happen overnight.

When I asked her how in the world she was able to retain business dealings with men who can be very set in their ways, or even get them to listen and not judge her by appearance,

Zuzana said it is important to overwrite that possibility from the start, and show great confidence that will be more aggrandized than theirs, which will leave no room for doubt in your ability. You must keep in mind not to waste any time on small talk; you have to start with showing your ***informational power*** because you could lose their attention fast. In the study of influence and persuasion, ***informational power*** is an advantage someone with valuable information possesses. Go straight to the paperwork, state the facts, and spare the fluff. Unnecessary chatter can dilute the perception of your competency. I guess, as the saying goes, there is a time and place for everything. Come prepared knowing your hard facts, so you can answer most important questions.

It may all seem like a lot of work, and it is, but that is the work of educating yourself in order to reach your desired, and even unexpected, results. Life is a game, and those who learn the rules have an easier time winning. It is that fine balance of not giving up trying to change the world, while at the same time playing the game not to get left behind in the process. Learn from those who have been showing results. Experience, plus constant learning, will provide you with a leverage to be able to actually work smarter and not harder. Sometimes hard work alone doesn't bring desired results, but leveraging hard work with making cunning changes to the slightest behaviours that you don't even realize that you're doing, can be magical. That's why hiring a life coach, who can point out the things that your dear friends won't tell you, has tremendous benefits. And reading this far into this book is already a great deal of work you have done to set your mind up for greater success. Let's keep going; we only have a little more work left to do!

CHAPTER 9

UNDER THE INFLUENCE

"Power is not an institution, and not a structure; neither is it a certain strength we are endowed with; it is the name that one attributes to a complex strategical situation in a particular society."

– Michel Foucault

9

What's With the Attitude?

C ongrats that you have made it this far, which puts you among the smaller group of people who actually complete the book they set out to read! I admire you for being diligent and eager to learn, so I saved the higher information for the end. I actually decided to remove another topic that was going to originally be in this chapter, and instead reinforce the basics of *attitudes* and *influence*.

What inspired me to do this is the recent increase of clever schemes and next-level manipulation tactics used on unsuspecting victims. Internet capabilities made it possible to reach larger numbers of people, and thus the game got turned up hard! The topic of influence really fired me up to start digging deeper into things that capture people physically, mentally, and/or spiritually by hijacking their deepest core, all while they don't even realize how much they are becoming subservient to someone or something.

The meaning of the word *attitude* does not just regard a person acting in an arrogant way. An *attitude* is a feeling or opinion about something or someone, or a way of behaving that is caused by this, as defined by Cambridge Dictionary. It can be a positive or negative evaluation of someone or something that you have constructed within your mind, or not constructed yet, but may put it together from the pieces stored in your memory when you're being called upon. Your attitudes, especially the ones that are more accessible in your mind, influence your behaviour and the way you process information.

One thing that all people do, all the time, is evaluate the world around them—what your eyes show you, your mind processes. To make things more complicated, you can also have an **ambivalent attitude**, which is when you both like and dislike something at the same time. I wrote earlier about how people typically agree that it's important for mothers to stay home to care for young children, and the same people also agree that mothers should be out of the house and taking up employment. Another example of ambivalent attitude, which often pops up in discussions, is that many people like naturopathic medicine because it provides natural ways of healing, but they also dislike it because it lacks regulation, and some companies can, and do, exploit that for profits while selling the so-called "snake oil."

There are three types of attitudes. One of them is the **behaviourally based attitude**, which is a strange one because, here, you are likely to base your attitude about something, on how you behaved towards it before. So if I was to ask you if you like to read books, and you think, "Well, I am reading a book right now, and I'm almost finished, so I must like reading," then you are coming from a behaviourally based evaluation of reading books.

My personal favourite is the **cognitively based attitude,** which is based on your belief in the properties of the attitude object, so I tend to seek out as much information about something before I decide on how to rate it. Things weren't always this mindful for me. Thankfully, the study of psychology, and of spirituality, along with participation in the stock market, has taught me the importance of digging deep for truth. In the market, investors constantly preach about doing your own due diligence, and not to rely on what someone tells you or what you read in media articles. In the esoteric communities, the quest for truth about this whole existence never stops, as it even goes far beyond the greatness of ancient Egypt; and in psychology, there are infinite hypotheses about our minds' operations to test and retest.

I used to make my decisions based on my emotions—like the time, as a teenager, I packed all of my stuff and moved from Canada back to Poland, because I missed the life that I had before I moved to Canada at the age of 12. I was often making decisions from **affectively based attitudes**, where "affect" comes from the word "affecting" or "moving" someone emotionally. Such attitudes are formed when you are thinking with your heart and not with your head. Research finds that most people use their emotions when making important decisions such as voting in political elections, and politicians are getting more skilled in catering to this fact, with their campaign strategies. Emotions are such strong forces of influence that voters are not just influenced by their deeply held values. Instead, in their research for Stanford Business School, Andrew Healy and colleagues found that voters appear to be responding to random short-term emotional stimuli.[163] Voters' choices depend on events that affect their emotional state, even when those events are totally unrelated to government activity, such as a football game. This finding puts citizen competence into question, and provides evidence about non-political criteria that affect voting behaviour. Let's keep an eye out for any major sporting, music, or other "events" happening before major elections, which could be an indication of the government trying to arouse specific emotions in people, especially ones that promote affinity towards a specific candidate or party, suggest how you should feel about specific issues or talking points, or whatever suits the **propaganda** of the source.

Propaganda is defined by *dictionary.com* as "information, ideas, or rumours deliberately spread widely to help or harm a person, group, movement, institution, nation, etc."[164] This tactic goes back to the 1600s, when the word was first utilized in the Christian religion in its efforts to propagate it onto others throughout the world. It is meant to change the common attitudes of people like yourself, within a specific group or society, who become a tool used by the source of propaganda to help shift perceptions of others. This information is designed to target emotional processes, and counts on shock value and hypnotic repetition of simple messages to get the point across. It is the type of messages that astound the minds of those who use more of their cognitive processes; or in other words, are more mindful of how they form their attitudes and beliefs, and their intellect is not as susceptible to such manipulation. It may very well be those people who don't fall for pranks, or are hard to hypnotize, but that's just my guess.

Not all propaganda is equal; some can be for a good cause, such as the promotion of animal welfare, or respect for nature. However, most propaganda is used to deceive people into thinking or behaving in a way that is not exactly part of their natural course, and the fact that so much effort is put into convincing them of something that someone else has come up with, speaks for itself. The growing research into psychology has surely contributed to the increasing potency of techniques used to change attitudes. Today, online "memes" meant to be humourous are definitely used as propaganda. The British Library writes about how propaganda was used to fuel World War One, and "unlike previous wars, this was the first total war in which whole nations and not just professional armies were locked in mortal combat. This and subsequent modern wars required propaganda to mobilize hatred against the enemy; to convince the population of the justness of the cause; to enlist the active support and cooperation of neutral countries; and to strengthen the support of allies."[165] After expressing that people are generally not that bright, World War Two's famous propagandist, and a

Nazi politician, Joseph Goebbels, is quoted coaching us on this deceitful practice, saying that "propaganda must therefore always be essentially simple and repetitious. In the long run, only he will achieve basic results in influencing public opinion, who is able to reduce problems to the simplest terms, and who has the courage to keep forever repeating them in this simplified form, despite the objections of intellectuals."[166] Isn't it interesting that people such as Goebbels openly tell us exactly how they are messing with us, and the public just falls for it?

By understanding the mechanism of propaganda, and what it's like to be under the influence of it, you will maintain your mind's sovereignty, and make sure your thoughts are really your own. You will also be more in control of your interactions with others, as you will be quicker in recognizing what drives that person's opinions, feelings, and behaviours. Often, people are not aware of how much of their opinions and beliefs are swayed by all kinds of persuasive messages from sources that are trying to do so, and they themselves are often in support of those sources. If a person idolizes a specific famous musical artist, they may mimic that celebrity's opinions on various topics, and not allow others to criticize them even when it's something commonly found to be concerning. This is why such artists are often used by politicians to spread propaganda on their behalf. They have great power to change attitudes of the masses, such as when unpopular presidential nominees ask pop stars to endorse them on their platforms. If you are quick enough to catch who the person listens to—

not just in music, but also news channels, podcasters, and YouTubers—you will have a slightly better idea of their attitudes. It will allow you to either work around that person's convictions, while maintaining your own stance, or if it's truly necessary, you may try to respectfully and skillfully help them see the bigger picture, and realize that they may have drifted away from the core of who they are, while taking on opinions and beliefs that may not be their own.

Emotions have always been running wild in our world. Whether it's on a macro (societal) or micro (personal) level, they can be the cause of much error, disorder, divisions, and hardship because of their strong connection to passion; and the fire of passion, fanned by the wind of deceit, can easily turn into an inferno. It is up to you to always keep the water of reason handy.

Bypassing the Conscious

The tricky part about attitudes is that once they're developed, they can exist on two different levels. ***Explicit attitudes*** are ones that you are conscious of, and can easily report; so if you were asked to give your opinion on whether you think schools should be teaching children to think for themselves, you'd likely say that you are in favour. ***Implicit attitudes*** are uncontrollable and unconscious. To really grasp what unconscious and uncontrollable means, think of it this way: If you hear a dish break at a restaurant, you will automatically move your eyes in the direction of the noise, and your body may jump, all being outside of your control—it's just part of your inner programming. ***Implicit*** attitudes are outside of your daily awareness, and most likely you don't even know you have them, but they will come out when you are in autopilot mode (or when drunk), and will affect your behaviour when a conducive situation arises. They are pretty much built from your life experiences and interactions; therefore, you have a possibility to change it if you decide to work on your inner self. This is why the ancient saying, "Know thyself," is such powerful advice for humanity.

During my studies, I came across a powerful tool used in assessing implicit bias. It isn't free of criticism, but it is still quite eye-opening and helps you feel what an implicit bias is and how it can hide within you so easily. It is the ***Implicit Association Test***,[167] a computer game that measures the strength of your bias or stereotype towards some objects, by testing how your subconscious mind associates things. I strongly recommend taking this quick test yourself online, on the *Harvard* website. Go to my website to find the link, or type into your search engine. As you play, you must sort words and pictures into categories as quickly as possible, such as "dark" = "negative," "light" = "positive," by pressing the corresponding buttons, and the associations keep switching up in many variations. If you are faster in connecting the word "dark" with "negative" than you are in matching "light" with "positive," then that reveals your hidden bias, which makes you act from a pre-learned assumption that something dark must be equal to something negative. For example, someone at some point in time put it out into the world that black cats are evil, and these poor little beings that are born black, have no idea why they are treated differently than cats of other colours. This misconception has lasted hundreds of years—by word of mouth or exacerbated by religious representatives, movies, and many other genres—and resulted in harm for many innocent animals, all because of what someone said, while others adapted that belief by allowing fear to suspend their reason. Such representations create implicit attitudes, then bring about unconscious behaviours, which we are trying to get better at predicting. Betting on people doing what they say, or even what they think, is not a very good bet. Someone may say that they love animals, but then may automatically shoo away a black cat when they encounter it on their path. You must keep in mind the implicit biases they may have. To do that, it is a good idea to think about things—how they were raised, where they grew up, who they associate with, what they do in their spare time, how they treat the coffee-shop attendant who got their order wrong—and watch for behaviours that don't really match what they say.

Many researchers have taken this journey into the hidden depths of the human subconscious biases. Alexander Green and colleagues used the IAT test to measure physicians' implicit race preference and perceptions of cooperativeness. They wanted to see whether doctors act out of their *implicit*

bias towards Black people who come into the emergency room with complaints of symptoms of coronary artery disease. Results suggest that physicians' unconscious biases may contribute to racial/ethnic disparities in use of medical procedures such as thrombolysis for myocardial infarction. This study represents the first evidence of unconscious (implicit, one that they are not necessarily aware of) race bias among physicians.[168] Similar studies included police officers, in order to know more about the concern of racial bias that leads to misidentification of objects held in suspects' hands or pockets. These computer game based studies found that even dark skinned officers displayed a bias when they were matching up dark figures with weapon-like objects, faster than they matched lighter figures.

Keep in mind, this test is not perfect. There have been many researchers who have found issues with it, such as that it is not a good predictor of behaviour, that it's not effective in changing this bias for the better, or that by blaming negative feelings towards some people or things, on something uncontrollable, it will provide an excuse for ignoring the issue. However, it is a good exercise that forces us to take a look deep within ourselves, and at how we were programmed to think, and at least encourages a more conscious effort to do some spring cleaning of our unconscious.

Why Would You Do That?

Wouldn't it be great to always know how someone else will behave? If all business owners knew what their potential clients are inclined towards, wouldn't it allow them to save time and money? Why many businesses fail is because their leaders are overconfident in their ability to read their clientele. Often, people assume they know what someone else will like, based on what they themselves like, forgetting that they should place themselves in the position of their clients. What makes things even more complicated is that people don't always behave based on what they say, or even what they think. Behaviour is separate from these things; it walks down its own path.

Robert Cialdini, a popular social psychologist who specializes in the topic of persuasion, wrote an article called "Crafting Normative Messages to Protect the Environment," where he dives deep into the psychology of influence in advertising.[169] What he brings to light helps us understand a puzzling trend: People often hold themselves high on the moral standard scale, but actually put very little action towards positive social or environmental change of some sort. Cialdini noticed an error in an award-winning anti-littering campaign, which actually turned out to be ineffective in persuading people to stop littering in that particular region, and it inspired him to look into this matter. In his advice to the pro-environmental advertisers, he specifies the difference between ***descriptive***

norms, which are norms that describe actions such as "many people litter," and ***injunctive norms,*** which refer to what is approved of, or prescribed, such as "please recycle to minimize pollution."

What the advertisers did wrong was use a **descriptive norm**, which had a psychologically overpowering effect. It sent the message to the audience's autopilots that everyone is littering, and that backfired by normalizing this action. If the parking lot by a fast food joint already has litter all over the ground, it's easier to feel like it's not really a big deal to throw out another wrapper or cup, rather than stashing it in the car, because everyone else has done it. If the parking lot is clean, and all the other people are seen walking up to the garbage bin to throw out their used packaging, it is going to feel strange being the only one throwing stuff on the ground. Unless, of course, the person is a real jerk. Advertisers should focus on presenting an ***injunctive norm***, such as, "In order to keep this beautiful lake clean, please don't litter," which is apparently much more effective.

This is good information for those who pay for any type of commercials and advertising for their company. Not many advertising producers have a deeper understanding of psychology; many focus more on the creative and artistic aspects of their work. There is a pretty good chance that an expressed attitude towards something may, or may not, lead a person to behave in a way aligned with that attitude. Even doing a poll doesn't really help predict behaviour. A positive response can be maximized to a shocking extent when the advertisement is delivered in a way that hits all the right notes and actually elicits a desired response from the audience.

There have been company leaders and politicians who advocate for the environment, but they themselves don't often walk the walk. In their article, Shane Gunster and colleagues acknowledge this phenomenon called **hypocrisy discourse**, which "is used to support both anti- and pro-climate change perspectives; its nature and function fundamentally differs depending on who is using it." They say that "hypocrisy discourse plays up the moral value that contemporary culture places on the individual's responsibility to act, while largely dismissing the idea that broad social, collective, and systemic practices may have any influence on those actions." They give an example from the American political context, mentioning how "less than a day after *An Inconvenient Truth* won an Academy award for best documentary, Al Gore was back in the headlines when a "free market" advocacy group—The Tennessee Center for Policy Research—revealed that the gas and electric bills for Gore's Nashville mansion were more than twenty times higher than the US average."[170] The game of politics summed up. No offence to politicians here; there are those who have dignity and are as honest as they can be. But most of them dramatize their front stage performance, and often don't want to leave the stage when the clapping has stopped long ago. In a recent example (within this action-movie of a year, year 2020) written about by *Fox News*, a democratic Pennsylvania lawmaker told the world exactly how the game of politics works. While unaware that the camera microphone was live, she made remarks to her colleague that she was about to do some "political theatre" in front of the news camera.[171] It sent a message to the public that they are so unimportant that all they deserve is lies.

So if people don't always act according to what they say, to their values or beliefs, how can we predict behaviour after all? Consider the concept of **authority**. Know who is in charge of the situation, or the rewards, and you will know how people are likely to behave. People comply with that which has some power over them. **Compliance** is when you obey an order, or a request of someone else's. It is a bit more of an aggressive factor of persuasion and influence. **Forced compliance theory**, according to *Wikipedia*, is the idea that authority, or some other perceived higher-ranking person, can force a lower-ranked individual to make statements or perform acts that violate their better judgment.[172] It focuses on the goal of altering an individual's attitude through persuasion and authority.

There is a famous study called "The Boring Task Study," by Stanford's social psychologists, Festinger and Carlsmith, who investigated the cognitive consequences of forced compliance and the resulting attempts to reduce **cognitive dissonance**. So the volunteers of this study were divided into two groups. They were told that they were going to be measured for performance by doing this cool and easy task. But they soon found themselves doing very annoying tasks, like putting spools on and off of pegs for an hour. Later, they were each asked if they would help the researchers present this process to the next batch of participants, and entice them to also go and do this annoying task. Long story short, the two groups were paid to recruit others to participate in something that was not very enjoyable. Group 1 got paid twenty times more money than Group 2 for convincing the newbies. People in both groups were risking their reputation or getting cursed-out by the person they recruited, because when the newbies realized how boring the task was, they would be mad at the person, who convinced them, for lying to them, or think that they lost their mind.

At the end, the original participants were tested for **cognitive dissonance**, to find out who felt worse about lying to others, and how they would try to resolve this feeling of friction within themselves, as most people think of themselves as honest and trustworthy, and would prefer to keep that attitude intact. Would you guess who felt worse? Was it Group 1, which received more money (let's say it was $200), or Group 2, who got less (let's say $10)? The group that was paid less felt the biggest dissonance! They shifted their belief to get their mind back to some state of balance, even if it was based on convincing themselves of some excuse. Their automatic processes led them to shift their belief regarding their enjoyment of the study, and convince themselves that it was actually kind of fun in a way—a very strange way. A person would often rather do that, than maintain a full realization that they themselves may potentially be a bad person, a liar, or someone who is capable of tricking other people. People may not want to admit to themselves that they may actually be naïve, and may so easily follow the orders of others without questioning anything, or thinking it through when being in the spur of a moment.

The people who got less money rated the task as pleasant, contrary to the people who got paid more. The people who were paid a good amount of money were able to reduce their dissonance by telling themselves that they're not a bad person because, most likely, anyone would have lied for that much money; it was more easily justified. The people who lied for a tiny amount of money had a greater reason to feel shame, although the lesson for both is priceless. When you actually realize what you are capable of, both good and bad, you will be able to recognize it faster when a situation arises, and remain in control. It can spare you from falling for worse influence in the future. Sometimes influence is so powerful that it can bend a person's values, often without them even knowing they're doing it, until later when they come out of "the moment."

Just like in the Milgram shock experiment (where the guy in the white lab coat was telling the participants to continue administering electric shocks to another alleged participant, in another room), Festinger's study shows how easily you can be influenced into compliance. It also shows an even tougher truth: that you can be influenced into convincing others to do something you know you did not enjoy or benefit much from, telling them to jump in, that the water is fine, while knowing it's actually quite the opposite. I can confess, I have done that when I worked in the cosmetics field. There were times when we were encouraged by our higher-ups to push specific items that were newly launched, just because the company spent money on the big launch and needed to report numbers to their higher-ups. We did have to suggest items that we didn't personally like, just because we had to. This type of counter-attitudinal work, or behaviour, when you have to pretend you align with something that you actually don't, because it is your job, can be very mentally and emotionally draining and can cause cognitive dissonance.

Improving your skill of predicting behaviour, by understanding what drives it, will help you in serious situations that can arise in your life. It will protect you from the conscious and unconscious agendas of others, give you more control over your own energy, and not allow anyone to take it hostage. People will come to you with all kinds of matters, but you must perfect your discernment not to waste time getting stringed along in the process, as you figure out where they're really heading.

I recently came across a large number of people advocating online against the harmful effects of signing up to multi-level marketing companies, which are like pyramid scheme scams; it's just that they involve a product sale, which allows them to escape that illegal category. An article in *Seeking Alpha*, an online investment news portal, has summarized this industry perfectly by saying "MLM's 'brand' is **not** based on products or on company culture, customer loyalty or on new technology, or social or political values. The brands of all MLM companies are one and the same, 'multi-level marketing' itself, the contradictory business model, involving recruiting your own competitors and 'being your own customer'".[173] They all effectively grasp the devotion of many people because of their psychologically tailored systems, which some people find hard to resist, and later escape. Recruits are mostly encouraged to recruit others, because that is where the biggest chance of earning money is. Interestingly, a study by American Association of Retired Persons Foundation, reported by CISION, states that "among the more than 20 million Americans who participate or have participated in multilevel marketing (MLM) organizations, 90 percent say they got involved to make money. However, nearly half (47 percent) lose money, and a quarter (27 percent) make no money." They also write that "of those that made money, more than half (53 percent) made less than $5,000" and that is per year.[174] The people who sign up under you, make you commission, if they happen to become devoted too, by buying, selling, and keeping the recruiting chain going. The consultants lose money because they are expected to buy the merchandise themselves, so that they can actually experience the products they're selling, and maintain their active status. They also end up paying for the parties they organize, and for travel, among other things, which they happen to find out about after signing up.

So why would people recruit others into a scheme, which they know is not as easy and profitable as they make it sound to others? There are many reasons, mostly due to a level of psychological entanglement that is perpetrated by the intricate design of this "game." What I found interesting is that "The Boring Task Study" explains some of what may be happening in this example. People who were recruited realize that it may not all be as peachy as they thought, and end up in a cognitively dissonant state. They try to make themselves like it. Now that they announced to everyone that they have found this exciting business opportunity, and many have showed off their often exaggerated or fake success on social media, they don't want to be seen as a quitter; they may think that beginnings are just hard, as in any business, and they want to stick around to at least get their sign-up investment back, and they often choose to talk themselves into continuing. They must recruit others as instructed by the company, so they convince others to sign up too, knowing that there is only a slight chance that they will make any money. Next, they try to convince themselves (cognitive dissonance reduction) that convincing that person was the right thing because it gives that person a chance to make money, and teaches them confidence. They may convince themselves that they are helping them to just get a good discount on these "miracle" products that will allegedly change their life. With this psychological formula perfected over many years by these companies, there seem to be no limits.

Spell on You

Throughout your life, you encounter many things that attempt to persuade you, and you will likely be persuading others too. All you have to do is open your cell phone, and there will be some advertisement flashing in your face, trying to convince you of something. But not all persuasion is "evil"; there is a scale to the moral aspect of it. For example, if you try to persuade someone to join you for a walk in the park, and there is nothing wrong with that (unless that person refuses more than once... well maybe twice, as some people do need to be given more of a nudge to get out of their comfortable state!). I would like to focus on the kind of persuasion that wants to sway you towards some goal of its source, and the psychological circumstances involved, which can leave you without much control over what's actually happening, unless you arm yourself with awareness of the psychology of persuasion and attitude change.

There is a system I want you to get familiar with, which defines factors that influence persuasion. It is the ***Elaboration Likelihood Model***, which of course, like any model, is not without flaws, but it is extremely helpful in understanding how people process information, how they elaborate on things, and what factors will or will not be strong enough to change their opinions or behaviours. Your mind is working within an ***elaboration continuum***, a scale that goes from the ***peripheral route*** to the ***central route*** to persuasion.

Probably the most widely used out of the two is the **peripheral route to persuasion**; it's your autopilot's favourite because it takes the least effort. When something is in the peripheral, it is outside of your central focus. When you take this path, you will be more influenced by the surrounding context of the message that you're receiving; the factors that decorate it will become the main ingredients of the spell. It could be the **credibility** of the source of the message that acts as a misleading factor. You may think that if the message came from a well-known person, then it must be true. Have you seen the commercials that use Hollywood actresses to advertise the benefits of some cheap skincare products, as if they really use them? Did you actually try to justify that in your mind, just a tiny bit, convincing yourself that maybe they actually like this $20 face cream, when they can clearly afford the $500 one? And, on top of that, you also know that they are obsessed with anti-aging.

You may focus on other superficial things, like **attractiveness** of the source, which is why the "sex sells method" has been used in advertising over and over, because it seems to be effective. The **music** playing in the background of a commercial can affect your judgment of the product advertised; so if it's a popular song from your school days, it may elicit emotions that you may transfer onto the object advertised. I really don't think we need any studies to prove that, in regard to the social media world. Whether the audience is consciously aware of the overinflated statuses presented by many influencers or not, something in them still cannot resist having some level of a cognitive reaction to the embellished front-stage presentations. When rappers throw fake money around in their music videos, you may know that it's fake, but you will still accept the entirety of the presentation with the symbolism of money, while registering it as real in your subconscious mind, which is enough to build a lasting schema. At some later time, you will be more likely to automatically associate rappers with cash-money. Simply the **amount** of times you have been presented with a message is a peripheral cue in itself; repetition causes you to start internalizing it as true, without much thought.

Short commercials are a peripheral wonderland because, in the few seconds, it's really hard to elaborate on the message too much. When the target audience is not expected to devote much effort to careful examination, or they don't have the **ability** or **motivation** to do so, they will be hit with that peripheral bomb. A YouTube advertisement has to be clever enough to grab your attention in the short time before you are able to press the skip button. You are likely not motivated to pay attention to what they're presenting in the ad, and you may not even have the ability to pay attention, because your friends are visiting, and you are waiting anxiously to be able to show them your chosen video. If you happen to pay for digital advertising, you may want to keep this in mind. Side note: I really don't know how YouTube ads pay off for the advertiser; they must be the most resented form of advertising, as everyone just wants to get to the video and is projecting an energy of annoyance towards it before it even starts.

In the earlier chapter, we talked about **exposure** and greater **familiarity** resulting in increased positive feelings towards that person. They are also tools in the "peripheral route to persuasion" belt. This type of effect can be a bit dangerous: When something feels familiar, you are less likely to question it. For example, there are marketers who take the "psychological blueprints" from religious organizations, and use them in their selling strategies. If you have ever seen marketing conventions, you will notice how much it resembles an evangelical mega-church service. It is all put together to feel like it was meant to be. The participants then feel a greater need to share their euphoria with others in order to recruit them, and use familiarity to chat up their target. So, for example, a new parent will get the pitch related to caring for their baby's future, or a student who recently graduated will be teased with the ability to pay off their student loans. A parasite usually likes to merge with the operations of the host to engrain itself into its natural flow, in order to take it over.

Fear appeals are very popular, and fear is also a peripheral cue as it distracts from intelligent investigation of the central details of the message. They grab attention more effectively than non-fear messages, but are they as effective in changing people's attitudes towards something? Do you think that scary advertisements on cigarette packages make people quit smoking? Campaigns with extreme or scary messages often equal to advertising dollars flying out the door of institutions, before researchers get to enter through them. Governmental health organizations spend millions on anti-smoking ads, but psychologists keep finding that they are a waste. A study, published in the *Journal of Media Psychology,* found that the disgusting images have a boomerang effect on smokers. Researcher Paul Bolls said that "simply trying to encourage smokers to quit by exposing them to combined threatening and disgusting visual images, is not an effective way to change attitudes and behaviours." He added that "effective communication is more complicated than simply showing a disgusting picture. That kind of communication will usually result in a **defensive avoidance response,** where the smoker will try to avoid the disgusting images, not the cigarettes."[175]

Fear messages that aren't that extreme can actually be effective, at least to temporarily get the desired response out of you, as they are designed to make you afraid that something bad may happen, and persuade you to change your attitude or behaviour. There are many sources that make fear the core of their business, even if it's something like the ***fear of missing out***. Entertainment event promoters like to say that they only have a few party tickets left, and you "better get them now because later you won't be able to get in," which entices those who are on the fence to buy the ticket ahead of time, just in case they sell out. Or what about those offers and special deals you may have come across somewhere, ones that only are valid today, because tomorrow the computer will reset, or the company will be on the other side of the planet... if they don't leave the planet all together by tomorrow... who knows. Of course, this doesn't apply to every case; it's up to you to do your due diligence so that you don't actually miss out on some early-bird offer that is actually beneficial.

Some sources will go as far as using the **problem-solution strategy**. They create a problem, or convince you that you have one, and present themselves as the only saviour in town. I recently saw a video from some multi-level marketing company's training seminar, which made me quite furious because humans are already bombarded by negative news, and those who want to purposefully contribute to that negativity in order to make a profit are like parasites to society and the economy. For the economy to flourish, it needs businesses that solve real problems and not made-up ones, while sucking people dry of their money that could be spent elsewhere, and robbing them of their time, which they could use more productively. This particular sales "guru," from the video, was telling consultants in the audience that in sales, you must create a problem, and sell the solution to that problem, while making it sound like you are the only one that can solve this issue because of how apparently "unique" your product is. He even went on to belittle the intelligence of potential clients, and told the audience to just say that their product is so great that it has a patent from God!

Sadly, negative information has more impact on attitudes than positive information; it seems to be easier to remember negative words. Messages that emphasize loss from not following the direction seem to be stronger than ones that emphasise gain, which seems illogical. So if I have a stock market group that I want you to sign up to, I would probably benefit more from advertising that you will lose more when trading alone without the support of a group, rather than advertising that you will make more money with our group's support. Speaking of the stock market, fear appeals and positive messages are strategically used with lots of reverse-psychology at play. The rich know the real meaning of fear, as the famous advice given by Warren Buffet cleverly explains it in relation to the mechanism of the financial world. He is famous for saying to "be fearful when others are greedy, and be greedy when others are fearful." When the market crashes and people are in fear, the news is in full doom and gloom mode, and that's when it's a good time for investors to be ready to put their cash position into action. When the market news is mostly positive for a while, it's time to take some profits. The most clever business minds find ways to capitalize in uncertain times. I guess this fits a quote I just saw someone post on Instagram: Smooth waters don't make good sailors. It may just be that we live in one big sailor training field—The strong are making waves while the rest are just trying to stay afloat.

Then there is the second, more effortful route to persuasion, the **central route**; the one that tries to zoom directly to the source of information and its relevant details. This route will take you on a longer but more scenic route, possibly through the mountains of mindful inquiry. Your motivation to process this information should be high, so when a stock market investor sees a paid promotion on *Twitter* about the stock they just purchased, the motivation to click on it will be much higher than if it was about a stock they never heard about. Low motivation clearly won't help much with engagement.

Your ability to pay attention is important to the processing of a central route type of message. Ability to **comprehend** the information presented, as well as low **distraction** or **pressure,** is needed in order to process a more detailed or important message; so that is why some sources create a time rush, urging you to buy now or lose out on this amazing opportunity. News media gives you fast-changing snips of information, intercepted by commercials, which decreases your ability to ponder each issue, though you may store and recall some of that information later when in a relevant conversation. Pressure can be used in order to distract you from elaborating, and make you act now. If you are at an important meeting, such as when you're about to sign something, always make sure you are not being distracted or in a rush, which will throw off your ability to focus on the central details. It may reset your vibe, and you may forget the important things you were going to ask about. A vibe too positive can make you more agreeable. Skilled negotiators will likely know this and may use it to their advantage.

Words Mean Things

In the powerful book of ancient knowledge, *Egyptian Book of the Dead: The Book of Coming Forth by Day*, translated by

Muata Ashby, it is written: "Never forget, the words are not the reality, only reality is reality; picture symbols are the idea, words are confusion."[176] A late graffiti pioneer from New York, artist Ramm Ell Zee, has explored the history and meaning of language, describing them through his cosmically veiled perspective as equations and formations that register in the unconscious. In his writings, he raises a deep question made of clever word play: "Who titled us off as the human 'race'; who put us in a race, and for what purpose are we racing?"[177] Good question!

When considering the perils of humanity, we can see how much negativity spirals out of words being misunderstood, twisted, or suppressed. Whole nations fell or rose because of a clever use of words that have affected the actions of masses. Words also embody their energy throughout time. Each word has a trajectory of meanings that go back all the way back to their origins, and its own unique journey through the various societal stages, channelled by people of the times. Deep knowledge of original word meanings can be found within the study of *etymology*. We tend to ignore the meanings of words as we move through our days in a cognitively economical vehicle, and don't even realize how the simple things we all say have a meaning that wasn't necessarily intended, but that doesn't stop them from having power over our reality. Take something as simple as days of the week, something you say so many times each day—could you name the meanings of these words other than the day they represent? The word "Friday" comes from the name of the Nordic Goddess, *Freya* (Freya-day).

I have looked up various meanings of my own name, and found that *Dominika* comes from the word "dominate," or "lord, master," and dates back to the ancient Roman period. But if you take parts of the name—Domi and Nika—separately, then we have a meaning of "Lord," or "Master" and "Good," so I guess I will accept it in whichever order; it suits me perfectly either way. Have you looked into your own name, or asked your parents what guided them to choose it? You may find out some interesting facts that can reveal more pieces to the puzzle that is you.

I was recently thinking of this ironic twist that language has played on the "self-help" community. Life coaches, motivational speakers, and people in the positivity movement often say that it's important to stay humble. People use the word "humble" like it's something really dignified, signalling good character. If you look up the meaning of that word, it actually means something that is not very desirable—well, at least in the real dictionaries. The Miriam-Webster Dictionary states that the word has its origin in the Latin word "humilis," meaning "low."[178] Their definition refers to reflecting, expressing, or offering in a spirit of deference or submission, ranking low in a hierarchy or scale, being insignificant. To humble means to destroy the power, independence, or prestige of someone. So if a motivational speaker talks about secrets of success,

315

and they say that you have to be proud, confident, independent, strive for greatness, look the part, know your worth, and then they tell you to also be humble, it will contradict the rest of what they just taught you. It's like telling someone to walk faster and remember to slow down, at the same time. An interesting example of why our societies are so confused and riddled with contradictions lies in the example from *urbandictionary.com*, which seems to just do its own thing by suggesting a top definition that glorifies this somewhat demeaning word, and saying that it means "to be kind and honest, showing equality to others."[179] I guess it's up to you to make your pick, but just remember: The energy and the substance of a word is what matters to the spirit of truth, and its social meaning is a societal twist constructed through random social interactions and influence of those with greater social authority.

Social psychology tries to decipher how words can be used in persuasion. Words can also become elements of the *peripheral route* when they are specifically manipulated to achieve some desired reaction from their receiver, other than just attempting to present dry facts. Word selection, word order, and context of the words being read or spoken, can affect people's thoughts, feelings, and behaviours, accidentally or purposefully, and change their response. That is why *questionnaires* or *polls* must be created carefully, with the focus on minimizing the possibility of *response biases*. There are many response biases that can cause participants of these questionnaires to give inaccurate answers. If I wanted to deliberately get a positive rating from people who read my book, I would benefit more from giving them a survey that asks them to circle the word "agree" or "disagree"—while answering the question, "Did you like reading the *Person to Person* book?"—than if I gave them a survey that asks them to rate how much they liked this book on a scale of 1–10. I would be then relying on a popular response bias—the **acquiescence effect**—which is this strange desire for people to just agree, rather than disagree.

The same words can also mean different things to different people. If your school gives you a questionnaire asking you to "rate the effectiveness of your instructor," you may not think much of it, and give some rating you think is appropriate. It would probably be somewhere in the high end of the scale, because often people want to be nice, and don't really intend to cause trouble for the other person. Most people actually tend to give a really good rating, even if their experience was just "alright" but not really good, or they give a really bad one if they happened to have a specifically bad experience. But what are they really measuring with such a broad vocabulary? What does that question even mean—effectiveness in what exactly? This can mean different things to different people, so the results of this questionnaire may not reflect anything meaningful in turn, and award false praise to the instructor.

If you think questionnaires and polls aren't important, think again, because they are used to change or create policies, and in many other deciding aspects of the world you live in. It becomes tricky because people often don't really know what they think about something, and the way a question is asked can totally change how the person answers. One of the researchers who decided to challenge faulty opinion polls and questionnaires, Stanley Presser, profoundly states that "findings are scientifically meaningless in the absence of an interpretive context describing how they were obtained."[180] A very surprising result came out of his study in which participants were asked to write down what they think are the most important skills for children to learn to prepare them for life. Only 5% of them wrote anything related to children learning to "think for themselves." The interesting part is that when they were given a chance to select "thinking for themselves" as one of the available pre-written options, a whole 62% selected it! Yes, these were the same people for whom this issue didn't come to mind as something of high importance earlier!

Something like the order of words or sentences may seem like nothing major, and who would really have time or energy to think about things like the order of all words we speak? We simply don't have the capacity to keep all of these rules in mind all the time, but starting at whatever point each of us is at, right here and in this present moment, and following with continuous refreshing of this knowledge, eventually it will stick more permanently. That is the path to mastery. *The order effect* can change how you rate things almost completely, and it works with what you are thinking about at the moment of being asked a question. Male participants of a study rated their marital satisfaction as much more positive when they were first asked to rate their life satisfaction, and then marital satisfaction second. Researchers then asked participants these same questions but in an opposite order, so the marital question was now first, and they got a much lower rating of life satisfaction in this scenario. This happened because, for some reason, a lot of men do not feel too positive about their marital satisfaction; it is quite likely that they could be fighting with their spouse, or may have a bad financial situation. Many young couples face lots of household bills, so it's more likely that the marital question primed these men with a negative mood, and then that mood affected their subsequent attitude and caused them to lower their rating for the next question about their general life satisfaction. This adds to the evidence of how emotions significantly affect opinions and actions.

S(p)elling

It is a common reality that a large part of our communication with others involves selling and buying. On social media, many posts are made with the intention to sell something, or change an attitude about something, which will give it a clearer path towards being sold. Ideas are also being sold. With the rise of entrepreneurship, or at least the attempts at it, the thing that drives pretty much any business is the ability to gain attention, and to do that, some form of communication must happen. Let's talk more about the psychological processes that are commonly utilized in the realm of sales.

Many retail businesses struggle with the decision about which strategy is more successful: representation of everyday low prices all the time, such as Dollarama, Winners, or Wal-mart to some degree; or a "special sale" every so often, with deep discounts, such as *Sephora,* which is famous for their discount event a few times a year. Events such as Black Friday, warehouse sales, and scratch and save, generate a lot of traffic and excitement for many reasons. They create the fear of missing out—if you don't get to the store in time, you may miss the sale and have to wait until the next big event, and who knows when that may happen. Stores with an everyday low price tend to have a low perception of quality in the minds of shoppers, and that may sometimes hurt them because they won't be able to raise prices as easily. Regular stores can jack up the prices and then have a sale event. Sales create a **contrast effect** that provides the human mind with a benchmark of comparison, which it seeks in order to make judgements. Things can be contrasted to something good or bad in order to change how it appears to our perception. If you see something that was $200 last week, on sale for $75, you will have the comparison of the two prices, and the difference between them will make it tempting to make the purchase. If a salesperson wants to be more effective, they should present the client with contrast so that the client won't have to look into their mind's storage to find something to compare the product to. If the salesperson compares the product they're buying, to something much pricier, suddenly what they're selling will appear more affordable.

What about the "buy one get one free" deal, versus "50% off?" Which one is more persuasive? It's apparently the first one. Many people don't consider mathematics; their minds just don't automatically go there, but those two things are kind of equal in value, just not equal psychologically! Words have great power, and the word "free" still continues to conquer our minds, although what's free may often come with invisible strings attached, which can potentially trip you up later. The **norm of reciprocity** may overcome you after taking that free sample, or gift, or campaign donation, and you may feel obligated to reciprocate by giving something in return. When politicians accept campaign donations, they're expected to reciprocate back to the donor later on.

Teenagers have to be especially reminded of this norm, and know when something is too good or generous to be true, because it may very well be. Teenagers don't yet know of the many intricate human relations that are weaved into the mechanism of our world, so this knowledge can be a life-saving reminder when they are faced with a decision to accept gifts from strangers. I recently watched a documentary that showed how young girls in Canada were coerced into being trafficked. The girls were explaining that what often happens is that they encounter some new friends, often older, who will offer to take them out, and pay for drinks and club entries, and when the fun is over, these new friends tell the girls that they owe them money. It's a sickening trick, and especially shocking to someone's emotional state when they are in a state of a fun rush, and all of a sudden this fun turns into a nightmare, just because they didn't even think to question the generosity of these people.

I recently had an opportunity to ask Kara Smith (aka Kara the Huntress) some questions about her work as a senior targeting analyst for DeliverFund, a non-profit private intelligence organization in the USA, which equips, trains, and advises law enforcement on how to combat human trafficking. She has the job that many people admire for being such a crucial and rare thing in our society, as she plays a major role in bringing traffickers and abusers to justice. In one of her Instagram posts, she writes about signs to look for, because human traffickers most often blend in and go unnoticed. Kara writes that pimps often have overly friendly young girls working for them as recruiters, who invite other teens to come and party with them, while giving them alcohol and drugs. They also tempt them with a lavish lifestyle and luxury items that are used in the grooming process.[181] In today's social media frenzy, many young girls want to show off luxurious things in their posts, so they get tempted by this desire to have access to such things.

After the freebie technique, there is one that is popular in sales, or charity requests, and that is the ***door in the face*** technique. Mowen and Cialdini, the researchers who specialize in the psychology of persuasion, decided to test something that is so simple when you think about it, but despite it seeming like common sense, many people fall for it regardless. When people were asked to complete a two-hour survey, most turned down this request. Then the second, smaller request was made, asking them to complete a fifteen-minute survey instead, and 44% accepted the smaller request after denying the first large request. These results were then compared to another time, when the participants were asked just to complete the smaller survey, without the first request, and 25% only accepted it. That means that when, for example, you want to borrow $50 from someone, the person will be more likely to lend it to you if you first ask for $100, and then when denied, ask for $50 instead.

That technique has a partner, which is a bit opposite but is meant to achieve the same thing, and that is the ***foot in the door*** technique. The foot represents the first step of the process of influencing someone to agree to something small, only to later make them agree to something bigger, because they are already in an agreement mode, and are feeling like they are in the situation together. There is a tendency for people to misattribute an interpersonal connection and spill it over to an action they may not have normally taken. Let's take a certain scheme whose representatives were recently sued by the Federal Trade Commission for selling courses on how to create an online business. They got people to sign up for a low fee, promising that they would learn how to run an online business if they took the course. Once someone signed up, they were prompted to pay for additional services and classes to be able to move further in the course, which barely had any educational value other than what you can easily google yourself. Many vulnerable people who recently retired, lost their job, or had to stay at home for personal reasons, which are often negative in nature, got sucked into this cycle and paid up until they realized that they fell for a clever system that used their own psychological processes against them. The schemers got their **foot in the door** with the new subscriber, and then knew that this person would not want to lose the sign-up fee, and the **justification of effort** would kick in, telling them not to be a quitter. Some things must be quit if they just don't feel right in your gut.

Hundreds of years have passed, and most people still haven't reached a level of mental mastery to avoid psychological traps set out by those who have learned them, as they get better at non-aggressive methods of gaining agreement. Researchers Freedman and Fraser studied compliance without pressure, and one of their studies involved two groups of women participants, where one group was asked to take a quick survey about their use of soap products.[182] The second group was the so-called "control group," which was not asked to do this survey. Later, they asked both groups if they would allow a few male researchers to come into their house and do a physical inventory of their soap products, as part of a study they were doing. They found that the group that received the small task of filling out a survey, was much more willing to agree to the big request, which was kind of an uncomfortable one. The participants who didn't receive the small request, but were just straight up asked to agree to have strangers come and check out their soap supply, were not as agreeable. It is very strange how **door in the face** and **foot in the door** work wonders while operating within the realms of your unconscious mind. Like a magician at play, they give you an illusion of owing something to someone. Regardless of what allows them to bypass our defence radar, it's good to practice spotting them in your daily life so that you can get used to how they sound and feel; and once again, not be steered into making lousy choices.

CHAPTER 10

AS WITHIN SO WITHOUT

"I love conquering my own weaknesses.
The basis for happiness is freedom,
and the basis for freedom is courage."

– Doda (Dorota Robaczewska)

10

Winners Gonna Win

So you made it to the last chapter—congrats! This section refreshingly rests in positivity, so take a deep breath, feel the energy of the Universe flowing through your body, energizing every cell, and exhale. Now, let's keep it moving for just a little bit longer, and then I'll let you go out into the world to enjoy your new and improved perspectives, and share them with others. Throughout the study of this book, we examined a lot of inconsistencies and disappointments regarding human nature, and that can sometimes feel overwhelmingly negative. But to be truly positive, you must first be willing to uncover all the negative aspects of your outer and inner world, bring them to light, and face them courageously. Be your own detective who brings deserving "criminals" to justice; bring out that which can jeopardize your spirit. Know the ways in which people get manipulated so that you can spare yourself from similar mistakes, and manoeuvre through the intricacies of their systems with greater skill to benefit yourself. Recognize all the past traumas and mini traumas hiding within your unconscious that affect your moves through your current life, as well as hold you back from fulfillment. Once you go through such a clearing, the power of negativity will be diminished, or transmuted into its opposite.

The focus on having a positive **mindset** is not new. It did not arrive together with Mr. Tony Robbins, or *The Secret*, or even Napoleon Hill, and I would bet that it is as old as humanity itself; but the first known happiness guru is no other than the famous ancient Greek philosopher *Aristotle*. He had a pretty simple message, which I must say that I wish everyone followed; it's quite aligned with the essence of this book. Aristotle proclaimed that ***happiness*** is an action more than a state. It is the ultimate goal of humans, which is achieved through conscious striving towards it, through the continuous fulfillment of our natural desires, with a big emphasis on the importance of maintaining balance.

In the academic world of social psychology, it wasn't until the 1990s when an American psychologist, Martin Seligman, apparently was the first one to express his frustration with the tendency of classical social psychologists to focus mostly on mental illness, dysfunctional behaviour, and negative thinking.[183] This gave way to a new scholarly movement of positive social psychology, focused on the study of positivity, happiness, and well-being. The topic of **luck** has puzzled many great minds, and it's maybe the hardest thing to explain. One curious psychologist seems to be confident in his rather simple explanation, a result of a not so simple study, which took years to conduct. Richard Wiseman decided to test why some people get all the luck while others just can't get a break. His study involved random volunteers who either considered themselves quite lucky in life, or ones who thought that they seemed to have bad luck. They were then interviewed, tested through special exercises, and their lives were monitored for the duration of this study.[184]

Wiseman concluded that thoughts and behaviour of the participants were largely responsible for their good or bad fortune. This aligns with many famous thinkers, such as Napoleon Hill, who stated that whatever the mind can conceive and believe, it can achieve. Napoleon applied this wisdom to how thoughts shape broader life outcomes, but this study shows how this concept of positive mindset works even on the micro levels of our daily situations, which of course contribute to the whole. He found that unlucky people have more tension and anxiety, and this anxiety disrupts their ability to notice the unexpected, while lucky people see what is actually there, rather than just what they are looking for, so they award themselves a better chance of noticing opportunities, and act on them. This was revealed in one of the exercises in which Wiseman gave the participants a newspaper and asked them to count all the pictures in it. Inside the newspaper, he placed a big message, which was not hidden in any way, and it said, "Tell the experimenter you have seen this, and win £250." The lucky people found the message more often than the unlucky ones.

It's an interesting topic, especially lately, because there has been a popular debate about the famous universal law, the

Law of Attraction, which states that like attracts like, that maintaining an optimistic and grateful mind state opens the way for a greater chance of attracting into your reality what you want, or need. Esther Hicks, who is famous for her teachings about this topic, often talks about the importance of recognizing and appreciating the little good things that show up along the journey to whatever destination you may be heading towards. People often want the journey, to wherever they're going, to be fast. They worry about what they will encounter when they get there, and whether they will get there on time, or what could go wrong. Such overthinking can create tension, which is blinding to the jewels scattered along the way. How would a student benefit if they just bought the diploma, without going through the specific learning process to earn it? You can ask the people working under a fake diploma, who were recently exposed by an investigative TV show, *CBC Marketplace*, how that is working out for them. The temptation to get somewhere fast is often the cause of loss, and often it happens to be tied to reputation. Treasure your reputation; it's something almost impossible to restore. And do not confuse leverage with cheating—skillful leverage is energetically aligned, but straight up cheating is not.

Esther's explanations of this process of energetic attraction are spiritually veiled, and force people to take a look deep within themselves to recognize the patterns and programs that spin tension, standing in the way of having an optimistically charged conduct that will open the flow to its match. The esoteric explanations are quite correlated to what psychologists often find about the concept of luck, or positive thinking, but they have a touch of energetic current weaving it all together—a unity that has been suppressed for too long in the scientific world.

Reward System

It seems to be the case that academic studies that deal with the social world, such as sociology, history, economics, political studies, and even marketing, can be quite depressing. I'm not sure if it's by design or by accident, but the way they portray the reality of our human nature is mostly focused on describing the bad and the ugly. Among the dozens of social science courses I had to complete in order to obtain my degree in social psychology, only one was about "positive psychology," and it wasn't on the required list. Coming from my world of motivational teachings, I always wondered about the potential danger of this precipitating doom and gloom overload, to the young students' mental health, as well as to societal progress.

The newly embraced politically-correct trends only seem to create more tension by punishing naturally occurring thought, forcing it to stay buried deep within the person, rather than giving an opportunity for free expression that can open a dialogue leading to an organic resolution of it. The people are not the ones benefiting from censorship and restriction of free speech, but the benefit goes to the few who are not to be criticized, and most often it happens to be some dictatorial powers, official or behind the scenes. It is possible that most social tensions and inequalities still exist because people seem to be stuck in a continuous cycle of digging up old dirt from hundreds of years of our warped history, taking attention and energy away from reaping the rewards of fixing the now and the future. How can you fix any issue if all involved are not able to freely talk about it in fear of punishment? It is an interesting human phenomenon that people often exhibit an outlandish craving for mere punishment over solutions of peace. It's much easier to criticize someone than praise them, and proof is in social media comments, where most people hide behind the keyboard and take out their anger on others. All class and proper manners went out the window of our increasingly digital society. In the world of the mainstream media's worship of click-bait, positive aspects of our world just don't get enough attention and don't get the circulation they deserve; or rather, us civilized humans deserve, in order to change this age-old cycle. By now, I can almost guarantee that throughout history, all cultures, countries, religions, and individuals have done something wrong to someone else out there. Certain cultural wars have continued for generations, just because both sides go back and forth blaming each other for old hurts, and just can't seem to find a way to stop the fast-spinning fireball of hate, as they keep playing a never-ending game of hot potato.

After all, as we mentioned back in the part about persuasion, fear messages seem to get more attention, especially in the media, or in eschatological contexts of religious prophecy, and therefore this natural attention to fear-based messages can cause a destructive cycle: fear gets attention; sources interpret this attention as a viewer's desire to watch negative things, so they bring out more material of such topics to satisfy the apparent demand. Just like a merchant in a retail store, they order stock based on what the clients tend to buy more of. Now, who is responsible for taking control of steering things back towards balance? Is it someone other than each one of us?

The year 2020 became a perfect example of what happens when you let fear go unchecked and unbalanced, without the jolt of mature reason smacking it back down to the depths of darkness where it came from. Unfortunately, such jolts of reason have been consistently muted by increasingly widespread digital and physical censorship. The built-up ball of fear messages, spun by the increasing number of its stakeholders, came smashing right through the digital screens worldwide, and infected the masses of unsuspecting and gullible everyday people, to the point of them being scared to leave their homes. I bet the author who wrote about the increased barricading of home life—the security culture, the inside-culture—is now stunned by seeing it all suddenly progress from a stage of higher precautions to near paranoia. Society has added fear of not just humans themselves, but also fear of invisible forces they may bring with them.

If our society seems to be slanted to the negative extreme, and that seems to be given a clear path, what if we were all to agree on taking it all towards the other extreme, and only listen to the positivity gurus, disproportionately highlighting positive news all over the place? Would that have a more beneficial impact on the general vibe of our world, and maybe extinguish the negative to the point of fading it away completely in real life? Sometimes it can be quite beneficial to sway to one side and get a little extreme, especially with positivity, just enough to force yourself onto a positive wavelength when life is not really allowing it to happen naturally. I personally found that deliberately talking myself into positive outcomes has helped me achieve them, and it helped me gain courage, which successfully cancelled out fear. Now, can extreme negativity be in any way beneficial? Yes, I guess it can in some cases be beneficial in order to spark the fire of action needed to change something in society, or in your personal life. I recently ran into protesters in downtown Toronto, who were Canadians of Chinese background, and they were raising awareness about the behaviours of the communist political party that rules China. Their fear of the same thing happening here in their new home country, and the fear for their family back in China, has caused the force within them to rise, giving them courage to go out and make their voices heard. It may seem like it won't change much, but when you look at examples from history, all it can take is just one person to get the ball rolling, or to spark major change, even as if by a fluke. That regime was toppled in Poland in the 1980s, thanks to the courage of some brave industrial workers led by their own colleague, Lech Walesa. When you look at the example from North American history, in the late 1800s, the Knights of Labour, a worker's organization with Terence Powderly in the front line, led the fight that got you the 8-hour workday. Back then, North American workers were expected to work long hours and were given just enough free time to sleep. Such societal changes wouldn't have been possible if not for the common people turning fear into divine force, and deciding that enough is enough. In critical situations, one must set passive positivity aside, face the beast, and with full confidence channel that fiery energy to bend the toughest iron (and iron curtains)! But you must also realize that in regular day-to-day circumstances, a balanced approach of purposefully considering the good and the bad in every situation, and then choosing your direction wisely while maintaining optimism, is your best bet.

I came across an interesting quote by a famous scholar, Abraham Maslov, and it made me laugh because he called Freud hopeless and pessimistic; and as you have seen throughout this book, it's hard not to take that route when we begin to peel back the layers and expose our true inner mechanisms. The more you learn, the easier it is to develop a view of humans as unsophisticated beings, incapable of upholding overall well-being, while destroying themselves and their world. Maslow also said that on the other hand, it's important not to get too positive, to become a deluded *Pollyanna*. It seems like he was also an advocate of balance.

There are numerous examples within levels of our societal systems that produce imbalance within the lives of people whom they are supposed to serve. It can happen when each child has to pay for their own school trip, or else they're not going; that is a system that could be made more inclusive, so that kids who can't afford the costs of the trip don't have to miss out on memorable learning experiences, and fall into an emotionally unpleasant exclusion from their peer groups. There are many beneficial, psychologically sound solutions out there. Universities around the world are exploding with research, but it is not being utilized to create positive changes in our society. It seems like leaders of our societies are driven by the interest of their lobbyists first, and the emotional demands of some citizens before elections. I rarely hear them implement policy changes based on sound research that is free from bias. Changes implemented in time can spare lots of societal damage that builds up when imbalances are ignored or not managed correctly. The same is true in business, especially in large organizations.

Could it be that the social science scholars, who tend to be unfairly disregarded as "pseudoscientists," could hold the key to finally bringing actual "civilization" to the so-called "civilized" world? Possibly so. Unfortunately, they are left behind for the sake of more biologically focused agents, who often enjoy a bit more recognition in our institutions. I would urge representatives of societies to ponder what matters more: the knowledge of how the areas of the brain react when a certain emotion is felt, or which medication can alleviate depression, versus a social-psychological method that figures out why the person is in a bad psychological state to begin with, and how to fix the root of that negative state which led to deeper mental health issues. And that root is often found in the external world.

Within the realm of socio-psychological study, and even in the darker side of it, there is an abundance of positive theories and concepts that can practically assist our world in reaching greater levels of interpersonal cooperation, collaboration, acceptance, and understanding. The study by researchers Toko Kiyonari and Pat Barclay examined how group members will punish or reward co-operators and freeloaders in a group setting. The randomly chosen participants of this study were placed in groups and given a specific game to play together. Throughout this game, they were able to award various amounts of money to other group members. After the results of this exercise were noted and analyzed by the researchers, it was concluded that ***cooperation*** among group members was more likely to be maintained by a ***reward system***, rather than a ***punishment system***. When people were using positive things like praise and rewards, they ended up being more pleasant to others. When they were made to use punishment, that was not the case anymore. Also, people who were more eager to give out punishments were evaluated negatively by other group members, and those who were more inclined to give rewards were evaluated more positively.[185]

This suggests that if we made it our goal to keep rewarding people for pro-social and positive behaviours, more than we are eager to punish people for negative behaviours, there would be a great possibility for positivity to become more in-grained within humanity as a habit, and could even carry over to the next generations. This effect does correlate to the effect we saw in the study about aggressive children, from the earlier chapter about family, where it was found that when caregivers respond positively to the aggressive child, it has a positive effect on the traits of the child for the future. Now, don't get me wrong; punishment for wrong behaviours must still be fairly applied, but the weight of our attention should be on spreading the joy of reward to amplify the good versus the bad. It seems logical that if social science was implemented into the mechanisms of our society, it could have the ability to restructure our environment, along with our whole biological matrix—and then paradise awaits!

What if there were more of such reward systems used within the correctional institutions? Inmates sometimes have the opportunity to grab certain "jobs" on the range, such as sweeping, cleaning, cooking, and so on, but the reward is often not much more than the ability to get out of their cell, have something to do, and possibly make a mere $1 per day, which gets them some mail stamps so they can write a letter to their loved ones, if they still have someone left on the out-side. The fact is that not every reward has the same effect, and more significant ones rather than small ones result in more cooperativeness. When a person who is already feeling like they have lost all status in the world, and no one cares about them, $1 a day in the Western world can contribute to the already present feelings of dehumanization, and make them feel like it's not even worth trying.

There is lots of evidence that college programs provided in these facilities—which award inmates with a possibility of having a title of a graduate, and a diploma held in their hand—greatly uplifts their sense of self and their desire to live and do better when they come out. We must not forget that more often than not, these people end up there because of some trauma endured in their childhood, and their inner spirit likely craves recognition, the bad or good, so we might as well provide them with the good. It is important to note that education is key to the social and psychological improvement among these individuals. The *Center for American Progress* website states that approximately 41 percent of incarcerated individuals do not hold a high school diploma, compared with 18 percent in the general population. It notes that individuals without high school education were rearrested at the highest rate of 60 percent, while those who had a college degree were rearrested at a rate of 19 percent.[186] Since holding a diploma makes such a difference in a person's life, it also makes a difference in society by reducing crime and human suffering, and eliminating housing costs of inmates.

The Voice of Energy

This book is largely concentrated on training your mind to shield you against being fooled. We talked a lot about the mind in a socio-psychological context, but now it's time to talk about energy, something that is not insignificant, and rather necessary to integrate. Do you sometimes say to yourself that you should have listened to that slight thought that quietly passed through your mind, but instead, you listened to something else and made a mistake? In that situation, you weren't connected to all possible sources of your power. For sources of power to work, a way must be cleared. As we have explored various systems of human interactions and their conflicting nature, I hope that you got used to dealing with ambiguity without ravelling in confusion, but rather you improved your ability to accept multiple realities existing in one construct. Through this process, you are training yourself to be more fluent in connecting your intuition with your brain, in order to interpret the entire situation correctly from a place of many perspectives, and then choose the right moves. Just like when a security guard has more than one camera screen, it is then easier to see more spots and therefore better protect the property, as well as make the right decision. However, the guard cannot do it with the screens alone but needs to listen to the gut feeling within, to properly judge whether what meets the eye feels suspicious, despite it looking like there's nothing to worry about. Discernment largely comes from the inner voice, not just from the analytical mind.

The jolts of energy you feel in your gut, or the shivery currents zapping across your skin, are the energetic effects of your whole being that are tuning in to the right frequency, which is meant to guide you. The more I have made the effort to recognize that state, the more I have learned to read between the lines written by the various situations I come across in life, and therefore I started to make better decisions. It appears to be undeniable that your energy introduces you before you even enter the room. This means that your inner state of being is continuously sending out signals to those whom you share your reality with, and they pick up your true energy, kind of like when someone you haven't talked to in a while pops in your head, and the next minute they are calling your phone.

As important as it is to be wary of people's hidden programs and intentions, you must know when it is okay and even necessary to engage in interactions with people you don't know, or have just met. Such encounters in my own life have often been very beneficial, which proved to me that the **law of attraction** works and is very powerful. How will you recognize the stranger who was sent to you by the energy to help you in some way, from someone who is an imposter or means harm? You have to trust your intuition and look past their appearance. Read their energy without letting your fear or excitement interfere. So many times, I randomly met someone new, and they held the key to something that was happening in my life at the time, or to a lesson I was about to learn, or simply to bring a fun experience. This reminds me of the adventure video games where your character meets another strange character along the path to the next level, who has something beneficial to offer, like a clue or an object, or just a fun experience.

One profound encounter like that happened when I was in Rome with my teenage daughter. We were sitting at a breakfast cafe, wondering which monument to visit next. We started chatting with the waiter to get more ideas, while a random gentleman overheard us and joined in with his suggestions. I couldn't help but notice that he was holding this huge book, which looked totally out of the ordinary, with a name that would intrigue any mystic: *Codex Seraphinianus*. I asked about this book, and he said that he wrote it—it was his book. As we looked through this book, full of out-of-this world images, and writings in an incomprehensible language, which didn't match anything on this Earth, he told us that he was an artist. Check out the book and you'll see what I mean, but you must have some artistic and spiritual spirit to appreciate the depth of this phenomenon. The artist, Luigi Serafini,[187] was lovely to talk to. As we thanked him for the tips, he mentioned that he has a home-studio by the Pantheon, which is a famous monument close by, and that we were welcome to come by and see his art. We thanked him and took his information, thinking that we probably wouldn't have any time to go there anyway, since our vacation was coming to an end, and we went on our journey through town. We couldn't get this invitation out of our heads though, and we kept debating whether we should go or not. Yes, we do have common sense, and we did consider the fact that it was a total stranger inviting us, two tourist women, to his house, something that anywhere else we would not really be considering. But something kept telling us to take that invite! We went to check out his building, and sure enough, it was a gorgeous old building right in the very centre of Rome, a couple of steps from one of the most popular tourist attractions. After a debate, we both came to the conclusion that we should ring the doorbell and see what's up, since we were already there and everything looked pretty legit. Luigi opened the door, and we both looked at each other, stunned at what we saw! We felt like Alice entering Wonderland! The place was full of wacky floors, optically illusive walls, enchanting artwork hanging all over the place, and shelves full of books. The entire visit was so pleasantly unique that we both couldn't come to terms with the experience; it was like culture shock within a lucid dream. When we left, we talked about how anyone else would have thought we were crazy for even considering this visit, but the vibes were screaming "all clear." We got to meet an awesome Italian artist and see a beyond-inspiring way of living that we had never seen before. It was an experience that really showed us the cultural differences that influence the mindset, and how important it is to consider it when dealing with people that come from a different school of thought than you. We were influenced by something that is a big part of the modern Western culture — the reservation towards strangers and the closed-off dynamics of increased perceived desire for privacy. Though, this Italian artist's genuine human character was socialized through living in a near fairy-tale location, where people are more open to socialize with each other on the streets than they are in North America.

Who is more correct—the psychologists who say that people who are more positive don't necessarily attract things, but they just tend to notice more opportunities, thanks to their lack of tension and open mindedness; or is it the mindfulness coaches and mystics who say your energetic mind connects to some universal energy, which by way of some mysterious mechanism sets the perfect things and situations onto your path, all in perfect timing? If you recognize them and take advantage, then you win. It seems like no genius has yet been able to physically grasp the concept of energetic connection that causes you to not only think of a specific person out of nowhere, and suddenly they call you, but also meet a perfect person in a totally coincidental spot. There are many studies that show the existence of energy within humans, as well as in our natural environment; it's just that the ways in which this energy guides us humans is still much of a mystery, and sometimes I think that maybe that's how it's supposed to be. Maybe we should just trust it, and master the use of this tool that helps us reach our life's purpose—not constantly question how it works or waste time trying to debunk it. It may very well be the kind of energy that just likes to be trusted and not questioned. It's probably saying, "You want this goodness or not, cause if not, I'm moving on to someone who's easier to deal with." The evidence of various hard-to-explain metaphysical experiences is abundant, and they happen to the most sophisticated as well as most simple of us.

It often happens that I run into just the right people at the right time, although sometimes I also run into the wrong people; it's just that I'm getting better at recognizing them before it's too late. One of such helpful encounters happened in a time of crisis when I really needed it, and it seemed like it was already written. I was just at the beginning of my university experience, and I had to face the dreaded statistics course, as it was mandatory. I was freaking out because I hadn't done very well with math in my early schooling. So I asked my advisor many times if there was anything I could do to avoid it—maybe switch my whole degree to something else—as failing would be way too costly. My advisor firmly assured me not to worry, to stay in my program and just try to get through it, and maybe seek a tutor. She was so serious about it that at first I felt like she could have been more understanding, but now that it's all over, I see why she was guided to instruct me specifically to keep going. Well, so I did. Little did I know, the Universe already had it all figured out for me.

I took my course, and two weeks went by as I realized that I had no idea how to even begin understanding what this particular economics professor, who was teaching our psychology statistics course, was saying. As I looked around the room, all I saw were other students that were also looking like they had just seen a ghost. I didn't know whether to feel better or worse. What was coming out of his mouth was like a new language—standard deviation, alpha level, variance, and P value—and all of it made me want to deviate the "F value" out of there while I still had the chance to cancel the class without penalty. I desperately needed a new plan, as the situation seemed hopeless; I would have no choice but to face this course again at some point in the next couple of semesters. I started looking for a tutor, with no luck. I begged the Universe to do something about this statistics course problem. I went to bug the advisor again, and again she said, "You will get through it; do not switch your program." Then one day I heard of a pizza party happening on campus, and various social sciences professors were going to be there to chat with students and answer questions. I thought, "Hmm, so far I've been a loner, and I haven't made many friends since I started. Maybe it would be a good idea to go network, and get some free pizza" (which rarely tastes as good as it sounds). Then the disruptive thoughts came in, which were bringing my attention to the expensive parking charges the longer I stayed, and that I had better go home and work on my assignments. "Screw the party; I'm picky with pizza anyway." So there I was, walking to my car, slowly, while a battle of polarized energetic forces was raging inside my head. One force was pushing me to go to the party, telling me that I'm hungry, and the other force was trying to overpower by bringing up worry of losing a few bucks, and reminding me of the comfort of continuing my lonely but efficient journey back towards home. That second one turned out to be a force of an adversary trying to mislead me, not just because it was based in fear or worry, but also just because it was simply an adversarial force, something that is extremely hard to recognize and block, because it can also come as something that appears good. The more you work on your self-mastery, the easier it becomes.

The pressure of making this seemingly simple decision was so unbearably annoying, and as I almost walked out the door of the Degroote Business School, where my car was parked, I remember that pivotal moment when I turned around on one leg, with the thought that I would regret it if I didn't go to that event, and if I had to think about it that hard, then I had better go! And off for the pizza I went. As I was there, I talked with some students, and it wasn't anything super exciting. Some professors started to trickle in, but the conversations were not really sticking, and groups of students hovered around them, so it was hard to get a word in. As I decided to make my way out, I noticed a sociology professor walking in, whom I already knew from one of my previous classes. I said hello, and as she asked how I was doing, right away I said, "Great, but I am faced with a huge challenge; maybe you would have some tips for me." That is when I explained my dilemma. Then a miracle happened! She told me that she would actually be teaching a statistics course in January, and I could take that one instead of the other one I tried before, and that hers would be much better. If you don't yet think this "coincidence" is energetically significant, listen to this: As she explained to me that I would need to ask the dean of my department for approval to switch into this particular course, a second later, she said, "Oh look, there she is right there." The dean walked into the room, all in perfectly divine timing, right past us, just as we mentioned her! You should have seen me then—I nearly exploded inside but had to keep it cool.

My new statistics professor, who comes from the sociology department, and that gentleman who was from economics, were like night and day! I feel bad for the students who had him, or someone like him—not because he's a bad person, but he surely needed to work on his sensitivity towards people who fear math. Math is something that has been ruined in the school system by those who are too confident in it, and expect others to follow at the same pace. The sound of "we have to move on now," coming from most math teachers I came across in my life, is still part of my little traumas that I may never forget. I even had a math teacher in Poland, from when I went to elementary school there, who called us randomly by our last names, asking us to come to the chalkboard and write out some equations. It was the most traumatizing experience because we never knew who was next up, and each time I got called, I stood there holding the tip of the chalk against the blackboard, staring right through it as if it was a dark hole sucking me into its vortex. Many math teachers have a hard time understanding the feelings of students who are not as fast in comprehending numbers in a conversation setting, because that's what I think it's really about. Math is something that requires practice, not so much hearing about it, and especially not under stress and pressure. I learned this through my statistics course. As amazing in explaining complex equations as my angel-professor was, my understanding of the concepts clicked as I figured out the things she talked about, while I was going through the exercises at home, all relaxed, and when I had a clear mind to think.

This professor's communication style was something that all math teachers should learn from. We would then potentially have more kids doing better in math. Poor math skills can block young people from choosing many professions that they may dream about, such as medical, technology, or architecture. Math and science are the key to the doors of such programs. This is one of the many socio-psychological imbalances that exist in the educational system, which requires teachers as well as students to be exposed to more social training. I am an example of a person who always had a hard time in math classes, in elementary and high school. Finally, with the help and encouragement of an educator who was a great communicator, who knew exactly what confused students, and didn't move on until she explained something at least in three various ways, I got almost 80% in her class—yes, university-level statistics! I always thought that I was terrible at math, but by pushing through this challenge, which cost me much sleep, I have achieved what I was so sure that I could not possibly do. With a touch of magic from the higher powers, no doubt, this was a healthy dose of some *law of attraction* right there, and it tasted damn good with that free pizza.

Motivational Noise

For many people who have engaged themselves in any success motivation, self-help, or spiritual growth teachings, things have not always turned out as expected. There may be many reasons for that, and some people like to blame many things, including themselves, without the understanding that they skipped the basics. The major keys to what I suspect is responsible for hindering advancement in this area, are held by Freud and Jung. They both rang the alarm about the importance of resolving the deeply rooted negative issues hiding in our inner world. They block the flow of that which you desire, and send out signals that attract things that match up with it.

Elevating spiritually, as well as physically, requires preparation. Just as you can't go into a gym for the first time and lift the heaviest weights, you also can't ascend into the higher spiritual levels without completing the prerequisites. The topic of success, motivation, or the ever so popular *law of attraction*, has become hugely popular lately, and with that comes the oversaturation of noise coming from a plethora of its hijackers, such as some network marketers, success experts, spiritual coaches, and gurus on unicorns (not saying that unicorns aren't cool, but they surely can be exploited), who are loudly sharing their recipe for their secret sauce while guaranteeing more success and satisfaction in your life. There can be huge benefits to such preaching; don't get me wrong. I myself am one example of the impact that success mentors can make on a person who finds themselves in a realization that it's time for a level-up, time to transform. Such powerful mentors—some more and some less legit—have definitely helped lots of people rediscover their sense of optimism, become more comfortable in implementing it into their personal journey, pick up new ideas, come out of their shell, or re-energize their life force energy. But we must recognize the challenges that are visible in the self-help community, which lies in the concerns of many individuals who took part in some of such activities, that after all this perceived effort, they still find it challenging to translate all of that information into their own lives. Esther Hicks, who preaches about the importance of positive thoughts, and that the Universe already holds what you need, and you just have to work on aligning yourself with its energy, also recognizes that it can be a challenge. She often jokingly acknowledges that the audience must be thinking, "How do I get this money out of the Universe and into my bank?" Or, "How do I get my perfect soulmate into my arms?" Many people who go to motivational events tend to say that once they get home, they step right back into their old reality, and have a tough time applying all this great learning into their daily lives.

Throughout my years of studying, as well as practicing psychology and esoteric spirituality, coaching clients on how to remove blocks and destructive cycles from their life's path, I came to the conclusion that became a catalyst for writing this book. In order to make higher concepts (such as the famous law of attraction) work in your life, you must understand the very basics of how the human mind operates. There are too many people who actively engage in spiritual, philosophical, or academic attainment, who are not in tune with their inner self, who hold imbalanced emotions, or who just really suck at person-to-person interactions, or even at simply understanding another person. Not to mention the basic psychological knowledge; you know, the knowledge of that major body organ that directs your whole life, and your whole body itself—although I have noticed that the theory of cognitive dissonance has been gaining lots of popularity. It's way too easy to snap right back into your automatic modes after learning great spiritual concepts or success strategies. You can maybe jump up high and taste the clouds for a bit, but without the knowledge of the basic inner and outer human processes, staying up or moving higher is unlikely. With all of that higher knowledge, many people still end up getting tricked by someone who is less sophisticated but who possesses some "street smarts." Individuals who crave the higher results, at some point will be forced to go back and fill in the blanks they've missed while rushing upward. Many people become frustrated and discouraged that concepts like the *law of attraction* are not working for them as they did for others, and may even risk slipping into emotional and mental imbalance, because they were unable to live up to their own higher expectations.

The god, *Hermes,* is known for the profound statement that "as above, so below; as within, so without; as the Universe, so the soul." This life on Earth is a university, and the goal is to complete your training by holistically elevating your mind, body (and its environment), and spirit. If we want to rise spiritually, what makes us think that we can be a physical mess and still be able to attain that? If there is no balance of focus on the psychological, physical/material, as well as spiritual attainment, then a complete mastery of self most likely cannot be accomplished. That is the mind-body-spirit alignment. What sense is there to learn the ways of the spiritual world, and lack the ability to manoeuvre through the constructs of this physical reality in which all of us humans have been placed, for some reason still unknown to us. The attempt to skip the first steps of your personal staircase, and try to start somewhere higher, is way too common—just like everyone wants to be a millionaire, but not many want to put in the work or take on the responsibility that comes with it.

Many well-meaning people who desire self-improvement and success, get lost in the noise coming from all kinds of success gurus, many of which are trying to lure people into their spider web with the overused positivity clichés, to the point of their total dilution. This may not be the best influence for some people, such as those who decide to start businesses without any professional guidance, or research, basing it mostly on emotions. I thought about this when I was going through my Instagram follows to make sure that I'm not following dormant accounts; and surely, so many small business accounts, which I followed a couple of years ago, appeared to have completely stopped activity. Many of them had spent money and effort to start it, to rent and decorate store locations, but didn't research the needs and wants of their target audience, or the nature of the location. Driven by their own dreams and the encouraging "A for effort," and the cheers of support from well-meaning friends and followers, they thought they knew it all until it became clear that their "dreams" clouded the reality, and important steps of due diligence were not taken to ensure success. But there is a good side to this story: Failure is also an outstanding teacher. I'm speaking from experience as well as observation. I have climbed this mountain without much equipment myself, in my early twenties, when I decided to open a pub back in my hometown in Poland. I was way over-confident in my knowledge, abilities, and friends at the time, which caused me a great deal of hardship.

Yes, everyone has their lessons to learn, but I'm sure there's nothing wrong with making them a little easier. Learning social psychology of interactions will sharpen your mind to help you do whatever you set out to do, in a much smarter way, and it will make way for positivity to serve you the way it is meant to.

The Cosmic Tool Belt

The study of social psychology desired to lean over to the scientific side, so it distanced itself from philosophy and metaphysics, which have been highly regarded since the ancient Egyptian and Greek times. I appreciate the desire of psychology to focus on scientific explanations of our human consciousness, but I also happen to believe that the spirit and the mind are deeply connected, if not the same, and that side has been shut off from the study of mental states, and the solutions to their issues. What if mental states of imbalance lie in the realm of the spirit? There are many psychologists that can't seem to get away from the thought that maybe there is something to this energetic world relating to our mental processes. And there are many neuroscientists and biologists who are beginning to realize that they also need to tap into the world of the unknown to complete the things they were never able to fully explain by biological science alone. Empirical research strictly advises against bias; researchers often get trapped within a box, and they rarely reach into the other boxes for pieces to their puzzle. Can't blame them; the transcendental realm is tough to study... and who actually cares to fund it?

Metaphysics is defined by *dictionary.com* as the branch of philosophy that deals with first principles, including **ontology,** which is the study of being, and **cosmology,** which is the study of the Universe, and is intimately connected with **epistemology**, which is the study of knowledge and how we acquire it. *Oxford* explains the origins of the word "metaphysics" as dating back to the times of ancient Greece, and describes its original meaning as the science of things transcending what is physical or natural. In the last few years, there has been a noticeable surge of people turning to unique ways of understanding that which links our inner spiritual bodies with the external universal frequencies, as well as engaging in the inquiry into that thing we call "energy." Is it a surge, though? Or has social media only given people a public platform to express their already energy-conscious personalities, and facilitate an easier connection with like-minded others? Nevertheless, I took it upon myself to bring up a metaphysical topic that I couldn't leave out of a book about human communication, connection, and mastery of your inner self.

Whether you believe that astrological descriptions of people are correct or not, astrological concepts have been widely used for the past 2500 years, if we stick with the Greeks; or possibly even longer if we go further back to ancient Egypt. Astrology's descriptions of the various archetypes are like painted pictures of the possible aspects you will encounter in people throughout your life's journey. I personally have noticed astrological patterns in people around me, and it often even happens that I'll meet someone new and just guess their sun sign based on some things they have told me about themselves, or their behaviour. Their reaction is priceless! Most mainstream psychologists will likely attribute theories like confirmation bias to things like astrology, stating that once you know that cancer signs are highly emotional, you will look for that evidence in the person, and likely find it while assuming it's due to astrology. Trust me, I have taken confirmation bias into consideration many times, and unfortunately, the evidence of astrological and numerological systems at play in my daily experiences greatly outweighs it, or any other psychological theory, no matter how hard I try to explain it. It's unbelievably prevalent that, for example, Scorpios are more likely to be emotionally dramatic than Capricorns, who more often than not seem to have no emotions at all. Scorpio is a water sign, so they can't help but dive deep into dark waters and likely pull others in with them, and Capricorn is an earth sign, so they are grounded and emotionally detached.

Of course, there are exceptions, which can be due to upbringing and socialization, and the influence of other systems, like numerology, which has meanings assigned to numbers coming from your birthdate. Our cosmic blueprint is probably the most intricate system ever created, physically and spiritually. Learning astrological meanings of the twelve signs and the four elements has greatly contributed to my understanding the personalities of other people, before I started studying psychology; and when both knowledge bases came together, they combined into a next level of understanding of the complex human system. Simply getting to know the various aspects of human personalities as described in astrology, numerology, the tarot, and even by the famous scholar Carl Jung, will expose you to the discovery of higher aspects of human beings by getting to know the possible tools we are all equipped with, which are needed to fulfill our journey through this life. Carl Jung was one of the greatest researchers of archetypal information; as described in *Wikipe-*

dia, he "has understood archetypes as universal, archaic patterns and images that derive from the collective unconscious and are the psychic counterpart of instinct. They are inherited potentials which are actualized when they enter consciousness as images, or manifest in behaviour on interaction with the outside world. They are autonomous and hidden forms which are transformed once they enter consciousness and are given particular expression by individuals and their cultures."[188]

Most of us come from a biased perspective when assessing other people, and even when assessing our own selves. The psychology researchers who build specific theories, as much as they try to be bias free, are human themselves and will naturally be more inclined towards people who are more like them. As Stephen Arroyo writes in his award-winning thesis, many of them lack **cosmic framework** to have a broader perspective on humankind, rather than just fit them into these limited theories (yes, even the ones that this book describes all throughout).[189] They are crucial blueprints to understanding how a human being operates, but as complex as they may seem to someone who is just discovering them, they actually are quite basic, and that "cosmic framework" is needed to make the understanding of the human complete. People are increasingly seeking a deeper understanding of themselves, and a recognition of things such as cycles of life, which scientific frameworks omit, but astrology explains so well.

I often think of the many people who have more unique psychological issues that seem to puzzle therapists, where traditional approaches just don't seem to fit. If a person cannot get the hang of their emotions, and there are no real issues in their life to blame, it is crucial to look into their astrological chart and see whether it is the water element that overpowers the chart. The water element, for example, represents emotions, and if a person has the majority of their planets in water signs, that often predisposes them to being overly emotional. Drake is a good example of someone who has lots of water signs in his chart, but it appears that something in his life—possibly the quality of parenting he received—has mediated that water weight, and he channelled that energy into the right direction, which is music.

Humans are a specifically structured design, like the evolutionary theory proves over and over when it shows us how men tend to desire to be admired by many women, and women desire the safety provided by one man, and that makes us all part of this one human family, predictable to each other as we are connected by similar biological drives. We are also individuals, with a unique network of cosmic energy, or spirit, flowing through our being and making us different from each other.

Arroyo advises that synthesizing the spiritual knowledge with the scientific is the new hope for the modern human's future. In his book, he couldn't explain more perfectly what I'm trying to say here, so I might as well quote: "... astrology is indeed a language that describes the very energies that activate a human being; it could very well be the most accurate way we have in describing what is truly the 'human nature' of each individual ... a means of understanding human personality, behaviour, change, and growth."

Love Thyself So You Can Love Others

Love is inescapable; it has been one of the main things on the minds and tongues of humans for ages. It is even a desire of those who don't think they need love, who resist it, or think they can replace it with material substitutes. They seek it even when they don't know it; it just comes out in a complicated way, kind of like the study of attachment taught us in the chapter about relationships, that the unfulfilled desire for mother's love can carry over to adulthood. "Love is the law, love under will," said a certain very controversial old time mystic, Alleister Crowley. He had a simple solution for the order of this world: Love others, but not like you want to love them, but as they want to be loved, under their will. Words have meaning, as we already mentioned in an earlier chapter, and the popular saying, "Do unto others as you would have them do unto you," is a perfect example of our robotic minds just repeating what we learn from our environment so mindlessly, just because the idea sounds pretty good. But the devil is in the details. The "devil," which actually means the adversary, wants us to focus and do a better job at paying attention to what we say and do. That's why we get tested over and over, until we learn the lessons that are meant to snap us out of idleness and make us more in control of our being and the world around us. When you actually think about it, the saying "do unto others…" basically translates to a pretty weird literal meaning: that your likings, pleasures, and desires are shared by other people, and that whatever it is that you like being done to you, will be automatically welcomed by other people as well. For example, older relatives like to react affectionately when they see their young grandchildren, and they pick them up, kiss them on the face and so on, although the child is quite often not very happy with such behaviour. When the child protests, they are guilt-tripped by the parents and the elders, though no one has considered how this child may feel about these sometimes-abrupt displays of affection, not to mention the scratchy beards, lipstick, or even germs. The saying needs to be modified to state, "Do unto others as they would like done unto them," and shall we add: "under free and conscious will of all involved."

It's hard to refute the idea that to truly be able to love others, and be able to give them your best version of yourself, you must first master the love for thyself. When you love yourself, you become more relaxed in your approach to others, which will allow the interaction to flow free from the grasp of your unconscious needs. Looking from an angle of reciprocity, you can't pour from an empty cup, so you must fill your cup with a self-love potion and drink up with delight. On an airplane, the crew always instructs that in case of emergency, passengers must put on their own oxygen mask first, then assist the children. Helping others is a noble thing, but there are those who deplete themselves by constantly helping others but forgetting about themselves. They often are the ones who get taken advantage of, and don't get much in return. It is crucial that you love yourself, and don't feel bad about it; don't diminish it when being around people who don't love themselves, and who will usually let you know, in various ways, that they don't appreciate your "who-do-you-think-you-areness."

But how do you know if you're dealing with self-love or narcissism? What is love for yourself really about? Love for the self requires a healthy level of self-esteem, and narcissism comes from lack of self-esteem, because it is desperate to constantly try to make up for what the person believes is unlovable about them, but they're shopping in the wrong department for solutions. They seem to have high self-esteem on the outside; but on the inside, they hold some insecurities. People with high self-esteem are most likely satisfied with themselves and don't need to go to these extremes to prove it.

The book Principles of Social Psychology states that positive effects of self-esteem are related to your actions or your behaviour.[190] In order to maintain or raise your self-esteem, it's good to find something you do well, and to try your best to get better and better at it so that you can see the positive results of it, and others can too. Being good at something—it can be that one thing you put your focus into—will lead to feelings of greater efficacy, accomplishment, and raise your self-esteem. You don't have to always be the best; if at times you happen to do more poorly, you will have the capacity to bounce back quickly from that failure because your confidence will already be built so strongly that a little wind won't topple it over. You'll still have your knowledge and skill to work with; that is what no one can take away. The book mentions another important factor in maintaining higher self-esteem, which is forming and maintaining satisfying personal connections with others. Not just those connections that can do things for you, but also those with whom you feel at ease, who you can trust, who aren't giving you strange vibes, and whose company doesn't feel like a struggle. Usually, such people are found among those who also figured out how to love themselves.

An American scholar, Chloe Valdary, founded the **Theory of Enchantment**, from the base of which she provides courses to corporate clients, which are designed to eliminate racism and discrimination within the organizations. Such training teaches clients "how to first develop healthy relationships with themselves, so that they can grow to develop healthy relationships with others. This makes it less likely that the conditions of scarcity will take root in a company's culture." The trainees benefit from learning about self-awareness, self-management, social awareness, relationship skills, and responsible decision-making. Trust me, I have seen big business fall because it was infested with negative human interactions enacted by big babies who somehow found themselves as the keyholders of the company's future. Their behaviours were left unaddressed for years and somehow became the prominent culture of the entire company. Such culture quickly spiralled into bankruptcy because management was too busy dealing with each other's emotional drama, possibly because it created a cover for their lack of competency. Something like racism, jealousy, manipulation, and abuse of power, are most often results of lack of love for oneself, which is when love for others has a much slimmer chance. Chloe's program is praised to be effective for organizations because it creates positive change at the core, the inner state of human beings, which make up the organization as a whole. When you see yourself as an individual in the world, without labels or boxes, and you learn to see others as human beings first, and not as "political abstractions," as Chloe states, then the positive butterfly effect you create will spread far and wide. Interestingly enough, most existing antiracism programs do not offer this type of training.

People who abuse others are often said to have low self-esteem, and don't love themselves. Such people very often have been abused in their early lives, and have grown in the direction of that vibe, and not against it, like many others who have gone through abuse. It is important to recognize the signs of potential aggression in others to protect yourself from unpleasant relationships with them. It often is the case that many people who don't love themselves, and have low self-esteem, will fall for all kinds of predatory interactions. It is important to look for warning signs in others. A troublesome interaction may be preceded by things like extreme boasting, always looking to benefit but not spare a penny, or plain disregard for the feelings or pain of others. I have looked around my environment for evidence of the saying, "You can tell the kind of person someone is by the way they treat animals," and I have found more than plenty. There are, of course, exceptions, and I have seen when someone was good to animals but quite nasty to other people. I do like to observe the approach towards animals when I'm meeting new friends, because chances are, if they are able to mistreat a living being such as an animal, then that shows lack of respect for the treasure that is life. Animals are true angels on earth; they are in tune with the divine natural order and are able to sense many things that humans cannot, as well as help them. Being able to understand and communicate with animals is a trait of kindness and high intelligence, because it requires imagination and compassion exemplified by the desire to go out of the way for their benefit.

Now that you have reached this point in the book, I am certain that the process of reading about all of these psychological aspects has sparked some introspection, and resulted in knowing thyself much more than before. As you begin to see other people's intricate patchwork of shadow and light aspects more clearly, don't let judgement tempt you. Be accepting of the fact that everyone has their purpose, and their "design" has some reason for being the way it is; maybe because we all have our unique path to travel through, so we each have various traits to enable us to withstand it, or suit the work we are here to accomplish. Just like in the animal kingdom, a fish has a different design and ideal environment, and so does a bee or a giraffe. A greater understanding of human psychology does give you a higher perspective, which will naturally feel a bit like you are above others. Do not allow ego to deceive you away from true mastery; a person with high knowledge must match it with high personal integrity, and treat others like they all have a spark of the divine within them, although not all are on the same level or heading in the same direction. Not all put in the same amount of effort or the same intensity of determination. So don't hesitate to celebrate yourself and your achievements.

Realize that you're standing on a much higher step of your stairway to the total MASTERY OF LIFE, and going back is not an option, because once a mind expands, it does not want to contract! Lead by example and pay this knowledge forward. Your intellectual status was attained by your desire to study, and your willingness to put in the work, so be proud of the levels you have earned, and feel free to firmly exalt yourself as an expert in it. The world needs you, though not as much as your spirit does. If you happen to become lost, always remember what comes first, and you will regain control again. Be well my friend, till we meet again.

"*The masses of people are carried along, obedient to their environment; the wills and desires of others stronger than themselves; the effects of inherited tendencies; the suggestions of those about them; and other outward causes; which tend to move them about on the chess-board of life like mere pawns. By rising above these influencing causes, the advanced Hermetists seek a higher plane of mental action, and by dominating their moods, emotions, impulses, and feelings, they create for themselves new characters, qualities, and powers, by which they overcome their ordinary environment, and thus become practically players instead of mere pawns. Such people help to play the game of life understandingly, instead of being moved about this way and that way by stronger influences and powers and wills. They use the Principle of Cause and Effect, instead of being used by it. Of course, even the highest are subject to the Principle as it manifests on the higher planes, but on the lower planes of activity, they are Masters instead of Slaves.*"

– The Kybalion

Endnotes

Endnotes

* Please refer to the book's website www.persontopersonbook.com for a complete and interactive reference list.

1   Jastrow, J. (1917). The psychology of conviction. *The Scientific Monthly*, 5(6), 523-544. Retrieved from http://www.jstor.org/stable/22499

2   Bond, C. F., Jr, & DePaulo, B. M. (2006). Accuracy of deception judgments. *Personality and social psychology review : An official journal of the Society for Personality and Social Psychology, Inc*, 10(3), 214–234. https://doi.org/10.1207/s15327957pspr1003_2

3   Wilson, T. D., Reinhard, D. A., Westgate, E. C., Gilbert, D. T., Ellerbeck, N., Hahn, C., Brown, C. L., & Shaked, A. (2014). Social psychology. Just think: The challenges of the disengaged mind. *Science* 345(6192), 75–77. https://doi.org/10.1126/science.1250830

4   https://wsiz.edu.pl/aktualnosci/wielkie-pytania-w-nauce-profesor-jerzy-bralczyk-gosciem-wsiiz/

5   https://en.wikipedia.org/wiki/Negotiation

6   https://smallbiztrends.com/2016/03/surepayroll-survey-word-mouth-job-candidates.html#:
~:text=The%20answer%20to%20the%20first,such%20as
%20Indeed%20or%20Careerbuilder.&text=Most%20agree%20that%20the
%20biggest,the%20job%20at%2048%20percent

7   https://www.goodreads.com/quotes/791609-people-will-love-you-people-will-hate-you-and-none

8   https://lucabosurgi.com/adult-emotional-dependency-aed/

9   Maslow, A. H. (1998, first published in 1962). *Toward a psychology of being.* (3rd ed.). Wiley.

10 https://hbswk.hbs.edu/item/the-subconscious-mind-of-the-consumer-and-how-to-reach-it

11 https://www.consumer.ftc.gov/blog/2015/07/faking-it-scammers-tricks-steal-your-heart-and-money

12 https://human-memory.net/memory-the-brain/

13 https://www.youtube.com/watch?v=cavoDYUgtmY

14 https://www.dictionary.com/browse/consciousness?s=t

15 https://www.health.harvard.edu/blog/unconscious-or-subconscious-20100801255

16 https://pure.mpg.de/rest/items/item_2273030_5/component/file_2309291/content

17 https://www.psychologytoday.com/ca/basics/heuristics

18 8) https://www.investopedia.com/terms/h/heuristics.asp

19 https://journals.sagepub.com/doi/ 10.1177/014616727800400309

20 https://www.youtube.com/watch?v=rag0Z1nTJOc

21 Ashby, M. (2000, first published in 1998). *The Egyptian book of the dead: The book of coming forth by day.* Sema Institute.

22 https://doi.org/10.1016/B0-08-043076-7/01688-0
23 https://www.bionews.org.uk/page_92221
24 https://hms.harvard.edu/news/what-grandma-ate
25 https://www.bionews.org.uk/page_92045
26 https://www.naeyc.org/resources/pubs/yc/may2017/caring-relationships-heart-early-brain-development
27 https://doi.org/10.4159/harvard.9780674060982
28 Thomas, D. S. (1928). The Methodology of Behavior Study. In W. I. Thomas, *The child in America: Behavior problems and programs.* (pp. 553-576). New York, NY: Alfred A. Knopf. Retrieved from https://archive.org/details/in.ernet.dli.2015.155699/page/n593/mode/2up
29 https://www150.statcan.gc.ca/n1/dailyquotidien/191030/dq191030a-eng.htm
30 https://www.ncbi.nlm.nih.gov/pubmed/2313078
31 Adams, S. (2017). *Win bigly: Persuasion in a world where facts don't matter.* New York, NY: Portfolio/Penguin.
32 https://www.nature.com/articles/nature13725
33 https://media4.manhattan-institute.org/pdf/_atlantic_monthly-broken_windows.pdf
34 Halle, D. (1993). *Inside culture: Art and class in the American home.* Chicago, IL: The University of Chicago Press.
35 Chapman, T., Hockey, J. (Eds.). (1999). *Ideal Homes? Social change and the domestic life.* New York, NY: Routledge.
36 van den Scott, Lisa-Jo K. (2016). Mundane Technology in non-Western Contexts: Wall-as-Tool. In Gillian Anderson, Joseph G. Moore, Laura Suski (Eds.), *Sociology of home: Belonging, Community and Place in the Canadian Context* (Pp. 33-53). Canadian Scholars Press International.
37 https://en.wikipedia.org/wiki/Berlin_Wall
38 https://www.ft.com/content/a22d04b2-c4b0-11e9-a8e9-296ca66511c9
39 https://www.youtube.com/watch?v=Wa-2fO5pMNM
40 https://en.wikipedia.org/wiki/Leon_Festinger#cite_ref-44
41 Goffman, E. (1959). *The presentation of self in everyday life.* Garden City, NY: Doubleday & Company.
42 Cooley, C. H. (1983, first published in 1902). *Human nature and social order.* Routledge.
43 Festinger, L., Riecken, H. W., & Schachter, S. (1964, first published in 1956). *When prophecy fails: A social and psychological study of a modern group that predicted the destruction of the world.* New York, NY: Torchbooks/Harper & Row.
44 https://www.everydayhealth.com/neurology/cognitive-dissonance/real-life-examples-how-we-react/
45 https://www.youtube.com/watch?v=pnzHIEOgr8Q

46 https://www.inc.com/marcel-schwantes/science-says-92-percent-of-people-dont-achieve-goals-heres-how-the-other-8-perce.html

47 https://www.marketwatch.com/story/employees-would-rather-make-less-money-than-tolerate-bad-office-vibes-2018-06-25

48 http://www.3dfit.ca

49 https://www.psychologytoday.com/us/blog/out-the-darkness/201307/the-power-purpose

50 https://ec.europa.eu/eurostat/statistics-explained/index.php/Social_protection_statistics_-_family_and_children_benefits

51 https://www.ncbi.nlm.nih.gov/

52 https://www.statista.com/statistics/612207/divorce-rates-in-european-countries-per-100-marriages/

53 https://www.ncbi.nlm.nih.gov/pmc/articles/PMC4240051/

54 https://www.researchgate.net/publication/272588938_Explaining_the_Higher_Incidence_of_Adjustment_Problems_among_Children_of_Divorce_Compared_with_Those_in_Two_Parent_Families/figures?lo=1

55 https://www.psychologytoday.com/ca/blog/livingsingle/201908/around-the-world-marriage-is-declining-singles-are-rising

56 http://dx.doi.org/10.4135/9781483349350.n11

57 Rothenberg, C. E. (2004). *Spirits of Palestine: Gender, society, and stories of the Jinn*. Lexington Books.

58 https://en.wikipedia.org/wiki/Narcissistic_supply

59 https://www.insider.com/children-of-narcissistic-parents-are-either-favourite-or-scapegoat-2019-1

60 Baldwin, M. W., & Holmes, J. G. (1987). Salient Private Audiences and Awareness of the Self. *Journal of Personality and Social Psychology*, 52, 1087-1098.

61 Myers, D. G. (2009). *Social psychology* (10th ed.). McGraw-Hill.

62 https://socialsciences.mcmaster.ca/people/clancy-sarah

63 https://www.youtube.com/watch?v=daVjWUCIbAc

64 https://www.pewsocialtrends.org/2016/10/06/3-how-americans-view-their-jobs/

65 https://www12.statcan.gc.ca/census-recensement/2016/as-sa/98-200-x/2016024/98-200-x2016024-eng.cfm

66 https://www.independent.co.uk/news/education/higher/one-in-three-university-students-wish-they-had-chosen-a-different-course-says-study-10295076.html

67 https://www150.statcan.gc.ca/n1/pub/11-008-x/2011002/article/11536-eng.htm#n1

68 https://en.wikipedia.org/wiki/Drake_(musician)#Early_life

69 https://ca.news.yahoo.com/blogs/north-stars/drake-didn-t-easy-growing-wealthy-toronto-neighbourhood-165446063.html
70 https://www.oldest.org/politics/members-us-congress/
71 https://en.wikipedia.org/wiki/List_of_current_senators_of_Canada _by_age
72 https://pagesix.com/2014/06/12/where-did-it-all-go-wrong-for-rob-kardashian/
73 https://www.biography.com/actor/sylvester-stallone
74 https://www.ncbi.nlm.nih.gov/pmc/articles/PMC5937874/
75 https://www.theguardian.com/commentisfree/2019/jan/31/kamala-harris-laughed-jailing-parents-truancy
76 https://dictionary.apa.org/temperament
77 https://www.sciencedaily.com/releases/2018/07/180709101117.htm
78 https://www.aacap.org/AACAP/Families_and_Youth/Facts_for_Families/FFF-Guide/Understanding-Violent-Behavior-In-Children-and-Adolescents-055.aspx
79 79) Thomas, A., & Chess, S. (1977). *Temperament and development.* (2nd ed). Brunner/Mazel
80 https://www.researchgate.net/publication/256475323_Coercive_Family_Process_and_Early-Onset_Conduct_Problems_From _Age_2_to_School_Entry
81 https://ejop.psychopen.eu/index.php/ejop/article/view/ 290/html
82 Darwin, C. (1859). *On the origin of species by means of natural selection.* New York, NY: Appleton and Company. Retrieved from http://darwin-online.org.uk/converted/pdf/1861_OriginNY_F382.pdf
83 https://youtu.be/hIq4UTgqDAc
84 https://wheatley.byu.edu/porn-gap-differences-mens-womens-pornography-patterns-couple-relationships/
85 https://www.researchgate.net/publication/227540333_A_Half_Century_of_Mate_Preferences_The_Cultural_Evolution_of_Values
86 Sroufe L. A., Duggal S., Weinfield N., & Carlson E. (2000). Relationships, Development, and Psychopathology. In A. J. Sameroff, M. Lewis, S. M. Miller (Eds), *Handbook of Developmental Psychopathology.* Boston, MA: Springer. https://doi.org/10.1007/978-1-4615-4163-9_5
87 Sroufe L. A., Duggal S., Weinfield N., & Carlson E. (2000). Relationships, Development, and Psychopathology. In A. J. Sameroff, M. Lewis, S. M. Miller (Eds), Handbook of Developmental Psychopathology. Boston, MA: Springer. https://doi.org/10.1007/978-1-4615-4163-9_5
88 Aronson, E., Wilson, T.D., Akert, R. M., & Fehr, B. (2012). *Social Psychology* (5th ed., p. 294). Toronto, ON: Pearson.
89 Sroufe L. A., Duggal S., Weinfield N., & Carlson E. (2000). Relationships, Development, and Psychopathology. In A. J. Sameroff, M. Lewis, S. M. Miller (Eds), Handbook of Developmental Psychopathology. Boston, MA: Springer. https://doi.org/10.1007/978-1-4615-4163-9_5

90 https://www.forbes.com/sites/katevinton/2016/06/01/these-15-billionaires-own-americas-news-media-companies/ #5ac563d6660a

91 https://www.statista.com/chart/20822/way-of-meeting-partner-heterosexual-us-couples/

92 https://www.psychologytoday.com/us/blog/sapient-nature/201201/familiarity-breeds-enjoyment

93 https://www.sciencedirect.com/science/article/abs/pii/0022103192900550?via%3Dihub

94 https://www.integrativemysticism.com

95 https://www.youtube.com/watch?v=DtoCw2iOTSc&t=1s

96 https://www.researchgate.net/publication/247562939_Social_desirable_responding_The_evolution_of_a_construct

97 https://doi.org/10.1007/978-3-319-28099-8_1349-1

98 https://www.researchgate.net/publication/232504886_Enhancement_and_Denial_in_Socially_Desirable_Responding

99 https://www.ncbi.nlm.nih.gov/pmc/articles/PMC4023461/

100 https://en.wikipedia.org/wiki/Freyja

101 Magnuson, M. J., & Dundes, L. (2008). Gender differences in "social portraits" reflected in MySpace profiles. *CyberPsychology & Behavior.* 11(2), 239-41. doi:10.1089/cpb.2007.0089

102 https://www.youtube.com/watch?v=SxVNOnPyvIU

103 Zurbriggen, E. L., Ramsey L. R., Jaworski B. K. (2011). Self and partner objectification in romantic relationships: Associations with media consumption and relationship satisfaction. *Sex Roles,* 64(7-8), 449-462. doi:10.1007/s11199-011-9933-4

104 https://www.ncbi.nlm.nih.gov/pmc/articles/PMC6917605/

105 https://www.theodysseyonline.com/bruno-mars-please-me-sexist

106 https://en.wikipedia.org/wiki/Ludacris#Personal_life

107 https://www.psychologytoday.com/us/articles/200011/the-science-laughter

108 Lieberman, M. D. (2013). *Social: Why our brains are wired to connect.* New York, NY: Crown Publishers.

109 https://www.psychologicalscience.org/observer/the-science-of-humor-is-no-laughing-matter

110 Carroll, N. (2014). *Humour: A Very Short Introduction.* (p. 84). Oxford. Oxford University Press.

111 https://www.instagram.com/tv/BzBVazyh1k1/?utm_source=ig_web_copy_link

112 https://www.psychologytoday.com/ca/articles/200011/the-science-laughter

113 https://www.verywellmind.com/what-is-the-halo-effect-2795906

114 Cialdini, R. B., & Goldstein, N. J. (2004). Social influence: compliance and conformity. Annual review of psychology, 55, 591–621. https://doi.org/10.1146/annurev.psych.55.090902.142015

115 https://www.imdb.com/title/tt2283748/

116 https://www.healthnewsreview.org/2018/02/pulling-back-the-curtain-on-the-doctors-and-the-dr-oz-show-what-our-analysis-reveals/

117 https://youtu.be/rdrKCilEhC0 https://youtu.be/UGxGDdQnC1Y

118 https://www.psychologytoday.com/us/blog/hope-relationships/201601/9-things-dependent-people-do

119 https://www.youtube.com/watch?v=MfZEDMsOrCk&t=4s
Look to the 1 minute mark.

120 Bielo, J. S. (2015). *Anthropology of religion: The Basics.* (p. 109). Routledge.

121 https://examples.yourdictionary.com/examples-of-groupthink.html

122 Schaller, M., Simpson, J. A., & Kenrick, D. T. (2006). *Evolution and Social Psychology.* (p. 319). New York, NY: Psychology Press.

123 https://opentextbc.ca/socialpsychology/chapter/social-categorization-and-stereotyping/

124 Tajfel, H., & Turner, J. C. (2004). The Social Identity Theory of intergroup behavior. In J. T. Jost & J. Sidanius (Eds.), *Key readings in social psychology: Political psychology.* (pp. 276–293). doi: 10.4324/9780203505984-16

125 Tajfel, H., & Turner, J. C. (2004). The Social Identity Theory of intergroup behavior. In J. T. Jost & J. Sidanius (Eds.), *Key readings in social psychology: Political psychology.* (p. 284). doi: 10.4324/9780203505984-16

126 Gaertner, L., & Insko, C.A. (2000). Intergroup discrimination in the minimal group paradigm: Categorization, reciprocation, or fear? *Journal of personality and social psychology*, 79(1), 92.

127 Gaertner, L., & Insko, C.A. (2000). Intergroup discrimination in the minimal group paradigm: Categorization, reciprocation, or fear? *Journal of personality and social psychology*, 79(1), 77.

128 Freud, S. (1989, first published in 1930). *Civilization and its discontents.* W. W. Norton. Retrieved from https://www.stephenhicks.org/wp-content/uploads/2015/10/FreudS-CIVILIZATION-AND-ITS-DISCONTENTS-text-final.pdf

129 https://www.theguardian.com/commentisfree/2015/may/07/ voting-irrational-emotions-politics-ideology

130 https://www.washingtonpost.com/news/the-fix/wp/2016/ 11/08/red-vs-blue-a-brief-history-of-how-we-use-political-colors/

131 https://toronto.citynews.ca/2006/06/23/violent-toronto-gangs-show-their-true-colours-leaving-many-youngsters-feeling-trapped/

132 https://en.wikipedia.org/wiki/Gang_colors

133 https://www.forbes.com/sites/stevedenning/2017/11/30/why-the-world-is-getting-better-why-hardly-anyone-knows-it/#767bcc887826

Endnotes

134 https://www.sciencemag.org/news/2017/12/why-human-society-isn-t-more-or-less-violent-past

135 https://www.nbcnews.com/think/opinion/trump-deserves-nobel-peace-prize-israel-bahrain-uae-deal-it-ncna1240363

136 https://www.whitehouse.gov/briefings-statements/president-donald-j-trump-brokers-historic-peace-agreement-israel-sudan/

137 https://www.sciencemag.org/news/2017/12/why-human-society-isn-t-more-or-less-violent-past

138 https://en.wikipedia.org/wiki/Frustration%E2%80%93 aggression_hypothesis

139 Radke, S., Volman, I., Mehta, P., van Son, V., Enter, D., Sanfey, A., Toni, I., de Bruijn, E. R., & Roelofs, K. (2015). Testosterone biases the amygdala toward social threat approach. *Science advances*, 1(5), e1400074. https://doi.org/10.1126/sciadv.1400074

140 Carré, J. M., Putnam, S. K., & McCormick, C. M. (2009). Testosterone responses to competition predict future aggressive behaviour at a cost to reward in men. *Psychoneuroendocrinology*, 34(4), 561–570. https://doi.org/10.1016/j.psyneuen.2008.10.018

141 Eisenberg, N., Damon, W., Lerner, R. M. (Eds.). (2006). *Handbook of child psychology: Social, emotional, and personality development.* New Jersey, NJ: Wiley.

142 https://www.bop.gov/about/statistics/statistics_inmate_gender.jsp

143 Aronson, E., Wilson, T. D., Akert, R. M., & Fehr, B. (2012). *Social Psychology* (5th ed., p. 346). Toronto, ON: Pearson.

144 Glavin, P. (2020). Multiple jobs? The prevalence, intensity and determinants of multiple jobholding in Canada. The Economic and Labour Relations Review, 31(3), 383–402. https://doi.org/10.1177/1035304620933399

145 https://www.opendemocracy.net/en/5050/indian-farmers-are-staring-suicide-modi-government-looks-other-way/

146 https://markets.businessinsider.com/news/stocks/farming-industry-facts-us-2019-5-1028242678#:~:text=While%20farmland% 20may%20stretch%20far,peaked %20at%20nearly%207%20million

147 https://www.pewsocialtrends.org/2013/12/11/on-pay-gap- millennial-women-near-parity-for-now/#the-balancing-act

148 Simon, R. (1995). Gender, multiple roles, role meaning, and mental health. *Journal of Health and Social Behavior*, 36(2), 182-194. Retrieved from http://www.jstor.org/stable/2137224

149 Bianchi, S. M., Robinson, J. P., & Milke, M. A. (2006). *The Changing Rhythms of American Family Life*. Russell Sage Foundation.

150 https://www.pewresearch.org/fact-tank/2015/10/01/women-more-than-men-adjust-their-careers-for-family-life/

151 https://pubmed.ncbi.nlm.nih.gov/21362611/

152 https://www.cbc.ca/marketplace/episodes/2015-2016/cellphones

153 Belfort, J. (2007). *The wolf of wall street.* New York, NY: Bantam Books.

154 https://psycnet.apa.org/doiLanding?doi=10.1037%2F0022-3514.62.3.469

155 Aronson, E., Wilson, T. D., Akert, R. M., & Fehr, B. (2012). *Social Psychology.* (5th ed., p. 257). Toronto, ON: Pearson.

156 Judge, T. A., & Piccolo, R. F. (2004). Transformational and transactional leadership: A meta-analytic test of their relative validity. *Journal of Applied Psychology, 89(5), 755-68. doi:10.1037/0021-9010.89.5.755*

157 https://www.pewresearch.org/fact-tank/2018/09/26/few-women-lead-large-u-s-companies-despite-modest-gains-over-past-decade/

158 https://dash.harvard.edu/handle/1/13030952

159 https://doi.org/10.1111/j.1755-618X.2010.01221.x

160 https://www.catalyst.org/research/women-in-financial-services/

161 Flett, C. V. (2007). What men don't tell women about business: Opening up the heavily guarded alpha male playbook. Wiley.

162 http://www.zuzanamisik.com

163 https://www.pnas.org/content/107/29/12804

164 https://www.dictionary.com/browse/propaganda?s=t

165 https://www.bl.uk/world-war-one/themes/propaganda

166 https://www.physics.smu.edu/pseudo/Propaganda/

167 https://implicit.harvard.edu/implicit/canada/selectatest.jsp

168 https://www.ncbi.nlm.nih.gov/pmc/articles/PMC2219763/

169 Cialdini, R. B. (2003). Crafting normative messages to protect the environment. *Current Directions in Psychological Science*, 12(4), 105-109. Retrieved from https://www.researchgate.net/publication/237301811_Crafting_Normative_Messages_to_Protect_the_Environment

170 https://doi.org/10.3389/fcomm.2018.00049

171 https://www.foxnews.com/politics/democratic-pennsylvania-lawmaker-masks-political-theater

172 https://en.wikipedia.org/wiki/Forced_compliance_theory

173 https://seekingalpha.com/article/4290812-multi-level-marketing-brands-are-taking-terrible-beating

174 https://www.prnewswire.com/news-releases/new-survey-reveals-73-percent-of-people-who-participate-in-network-marketing-opportunities-lose-money-or-make-no-money-300727716.html

175 https://www.sciencedaily.com/releases/2011/08/ 110822121721.htm

176 https://www.goodreads.com/book/show/199726. The_Egyptian_Book_of_the_Dead_

177 https://post.thing.net/node/3086

178 https://www.merriam-webster.com/dictionary/humble

179 https://www.urbandictionary.com/define.php?term=Humble

180 http://citeseerx.ist.psu.edu/viewdoc/download? doi=10.1.1.881.5827&rep=rep1&type=pdf

181 https://www.instagram.com/p/CGBRp53JcSu/?
utm_source=ig_web_copy_link

182 Freedman, J. L. & Fraser, S. C. (1966). Compliance without pressure: The foot
in the door technique. *Journal of Personality and Social Psychology,* 4(2). 195-
202.

183 https://en.wikipedia.org/wiki/Positive_psychology#Initial_theory:_
three_paths_to_happiness

184 http://news.bbc.co.uk/2/hi/3335275.stm

185 https://www.academia.edu/20837236/Cooperation_in_social_
dilemmas_Free_riding_may_be_thwarted_by_second-order_reward_
rather_than_by_punishment

186 https://www.americanprogress.org/issues/education-k-
12/news/2018/03/02/447321/education-opportunities-prison-key-
reducing-crime/

187 https://www.amazon.ca/Codex-Seraphinianus-Luigi-
Serafini/dp/0847842134

188 https://en.wikipedia.org/wiki/Jungian_archetypes#:~:text=
Jungian%20archetypes%20are%20defined%20as,the%20psychic%
20counterpart%20of%20instinct

189 Arroyo, S. (2018). *Astrology, psychology & the four elements: An energy
approach to astrology and its use in the counseling arts.* (Ch. 1). Sebastopol,
CA: CRCS Publications.

190 https://opentextbc.ca/socialpsychology/chapter/the-feeling-self-self-
esteem/